英文ビジネスメール
200の鉄則

Iron Laws
with 200
Techniques
for Effective
English
Business
Emails

倉骨彰、トラビス・T・クラホネ 著

日経BP社

■はじめに

　ビジネスのグローバル化とインターネットの普及の結果、外国人の仕事相手や同僚から英文メールが直接届いて、ちょっとした返事を書いているビジネスパーソンやエンジニアは増えているだろう。資料なら英文で読める、日常会話なら英会話もそこそこにこなせるという人でも、ビジネス上の用件を伝えるメールをいざ英語で書くとなると、すぐに役立つ参考例満載の手引書が手元にあれば、と思えてくるはずだ。本書には、こうした時代のビジネスの現場で、そのまま使える英文メールの基本例と、そのバリエーションが数多く採録されている。そして、ビジネスパーソンやエンジニアを対象に、英文メールで頻繁に使われる表現が、分類・整理されている。

　我々が情報を伝えるときに使う文章には、実はある種の枠組みがある。和文であれ英文であれ、ビジネス文書であれ技術文書であれ、とにかく何のためのものであれ、「書き出し」「展開」「締めくくり」の3つのパターンで表したものが、実際にはほとんどではないだろうか。そして、これらのパターンには、決まった言い回しや語句が多用されている。たいていの場合、伝えたい内容が多少異なっても、目的や用途が似通っていれば、同じような表現を含むことが多い。

　そこで本書では、現代の企業で遭遇するであろうビジネスシーンを考え、そこで実際にやりとりされる英文メールはどのようなものかという観点から、平易で明瞭、かつ効果的に意思疎通が図れるメッセージのパターンを検討し、1ページ1項目としてまとめた。採録した例文は、英語を共通言語とするビジネスの現場で実際に使われているものであり、シンプルだが、ちょっと気がきいた表現が満載である。

　本書は2003年に発行し好評をいただいた『説得できる英文Eメール200の鉄則』を見直し、時代に合わせて改題、再編集したものである。例文に取り上げた事例で古くなった内容を刷新するなどして、初版で人気が高かった「そのまま使える」実用性をさらに高めている。

詳細に分類・整理された基本パターンは200項目にのぼり、例文の数は1200を超えている。ビジネスシーンのリアリティを高めるため、日本と米国西海岸に拠点をもつ仮想的なIT企業を舞台として例文内容を統一してあるが、本書に掲載された表現のパターンのほとんどはどんな業種にも適用できるものと信じている。

　辞書的に「引いて使える」実用性を考え、見出しや強調書体による検索性に配慮し、索引も「用例索引」「用語索引」の2種類を用意した。多忙なビジネスパーソンのニーズに対応するため、必要とする例文にできるだけ短い時間でたどり着けるように工夫した。

　各項目の見出しはキーワードと指針・応用シーンからなっている。本文は、「簡単な解説」「EXAMPLE」「VARIATIONS」で構成した。「EXAMPLE」は、その項目の最も主要で基本的な例文である。「VARIATIONS」には各種参考例を短文で列挙した。項目によっては解説や「EXAMPLE」を割愛し、「VARIATIONS」をできるだけ多数記載したものもある。

　なお、本書に参考例として採録した1200を超える英文は、キャロル・イヌガイ＝ディクソン氏が複数回にわたりチェックしてくださり、彼女の精査なくして本書の完成はあり得なかったことをここに明記し、深く感謝の意を表したい。

　本書が読者の座右にあって、英文メールでの円滑なコミュニケーションの一助になれば幸いである。

2018年3月

著者

※本文中に出てくる企業名や人名、電話番号やメールアドレスなどの連絡先はすべて架空のものです。

英文ビジネスメール 200 の鉄則

目 次

第1章 英文メールの基本 ……………………………………………… 9

仕事の英文メール
- ① 要は簡潔に用件を伝える ………………… 10
- ② 例文を参考にして書く ……………………… 11
- ③ 平易で丁寧な表現を心がける …………… 12
- ④ 不用意にくだけた表現は使わない ……… 13
- ⑤ 軽い提案が尊大な表現にならないように … 14
- ⑥ 依頼は命令口調にならないように ……… 15

メールの要素
- ① 起筆と結尾を使い分ける ………………… 16
- ② 件名は用件が分かるように ……………… 17
- ③ 本文は単刀直入でよい …………………… 18
- ④ 英文用の署名を用意する ………………… 19
- ⑤ 句読点や空白の使い方 …………………… 20

日時の表現
- ① 日時を正しく伝える ……………………… 21
- ② 時間関係を示す表現……………………… 22

第2章 ビジネスメールの書き出しと結び ……………………… 23

書き出しの表現
- ① 最初に謝意を示す ………………………… 24
- ② 返事として送る …………………………… 25
- ③ 続報で知らせる …………………………… 26
- ④ 返事が遅れたとき ………………………… 27
- ⑤ 久しぶりのとき …………………………… 28
- ⑥ 主題や経緯を最初に述べる ……………… 29
- ⑦ 好ましいメールを出すとき ……………… 30
- ⑧ 遺憾なメールを出すとき ………………… 31
- ⑨ 業務連絡でよく使うフレーズ …………… 32

結びの表現
- ① 返事を期待する …………………………… 33
- ② 情報を提供したとき ……………………… 34
- ③ 何か依頼したとき ………………………… 35
- ④ 申し訳なかったとき ……………………… 36
- ⑤ 最後にもうひと言謝意を示す …………… 37
- ⑥ 期待感を示す ……………………………… 38
- ⑦ 「よろしく」と伝える …………………… 39
- ⑧ どうぞご遠慮なく ………………………… 40

第3章 メール特有の表現 …… 41

- 送受信
  - ① 添付ファイルで送る …… 42
  - ② ファイルの圧縮／解凍 …… 43
  - ③ 送付ミスがあったとき …… 44
- レイアウト
  - ① 箇条書きで情報を整理する …… 45
  - ② コロンを使って箇条書きにする …… 46
  - ③ インデントで区別する …… 47
  - ④ 罫線を使う …… 48
- 読み手への配慮
  - ① 宛先複数のメールをわかりやすく …… 49
  - ② 返信しやすいように本文を書く …… 50
- 引用と転送の表現
  - ① 引用文の間にコメントを書く …… 51
  - ② 必要のない部分は削除 …… 52
  - ③ 返信文が短いときは冒頭に …… 53
  - ④ Quote と Unquote で引用して転送 …… 54
  - ⑤ 転送であることを明記する …… 55
  - ⑥ 元の発信者に転送した旨を通知する …… 56
- メールの作法
  - ① 初めてメールを送るときの自己紹介 …… 57
  - ② ひと言でもよいからすぐ返信 …… 58
  - ③ 感情的な表現には要注意 …… 59

第4章 定型的な業務連絡 …… 61

- 送る・受け取る
  - ① 資料や物品を送る …… 62
  - ② 送付物の内容を伝える …… 63
  - ③ 送付先を確認する …… 64
  - ④ 送付の目的を述べる …… 65
  - ⑤ 受け取り確認 …… 66
  - ⑥ 後日／別便で送る …… 67
  - ⑦ 情報／資料を提供できない …… 68
- 通知する
  - ① 報告する／伝える …… 69
  - ② 各種お知らせの表現 …… 70
  - ③ 知らせてもらう …… 71
- オフィス関係
  - ① 開設や移転を知らせる …… 72
  - ② 住所・連絡先の変更 …… 73
  - ③ 住所・連絡先の変更（応用） …… 74
- 不在の通知
  - ① 出張の連絡 …… 75
  - ② オフィスの休業の通知 …… 76
  - ③ 休暇の連絡 …… 77
- 会議・イベント
  - ① 開催を通知する …… 78
  - ② 出欠を確認する …… 79

	③ 招待を受諾する／断る	……………	80
	④ 要人の訪問を通知する	……………	81
	⑤ 議題を通知する	……………	82
	⑥ 議事録を作成する	……………	83
	⑦ 議事録を送付する	……………	84
	⑧ 歓迎会・懇親会を知らせる	……………	85
	⑨ 宿泊を手配する	……………	86
社内掲示板	① 共有設備について	……………	87
	② 社内に情報を求める	……………	88
	③ 探し物があるとき	……………	89
	④ 紛失物があったとき	……………	90
	⑤ 告知（社内公募）	……………	91
	⑥ 告知（研修その他）	……………	92

第5章 ビジネスに役立つ表現 …………… 93

情報収集	① 情報を送ってもらう	……………	94
	② こちらの興味を示す	……………	95
	③ 追加情報を求める	……………	96
	④ 紹介してもらう	……………	97
	⑤ 情報源を尋ねる	……………	98
	⑥ 紹介元を説明する	……………	99
	⑦ 適任者を紹介する	……………	100
	⑧ 使用許諾を求める	……………	101
アポイントメント	① 面会を申し込む	……………	102
	② 来社してもらう	……………	103
	③ 面会の目的を述べる	……………	104
	④ 他人を紹介する	……………	105
	⑤ 面会を承諾する／辞退する	……………	106
	⑥ 会合場所を調整する	……………	107
	⑦ 別の日時を打診する	……………	108
	⑧ 当日の面会手順	……………	109
	⑨ 約束を変更する	……………	110
	⑩ 約束を取り消す	……………	111
	⑪ 面会のお礼を述べる	……………	112
スケジュール管理	① 日程を伝える	……………	113
	② 進捗状況を確認する	……………	114
	③ 進捗に問題があるとき	……………	115
各種用件の表現	① 注文／予約する	……………	116
	② 各種の問い合わせ	……………	117

	③ 問い合わせに答える	118
	④ 中止／取り消し／変更	119
	⑤ 原稿／投稿を依頼する	120
	⑥ 関係者の協力を請う	121
	⑦ 連絡先を知らせる	122
	⑧ 申し出を断る	123
	⑨ 申し出を承知する	124
	⑩ 指示を求める	125
	⑪ 指示を知らせる	126
	⑫ 誤解がないか確認を求める	127
	⑬ 念を押す	128
	⑭ 相手の理解を確認する	129
	⑮ 伝言する	130
	⑯ 希望や期待を伝える	131
	⑰ 返事を催促する	132
	⑱ クレーム対応	133

第6章 人事や社交の表現 … 135

異動や転職	① 転職／転勤／帰国の挨拶	136
	② 送別会開催の通知	137
	③ 転勤者からのお礼	138
人材採用	① 人を推薦する	139
	② 採用／不採用を通知する	140
病気や訃報	① 病欠の連絡	141
	② 社員／元社員の訃報	142
	③ 葬儀の献花／寄付	143
個人的なお見舞い	① お悔やみ	144
	② 元気づける	145
	③ お悔やみ／励ましへの返信	146
好意を伝える	① クリスマスや新年の挨拶	147
	② 好意／尽力に感謝する	148
	③ 賞賛する	149
	④ 祝い状	150

第7章 説得・交渉の表現 … 151

相手に何かを求める	① 援助を求める	152
	② 婉曲に許可を求める	153
	③ 何かの行動を依頼する	154
	④ 催促する	155

助言	① アドバイスを請う	156
	② アドバイスする	157
	③ 強く勧める	158
	④ アドバイスを採用する	159
意向を伝える	① 要望を婉曲に伝える	160
	② 売り込む	161
	③ 計画／目標を伝える	162
	④ 援助を申し出る	163
	⑤ 懸念／不安があることを伝える	164
	⑥ 婉曲に疑問や質問を提示する	165
	⑦ 約束する／請け合う	166
	⑧ 承認／許可する	167
	⑨ 承認しない	168
	⑩ 必要性を訴える	169
意見を交換する	① 相手の意見を求める	170
	② こちらの意見を述べる	171
	③ 断定的／曖昧に意見を述べる	172
	④ 意見を述べるのを控えたい	173
	⑤ 注意を喚起する	174
	⑥ 理由を示す	175
	⑦ 重要性を指摘する	176
	⑧ 重要性を強調する	177
	⑨ それほど重要でないと言いたいとき	178
	⑩ 確実性が高いとき	179
	⑪ 可能性が高いとき	180
	⑫ 可能性がほとんどないとき	181
同意する表現	① 賛成する	182
	② 部分的に合意する	183
	③ 提案を全面的に支持する	184
	④ 提案を基本的には支持する	185
反対する表現	① 意見の不一致を表明する	186
	② 意見の不一致を強調する	187
	③ 反対意見を巧みに表現する	188
	④ 提案／対案を出す	189
	⑤ 提案に対する不支持の表明	190
	⑥ 全面的な不支持の表明	191
	⑦ 再考を求める	192
妥協の表現	① 妥協案の提示／受け入れ	193
	② 妥協案を受け入れられないとき	194

問題が生じたとき	③ 要求を条件付きで受け入れる	195
	① 警告を発する	196
	② 落胆の意を表明する	197
	③ 驚きを伝える	198
	④ 苦情を述べる	199
	⑤ 陳謝する	200
	⑥ 間違いを通知する	201
	⑦ 問題点を指摘する	202
	⑧ 誤解を解消する	203

第8章 エンジニアがよく使う表現 ... 205

概要を打ち合わせる	① セールスポイントを強調する	206
	② 具体的効用を訴える	207
	③ 何が効用かを尋ねる	208
	④ 技術的詳細を確認する	209
問題解決策を探る	① 状況を知る	210
	② 要望や回答を述べる	211
	③ 機能の追加や変更	212
	④ 期限の延長を求める	213
環境や条件	① 動作環境について	214
	② 開発環境について	215
	③ 開発者のスキルや資格	216
ユーザーサポート	① 一般消費者からの問い合わせ	217
	② 技術的な対応	218
個別技術で使う表現	① Webアプリケーション関係	219
	② データベース関係	220
	③ ネットワーク関係	221

用例索引 ... 222
用語索引 ... 256

1

第1章
英文メールの基本

仕事の英文メール　》》P.10 - P.15

メールの要素　　　》》P.16 - P.20

日時の表現　　　　》》P.21 - P.22

仕事の英文メール① ┃ 要は簡潔に用件を伝える

　ビジネスの現場において、英文メールの第1の目的は「用件を簡潔に伝えること」である。日常の平易な文章で書けばよい。郵便に比べ、文章表現の簡略化も進んでおり、何よりもスピードが重んじられる。要領を得ない文面を長々と書き連ねられたら、忙しい相手はかえって迷惑である。

EXAMPLE

Subject: About your bug report regarding the Format module

Dear Mr. Ramsey,

Thank you for emailing us a bug report regarding the Format module.

You are entirely justified in expecting us to fix it right away.

I am sorry that you were inconvenienced and I hope to have your continued patronage.

Sincerely yours,
Akihiko Yamada
Technical Department

ラムジー様

フォーマットモジュールのバグレポートをメールしていただき、ありがとうございました。

弊社がこのバグを直ちに修正すべきであるのは、ご指摘の通りでございます。

ご不便をおかけしたことをお詫び申し上げます。引き続きご愛顧いただけますようお願い申し上げます。

敬具
山田昭彦
技術部

仕事の英文メール② 例文を参考にして書く

　学校の英作文のように、まず日本語で考えていちいち文章を和訳していては、仕事の生産性は上がらない。ビジネスの現場で使われる表現のパターンは必ずしも多くない。例文を真似したり、英語を母語とする人からもらったメールを参考にしたりして書き、大切な時間を節約するのが、忙しいビジネスパーソンの仕事の極意といえる。

先方から来た文面

I am inquiring about the ABC123 series that is listed on your product catalogue.

According to the distributor that I talked to, **this series has already been discontinued**. Is it true? If you still **have some of them in your inventory**, please let me know because I would like to place an order.

If you **have some alternatives to them**, please send me the catalogue(s) because I would like to consider them as well.

EXAMPLE（返信の文面）

Thank you for your email inquiry dated July 21, in which you expressed your interest in our ABC123 series.

Unfortunately, **we have already discontinued this series and have none left in our inventory**. However, we do **have two alternatives to them**, the ABC3456 series and the ABC5500 series.

The ABC3456 series are functionally almost equivalent to the ABC123 series. Of the two alternative series, the ABC3456 is the cheap version and the ABC5500 is the high-grade version. For technical details, please check the attached file.

仕事の英文メール③ 平易で丁寧な表現を心がける

英語でも日本語同様、くだけた表現と丁寧な表現がある。英文の微妙なニュアンスがよくわからないなら、平易かつ丁寧な表現を心がけた方がよい。

くだけた表現

Hey Scott, about the new email delivery server you told me about the other day. I wanna meet you in person and ask you about its details and all, you know? How about some time this week? I can come over.

スコット、この間話してくれた、新しいメール配信サーバーだけど、もう一度会って細かいことをいろいろ聞きたいんだけど、どう？ できれば今週中がいいな。こっちから出向くよ。

EXAMPLE（平易かつ丁寧な表現）

Mr. Scott Cladwell, if you have time to spare, I would like to meet you again and listen to your explanation on the new email delivery server that you described to me the other day. What time will be convenient for you? If it is all right with you, I would like to come visit your office sometime this week.

スコット・クラッドウェル様、先日説明していただいた新しいメール配信サーバーについて、もう一度お会いして詳細をうかがいたいのですが、ご都合はいかがでしょうか。もしよろしければ、今週中に御社にお邪魔できればと思います。

仕事の英文メール④ 不用意にくだけた表現は使わない

　いくら日常の平易な言葉を使うといっても、送る相手をある程度はわきまえる必要がある。ビジネスライクな文面の中にいきなり口語的でくだけた表現が出てきては、読み手に奇異な感じを与える。

不用意に使うと変な感じを与える、くだけた表現の例

Hey John! **What's happening** these days?
ヤァ　ジョン、近頃どうだい。

Are you making big bucks these days**?**
最近もうかってる？

Hey brother!
よう　兄弟！

Hey you!
やい　お前！

I don't know **what the heck** you are talking about.
何のことやら**皆目**見当がつかない。

Who do you think you are, making that kind of assertion?
何様のつもりで、そんなこと言ってるんだ。

A smart guy like you should be able to take care of it before lunch.
あんたみたいな頭の良い人だったら、そんなの朝飯前だろう。

Too bad. I can't let you have that information.
悪いけど、その情報は出せないな。

You saying so puts me in an awkward position.
そんなこと言われても困るんだが。

Don't you wanna do it with us?
うちと一緒にやってみる気はないか。

Have mercy! Just wait for three days. **Come on!**
お願いだ、3日だけ待ってくれ。**頼むよ**。

仕事の英文メール⑤ | 軽い提案が尊大な表現にならないように

　学校での英語の時間に柔らかい口調の表現と教えられた語句が、実は落とし穴となることもある。軽い提案のつもりが、命令口調になってしまうからだ。

had betterは主語に注意！

　「had better」は「I」以外が主語になると、「〜した方がよい」という柔らかい意味ではなく、尊大で高圧的なニュアンスに聞こえてしまいかねない。

Yes, **I had better** fix this bug by next week.
そうだ、このバグ、来週までに解決**しなければ**。

Yes, **you had better** fix this bug by next week.
そうだ、このバグは、来週までに解決**するようにしてくれ**（このバグの解決は来週までに解決せよ、ということだ）。

軽い提案はshouldでなく、why don't you 〜 ?

　「〜すべきだと思います」と軽く提案するつもりで「should」を使うのも避けた方が無難だ。こういうケースではできるだけshouldは使用せず、「Why don't you 〜 ?」を使うようにすれば、過剰な反応が避けられる。

I think that you **should** leave San Francisco next week.
来週、サンフランシスコを発っ**た方がいい**、と思います。

Why don't you leave San Francisco next week**?**
来週、サンフランシスコを発っ**てはいかがですか？**

仕事の英文メール⑥ 依頼は命令口調にならないように

「(あなたから誰々に)〜するように伝えてください」と言って、間接的に何かしてもらうことを依頼するとき、「伝えてください」を直訳して「please tell」と書くのはよくない。「tell」だと命令口調になってしまうからだ。この場合、「ask」を使った方が響きを和らげることができ、不要な誤解を招かない。疑問形にすれば、響きをさらに和らげることができる。

tellとaskはどちらがふさわしい？

If you are visiting our office next month, **please tell** John to call me at 81-3-5555-1234.
来週あなたが我々のオフィスを訪ねるなら、あなたからジョンに、私のところに電話するように言ってくれ。

If you are visiting our office next month, **please ask** John to call me at 81-3-5555-1234.
来週あなたが我々のオフィスを訪ねるなら、あなたからジョンに、私のところに電話するように伝えてください。

If you are visiting our office next month, **could you ask** John to call me at 81-3-5555-1234?
来週あなたが我々のオフィスを訪ねるなら、あなたからジョンに、私のところに電話するように伝えてもらえますか？

メールの要素① 起筆と結語を使い分ける

日本語の「拝啓」「前略」に当たる起筆（Salutation）と結語に注意しよう。相手が親しいときとフォーマルなとき、男性のときと女性のときなどで、使い分ける必要がある。

起筆の例

Dear Mr. Gatesbox, ――― 相手の姓だけを使うのが最も一般的。女性の場合は、Mrs.、Miss、Ms. があるが、最近は独身、既婚を問わず Ms. を使うことが多い。Mrs. や Miss を不用意に使うとセクハラと言われたりするので注意したい

Dear Bill, ――― よく知っている親しい相手に対して出す場合は、相手の名前（ファーストネーム）を使う

Dear Professor Thomas, ――― Mr. や Mrs. といった敬称ではなく、Professor（教授）や Dr.（博士／医師）、Manager や Director といった役職名を使う場合も多い

結語の例

Sincerely,
Sincerely yours,
Best regards,
Best wishes,
――― 以上は知っている相手だけでなく、よく知らない相手に使っても大丈夫なので、適用範囲が広い

Regards,
Best,
――― ファーストネームで呼び合えるような、よく知っている相手のとき使う

Yours truly, ――― 改まった感じがする

Respectfully,
Respectfully yours,
――― フォーマルな感じがする

メールの要素② 件名は用件がわかるように

件名（Subject）は用件が伝わりやすいように工夫しよう。単なる「お知らせ」といったあまりに漠然とした件名では、それでなくても多忙な相手に見落とされるかもしれない。特に、緊急メール・重要メールは、その旨を件名欄で知らせるとよい。

VARIATIONS

Regarding the meeting, could we reschedule to 3:00 please?
打ち合わせの件、時間を3時に変更できますか

Please send your progress report by the end of the day
今日中に進捗状況を送ってください

Some questions on your resource distribution list
資源配分リストについての質問

Sending you the errata
訂正リストの送付

About the next meeting
次回会議の連絡

About the study group meeting on marketing
マーケティング勉強会のお知らせ

Would like to discuss my/your/our/their/his/her scheduling
スケジュールについてのご相談

[Important Notice] The shared file server will be down this weekend
【重要】ファイル共有サーバーが週末停止します

[Urgent] The bug fix doesn't work properly
【緊急】バグ修正がうまく機能しません

[Resent] The latest inventory list
【再送】最新在庫表の送付

メールの要素③　本文は単刀直入でよい

　日本語のビジネスメールでは、「〜社の○○です。いつもお世話になっています」といった挨拶を冒頭に入れることが多いが、英語にはその習慣はない。社会人としてのマナーをわきまえた文面であれば、いきなり用件から入っても失礼ではない。長文にしすぎないことも大事だ。1通のメールでの用件は1件に絞ると、後日メールボックス内を参照する際にも、用件を探しやすい。

EXAMPLE

Mr. Yamanaka,

About the bug found in the the Message_Format module, please check the cut_elements_out function at line 15.

struct rec *cut_elements_out (struct rec *root, char line)

As you can see, the third argument is missing, which has to be pointer argument *delimiters. Therefore, please add it as in the following code.

struct rec *cut_elements_out (struct rec *root, char line, char *delimiters)

Please send the fixed file to Mr. Smith by 3:00 p.m. today (August 4). Thank you very much for your help.

山中さん

伝文フォーマットモジュールのバグですが、format_message.cファイルの15行目のcut_elements_outという関数を見てみてください。

struct rec *cut_elements_out(struct rec *root, char line)

第3引数であるべき*delimitersというポインタが欠落しています。従って、以下のように引数を加えてください。

struct rec *cut_elements_out(struct rec *root, char *delimiters)

本日（8月4日）の午後3時までに、修正済みファイルをスミスさんにメールしてください。よろしくお願いします。

メールの要素④ 英文用の署名を用意する

　本文の末尾に挿入するいわゆる「署名」は普通、メールソフトに複数のパターンを登録できる。英文用の署名を用意しておくとよい。また、日常使っている日本語の署名を誤って送らないよう注意したい。

VARIATIONS

Steve Meridan
CrossWay Co.
　— 氏名と会社名だけのシンプルな署名

Spiky Rogers, Chief Engineer
System Development
BitPower Co.
　— 氏名、役職、所属部署、社名からなる一般的な署名

Yutaka Nikkei
Chief Research Associate
Network Development Group
R & D Center Communication System Division
AquosTech Co.
+81-1-5804-4321 (direct)
+81-1-5804-9876 (cellphone)
+81-1-5804-5555
+81-1-5804-0123 (fax)
yutaka.nikkei@AquosTech.com
http://www.AquosTech.com
　— 会社の電話番号やURL、メールアドレスまで加えた名刺代わりの署名の例

COLUMN　英文メールで使われる略語

外国人からのメールでは、タイプ入力の手間をはぶいたり、文章を短くしたりするために略語が使われていることがある。日本のビジネスパーソンがあえてこうした略語を使う理由はあまりないだろうが、意味ぐらいは知っておきたい。

略語の例

ASAP = as soon as possible	Attn. = attention
BFN = bye for now	BTW = by the way
CU = see you	FYI = for your information
MSG = message	NRN = no reply necessary
TNX = thanks	TTYL = talk to you later

メールの要素⑤ 句読点の使い方

　カンマ（,）、セミコロン（;）、コロン（:）、ピリオド（.）の使い方にはルールがある。起筆（Dear ～）と結語（Sincerely yours など）の後にも、カンマを付けるのが一般的である。コロンは項目を列挙する場合のほか、引用する場合、前の文を受けて説明する場合などにも使う。セミコロンは、and などの接続詞の代わりに同格のフレーズや文をつなぐときに使う。また、パラグラフ間は1行空きにするのが原則だ。

EXAMPLE

Dear Mr. Conner, ——————————————————— 起筆の後には
　　　　　　　　　　　　　　　　　　　　　　　　　　　　カンマを付ける

My name is Rintaro Yamaguchi. Currently I am working for XacBit Co. I am writing this email because I was introduced to you by Mr. Oscar Lawrence.

　　　　　　　　　　　　　　　　　　　　　　　　　　　　項目列挙には
Before I started working for XacBit Co., I was a senior　　　コロンを使う
programmer at WiFiPlus. My responsibilities included: ——┘
managing a team of five programmers for system
development; coordinating development of multi-team
projects; supervising in-house open source projects. I
attended Brown University and graduated in June 1995
with a B.S. in Computer Science. I am proud of the skills
and experience I have as an engineer; I am confident that　　セミコロンで同
I can be an asset to your organization. └——————————— 格のフレーズを
　　　　　　　　　　　　　　　　　　　　　　　　　　　　つなぐ

I am attaching a detailed resume of mine and hope you will consider me for the position of Chief Engineer.

I look forward to hearing from you.

Sincerely yours, ——————————————————————— 結語の後には
Rintaro Yamaguchi　　　　　　　　　　　　　　　　　　　　カンマを付ける

日時の表現① 日時を正しく伝える

　ビジネスメールでは、日時を正しく伝えることが非常に重要だ。時刻や日時の書き方には、よく使われる表現があるので覚えておきたい。

VARIATIONS

今年の初め／半ば／終わり頃：
at the beginning of this year/in the middle of this year/around the end of this year

来月上旬に／中旬に／下旬に：
in the early part of next month/in the middle of next month/in the latter part of next month

今日中には／来週中には／数日中には：
within today/within next week/within the next couple of days

10月10日以降（10日を含む）／11月11日より後に（11日を含まない）：
on or after October 10/after November 11

昼前後に：sometime before or after 12:00（sometime before or after noon）

夕方6時以降／朝8時まで：after 6:00 in the evening/until 8:00 in the morning

朝10時から夜9時まで：
from 10:00 in the morning till 9:00 in the evening（from 10:00 a.m. till 9:00 p.m.）

月初／月中／月末：
at the beginning of the month/in the middle of the month/at the end of the month

第1四半期の初め／末：
at the beginning of the first quarter/at the end of the first quarter

年初／年末：at the beginning of the year/at the end of the year

年度始め／末：at the beginning of the fiscal year/at the end of the fiscal year

上半期／下半期：the first half of the fiscal year/the second half of the fiscal year

就業時間：operating hours

日本時間／中国時間／現地時間：Japan time/China time/local time

米国東部標準時間／米国中部標準時間／米国山岳部標準時間／米国太平洋標準時間：
EST/CST/MST/PST

そちらの時間で／こちらの時間で：at your (local) time / at our (local) time

日時の表現② 時間関係を示す表現

VARIATIONS

Please fix this bug **as soon as possible**.
このバグを**できるだけ早く**修正してください。

Please get the no. 3 meeting room ready 5 **minutes before** the project meeting.
プロジェクト会議開始の**5分前**には、第3会議室の準備を整えてください。

Please call me **as soon as** everybody **is ready**.
全員の**準備ができ次第**、電話をください。

Please get the handouts ready **before** the development meeting **starts**.
開発会議の**前までに**、配布資料を整えてください。

When you are done with the meeting, please email me the minutes within the day.
打ち合わせ**が終わったら**、その日のうちに議事録を私にメールしてください。

We will let you take a look at our technical documents **as soon as we receive** your NDA (Non-Disclosure Agreement).
御社の秘密保持誓約を**受け取り次第**、技術文書をお見せします。

時間関係を示すその他のフレーズ

今週一杯かかる：take till the end of this week

年内には完成：complete by the end of the year

時間的に許せば：if time permits

新製品をリリースするまでは：till (until) the release of the new product

他社に遅れないように：not fall behind the other companies

他社に先んじて：ahead of the other companies

現時点では：as of now

近い将来：in the near future

2

第 2 章

ビジネスメールの書き出しと結び

書き出しの表現　≫ P.24 - P.32

結びの表現　　　≫ P.33 - P.40

書き出しの表現① | 最初に謝意を示す

　英文メールでは書き出しの表現が自由なだけに、逆に迷ってしまう人は多いだろう。とはいえ、書き出しのパターンはいくつかある。例えば「～いただき、ありがとうございます」などと謝意を示すのはごく一般的だ。

EXAMPLE

Thank you for letting us know of problems with our server software yesterday. About the bugs you pointed out, please give us a couple of months because we will certainly fix them when we release the next version.

昨日は、弊社サーバーソフトウェアの問題点をご報告いただき、ありがとうございました。ご指摘のバグについてですが、次回バージョンリリース時に必ず対応させていただきますので、2、3カ月お待ちください。

VARIATIONS

Thank you for sending the information that I inquired about in my email of August 12.
8月12日付のメールで問い合わせた資料を**送っていただき、ありがとうございます**。

Thank you for your prompt reply to my suggestion of setting up a project meeting.
プロジェクトグループ会議開催の提案に対して**早速お返事いただき、ありがとうございます**。

Thank you for your email in which you **gave me important pieces of advice**.
メールで**貴重なアドバイスをいただき**、ありがとうございます。

Thank you for your email of March 8, in which you suggested a project group meeting.
3月8日付の、プロジェクトグループ会議開催を提案いただいた**メール、ありがとうございました**。

I really appreciate your suggestion on which network system would be best for the business model of our company.
弊社のビジネスモデルにとって、どのネットワークシステムがいいかの**ご提案、大変感謝しております**。

Thank you for your call. I will discuss the question you raised with my immediate superior and respond to you by email as soon as possible.
お電話ありがとうございました。ご質問の件、上司と相談し、できるだけ早くメールでお返事させていただきます。

書き出しの表現② | 返事として送る

「〜日付けのメールについてお返事します」というように、どのメールへの返事かを最初に明記すると、用件が相手にわかりやすい。

EXAMPLE

I am writing this message to reply to your email dated July 10. We agree with your plan and would like to visit your New York office on Friday, August 15. It would be great if we could discuss how we should proceed with the development project.

7月10日付けのメールについてお返事します。私どもはあなたのプランに賛成でして、8月15日（金）に貴社のニューヨーク・オフィスを訪問したい、と思っています。その際、開発プロジェクトをどのように推進すべきかについてご相談できれば幸いです。

VARIATIONS

This is to reply to your email of July 21. As you have guessed, your network maintenance service charge is scheduled to increase in October.

これは、7月21日付けのメール**に対する返信**です。ご推察の通り、ネットワークメンテナンス費用は10月から値上げされます。

I have received your email of July 21 about the increase in your maintenance service charge which is scheduled to start in October, **about which I have some questions**.

10月からのメンテナンス費用の値上げに関する、7月21日付けのメールを受け取りましたが、**この件に関して質問があります。**

In reference to (about, with regard to, with reference to, with respect to) **your email of** June 5 about a compilation error in the CreateAction.java program, please wait (for our answer) a couple of days because we are now checking the program.

CreateAction.javaプログラムのコンパイルエラーに関する、6月5日付け**のメールに関し**、現在、プログラムをチェック中ですので、回答は2、3日お待ちください。

I have received your inquiry of June 5. About the compilation error of Control_User.c, I think our Tokyo office can handle it. Please send your email to our Tokyo office.

6月5日付け**のお問い合わせを受け取りました。**Control_User.c プログラムのコンパイルエラーに関するご質問ですが、当社の東京事務所が対処できると思いますので、東京事務所にメールでお問い合わせください。

書き出しの表現③ 続報で知らせる

先に送ったメールを補足したり、事態に何か進展があったり、後日送付となっていた情報を送ったりするときには、書き出しでその点に触れてもよい。

EXAMPLE

As I touched upon in my latest email, we are starting up a new section specializing in Web marketing next month.

前回のメールでも触れましたが、弊社はWebマーケティングの専任部署を来月から立ち上げることになりました。

VARIATIONS

This is just a follow-up to the message I sent earlier regarding your August 11 inquiry about our E300 system series.
先程お送りした、弊社のE300システムシリーズに関するあなたからの8月11日付けのお問い合わせに**対する**メールの**フォローアップです**。

This is just a follow-up mail to yesterday's mail, **clarifying a few things**.
昨日送ったメールの続報です。**2、3の点を整理させてください**。

I thought I would send you this brief email **as a follow-up to remind you that** we want you to keep us posted on any developments.
この件で何か進展がありましたらご連絡いただきたいと思っております**ことをお知らせしたく**、この短いメールを**続報として差し上げました**。

This email is **to provide the details** regarding the price changes that we informed you of (discussed, announced) the other day.
このメールは、先日お知らせした価格改定について、**詳細をお知らせするためのもの**です。

As I have already informed you, Mr. Jones, the manager of the San Jose office, will visit us on business next week.
すでにお知らせしたように、今週、サンノゼ・オフィス所長のジョーンズ氏が出張で訪ねてきます。

書き出しの表現④　返事が遅れたとき

受け取ったらすぐ返信するのがメールの鉄則。返事があまりに遅れた場合はひと言謝るのがマナーだろう。

EXAMPLE

Your email dated July 20 was forwarded to me today. My apologies to you for not responding to your email in a more timely fashion.

本日、あなたからの7月20日付けのメールが私のもとに転送されてまいりました。お返事が遅れてしまったことをお詫びいたします。

VARIATIONS

Because I was out of my office on a business trip for a couple of days, I am sorry **I could not respond to your email right away**.

数日間出張しておりまして、オフィスを留守にしていたため、**すぐに返事をすることができず**、申し訳ありませんでした。

Thank you for emailing me your proposal. I am sorry that **I was unable to reply sooner** because it took us longer to review than we thought.

ご提案をメールしていただきありがとうございました。検討に予想以上の時間がかかり、**すぐにお返事することができず**、申し訳ありません。

As promised the other day (in my email), we have reviewed your proposal and I am sending a summary to you now. **It took us a couple of days longer than expected** to complete the review. Please accept our apologies.

先日のメールでお約束しました通り、あなたからの提案を検討しまして、要約を送付いたします。**検討に数日余計にかかってしまいました**。お詫びします。

書き出しの表現⑤ 久しぶりのとき

久しぶりにメールを送るとき、日本語では「ご無沙汰しております」などという便利でよく使う表現がある。英語にもいくつかの決まり文句があるので、相手との関係により使い分けるとよい。

EXAMPLE

I trust this email finds you well. I will be transferred to the valley this September. It would be great if we could meet for a dinner somewhere between our offices in Palo Alto and Sunnyvale. Please let me know what you think.

お元気でお変わりないことと察します。私はこの９月からシリコンバレーに転勤となります。お時間のある時に、パロアルトとサニーベールのオフィスの中間点のどこかで食事でもご一緒できると素晴らしいのですが、いかがですか。

VARIATIONS

I haven't seen you for a long time; how is everything with you these days? Right now, I am working as a programmer for DynaGrid in Santa Clara, California.

長いことご無沙汰しておりますが、お変わりありませんか。現在、私はカリフォルニア州サンタクララにあるDynaGrid社でプログラマーをしております。

Bill! **I haven't seen you for ages** and am interested in finding out what you have been up to since our last meeting. How have you been?

ビルさん、**久しぶりです**。最後にお会いしてから、いかがお過ごしでしたか。

If I can recall correctly, it seems like it has been at least a couple of years **since I saw you last** in San Jose. Doesn't it?

もし私の記憶が正しければ、サンノゼで**最後にお会いしたのは**、少なくとも２、３年前、そうじゃありませんでしたっけ。

Was it a year ago **when we exchanged our emails** last? It has been a long time since we had dinner together back in San Francisco China Town, hasn't it?

メールを最後に交わしたのは１年前でしたか。サンフランシスコのチャイナタウンで夕食をご一緒したのは、かなり前のことでしたね。

Hi, **long time no see**. Do you like it there in Menlo Park? Guess what? I will be visiting our Cupertino branch next month. Can you find time to get together?

よっ、**久しぶり**。メンローパークの生活、気に入ってる？　でね、そうなんだよ、来月、クパチーノ支社を訪ねることになってさ。会える時間あるかな？

書き出しの表現⑥ 主題や経緯を最初に述べる

ビジネスメールでは、そのメールが何のためのものか、主題やこれまでの経緯を最初に述べることが多い。

EXAMPLE

I am sending this email with respect to the Calculate_Data_Size.c program that your company developed. I would like to report that our engineers have found several bugs while they were testing the program.

このメールは、御社が開発したCalculate_Data_Size.cプログラムに関するものです。弊社の技術者がプログラムをテスト中にバグをいくつか発見しましたのでご報告いたします。

VARIATIONS

I am writing this email about the recent proposal to trim the program size by 10％.
プログラムサイズを10％削るという最近の提案**に関して、このメールを書いています**。

I am writing this email to express my complaint about the way that your company carries out software development.
御社のソフトウェアの開発のやり方にクレーム**を申し上げたく、このメールを書いています**。

This email is to inform you that we are willing to grant you a reduction.
このメールは、値引きのご用意が弊社にある**ことをお知らせするためのものです**。

This email is in reference to the source code of the CallAction.java program that your company sent to me 3 days ago.
このメールは、3日前に御社が私に送ったCallAction.javaプログラムのソースコード**に関するものです**。

The reason (why) I am writing this email is to tell you that we have encountered some problems with the Cancel_Application.c program.
このメールを書いている**理由**は、Cancel_Application.cプログラムにいくつかの問題があることをお知らせするためです。

This brief email is just to inform you that our company has finished developing the database.
このメールは、弊社がデータベースの開発を終えたことを**取り急ぎお知らせするためのもの**です。

書き出しの表現⑦ ┃ **好ましいメールを出すとき**

相手にとって喜ばしい用件の場合には、「〜をお知らせできてうれしく思います」などと、最初にそれを伝えるのもよい。

EXAMPLE

We are pleased to inform you that you have been awarded the contract to develop a major Web system for our marketing division.

弊社マーケティング部門向け大規模Webシステムの開発契約の発注先が御社に決定したことをお知らせできて、うれしく思います。

VARIATIONS

I have the pleasure of informing you that I have transmitted your message to my immediate superior and shall keep you informed of whatever action must be taken.

あなたからのメッセージを直属の上司に伝達し、今後の対応に関して逐次**お知らせできる**ことを**うれしく思います**。

We are happy to inform you that you have been hired as a chief programmer at Livermore Cluster Tech, Co.

あなたが、Livermore Cluster Tech社の主任プログラマーとして採用された**ことをお知らせでき、うれしく思います**。

We will be glad if your company can join us in developing a telephony system for the City of San Mateo.

サンマテオ市庁向け電話システムの開発に、御社が弊社とともに参画していただけると**うれしいのですが**。

We are pleased to learn that Professor Austin is positive about assisting your company's R&D efforts.

オースティン教授が御社の研究開発をお手伝いすることに非常に前向きである**とお聞きし、うれしく思います**。

We are very pleased that your company has succeeded in developing the search_info program.

御社がsearch_infoプログラムの開発に成功した**ことを大変喜んでおります**。

We had the great pleasure of receiving your software architect at our office yesterday. His insight into our Web system was very educational.

昨日、弊社に貴社ソフトウェアアーキテクトをお迎えしたことを、**大変うれしく思いました**。弊社Webシステムに関する彼の指摘は非常に勉強になりました。

書き出しの表現⑧ 遺憾なメールを出すとき

相手にとって必ずしも好ましくない内容のメールを出すのは心苦しいもの。失礼にならないよう、定石を踏まえて文面を工夫したい。

EXAMPLE

Please accept our apologies for the delay in identifying the exact cause of the bug that you reported to us in your email yesterday. We will keep working on it and will let you know by email as soon as we find something.

昨日ご報告いただいたバグの真の原因の特定が遅れており申し訳ございません。引き続き作業を継続し、何かわかり次第、メールでご連絡申し上げます。

VARIATIONS

We are very sorry to inform you that we have overlooked your email of July 11 in which you reported to us that we were in error in calculating the exact size of the customer database.

我々が計算した顧客データベースのサイズに誤りがあったとのご指摘を連絡してくださった、7月11日付けのあなたからのメールを見過ごしてしまった**ことをお詫びし、ご報告いたします**。

Please forgive me for taking so long to write the Get_User_Application.c program.

Get_User_Application.cプログラムの開発が遅れている**ことをお許しください**。

I am sorry to hear that the R & D division of your company is going to be shut down.

御社の研究開発部門が閉鎖される**と伺い、とても残念です**。

About your inquiry of August 9, **we are sorry** that the product you ordered is currently out of stock. We would appreciate it if you could wait another week as we will ship your order as soon as we get it.

8月9日付けのお問い合わせについてですが、**あいにく**ご注文いただいた製品はただいま品切れ状態になっております。ご注文の品は入荷次第、出荷いたしますので、あと1週間ほどお待ちください。

書き出しの表現⑨ | 業務連絡でよく使うフレーズ

社内宛ての業務連絡などでは、儀礼的な書き出しは省略し、用件から直接入ることが多い。そのような場合に役立つ表現が各種ある。

VARIATIONS

I would like to report that it has been brought to our attention that somebody forgot to lock the server room door when he/she left the room last.

どなたかがドアを施錠せずにサーバー室を最後に出てしまったとの連絡がありましたので、**お知らせいたします。**

As you already know, it has been decided that the deadline for developing a new data mining function is May 10, 2018.

すでにご存じのように、新データマイニング機能開発の締め切りは、2018年5月10日と決まりました。

As you are probably aware, this problem has to be taken care of by the next version release.

たぶんお気づきでしょうが、この問題は次回のバージョンアップまでに必ず対応してください。

It looks like Alex Bertland will be called back to the Saratoga office this summer because they need a UML specialist.

この夏、アレックス・バートランドがサラトガ・オフィスに呼び戻されるのは、UMLのスペシャリストが必要とされていることが理由**のようです。**

Everybody, I would like to draw your attention to the fact that we lost a big contract to DataZone Co. again.

またDataZone社に負けて大きな契約を取られてしまったことを、**皆さん、心にお留めおきください。**

This message is to let you know that it has been decided that Mr. Anton Montague will be promoted to project manager.

アントン・モンタギューさんがプロジェクトマネジャーに昇進することが決まりましたので、**お知らせいたします。**

We are writing with the hope that our server group has already sealed the system development contract with PhoneComm Co.

サーバーグループがすでにPhoneComm社とシステム開発契約を取り交わしている**ことを期待して、このメールを書いています。**

We are writing to request your attendance at the project group meeting scheduled in Tokyo next week.

来週、東京で予定されているプロジェクトグループ会議への出席を**お願いしたく、連絡を差し上げています。**

結びの表現① 返事を期待する

　メールでの結びの文句は特に必要なわけではないが、ひと言こちらの気持ちを付け加えたり、念を押したりすることは多い。一般的でよく使われるのは、「お返事お待ちしています」などと返信を期待する表現だろう。

EXAMPLE

We are sorry to trouble you with design changes of the authentication module, but we look forward to your reply to our inquiry.

authenticationモジュールの設計変更についてご迷惑をおかけするのを遺憾に思いますが、我々の問い合わせに対するお返事をお待ちしております。

VARIATIONS

I look forward to your reply to our inquiry of July 12.
7月12日付けの問い合わせに対して**お返事をいただきたく、お待ちしております。**

We look forward to hearing from you about design changes of the BayTech module as soon as possible.
BayTechモジュールの設計変更について、できるだけ早い**お返事をお待ちしています。**

Approximately when will you complete the check data module; **Please let us know by email promptly**.
check dataモジュールがいつ頃完成するかですが、**早急にメールでお知らせください。**

Please let us know by return email right away who will be replacing Bill Hansen in the R & D division.
研究開発部門のビル・ハンセンの交代要員について、**メールで直ちに折り返しご連絡ください。**

About bugs in the Data acquisition module; **You need to reply by return email ASAP**.
Data acquisitionモジュールのバグについて、**大至急、折り返しメールで返事をください。**

結びの表現② ▍情報を提供したとき

何か情報を提供してあげたとき、「喜んで〜いたします」などと結びでこちらの好意を表現すれば、相手に良い印象を与える。

EXAMPLE

I am pleased to send you the names of files and directories that you requested in your last email. If you need further help from us with this matter, please let us know and we will be happy to assist you.

直近のメールでご請求のあった、ファイル名およびディレクトリ名をお送りします。この件に関しまして、さらなるご要望がございましたら、どうぞお知らせください。喜んでお手伝いさせていただきます。

VARIATIONS

In regard to the damaged files, if you need our help in recovering them, **please do not hesitate to call us any time**.

壊れてしまったファイルですが、復元するのに我々でお役に立てることがあれば、**どうぞ遠慮なく、いつでもお電話ください**。

Concerning your question about hiring a couple of programmers in Tokyo, **if we can be of any assistance, please do let us know**.

東京でプログラマーを数人採用する件ですが、**もし我々でお役に立てることがあれば、ぜひお知らせください**。

As for holding monthly project manager meetings, if you have any questions about this matter, **please do not hesitate to contact us by email** at monthly-project-managermeetings@opentechweb.co.jp.

月例プロジェクトマネジャー会議の開催に関してご質問がある場合は、monthlyproject-manager-meetings@opentechweb.co.jp までメールにて、**ご遠慮なくご連絡ください**。

In response to your inquiry about our development project, if you need any information, please do not hesitate to get hold of us because **we will be happy to provide you with** any sort of technical information you want.

弊社の開発プロジェクトに関するお問い合わせの件、もし情報を必要とされる場合は、どうぞ遠慮なくお知らせください。ご希望の技術情報はそれがいかなる種類のものであれ、**喜んでご提供いたします**。

結びの表現③ 何か依頼したとき

相手に何かを頼んだときは、言いっ放しではなく、最後にこちらの依頼について婉曲的に念を押す表現を使ってもよい。

EXAMPLE

We thank you in advance for your usual kind attention to an estimate on setting up a Web server at our Yokohama branch office.

弊社の横浜支社にWebサーバーをセットアップする件の見積もりについて、いつもの親切なご配慮をいただけるものと、前もってお礼申し上げます。

VARIATIONS

About the source code of the program you showed me the other day, as it is not available in the Japan branch, **I would be grateful if you could** send me a copy soon.
先日見せていただいたプログラムのソースコードは日本支社では手に入らないので、すぐに**コピーをメールしていただけると助かります**。

Now that Yamamoto of my division will visit Los Alotos next week, **please give your attention to** having somebody introduce her to the chief engineer of your company when she is in the Bay Area.
私の部署の山本が来週ロスアルトスに参りますので、彼女がベイエリアに滞在中に、御社の主任技術者に御紹介していただく件**を、ご配慮ください**。

We would appreciate your attention to having someone meet Dr. Yamada at SFO.
サンフランシスコ空港で山田博士を出迎えていただく件**へのご配慮に、感謝いたします**。

Your prompt response to the claim from the San Jose office **will be appreciated**.
サンノゼ・オフィスからのクレームですが、**すぐにご対応いただければありがたく存じます**。

We appreciate your favorable consideration to the issue of overtime pay for our programmer who is taking care of network maintenance at your office.
御社でネットワーク保守を行っている弊社のプログラマーの残業手当の問題に対する、**好意あるご配慮に感謝いたします**。

As I email our requirements for the new network system that your company will be constructing for us, **I hope you will give them your consideration without delay**.
御社が構築を担当する新ネットワークシステムに関して、当方の要件をメールいたしますので、**すぐにご配慮いただけることを望んでおります**。

結びの表現④ 申し訳なかったとき

こちらに落ち度があった場合、結びでもうひと言詫びるケースも多い。

EXAMPLE

We are sorry that we failed to send you the bug report earlier and hope that it did not cause you too much inconvenience.

バグレポートをもっと早くお届けできなかったことをお詫び申し上げますとともに、ご迷惑をおかけしなかったことを願っております。

VARIATIONS

It appears that I have overlooked a few critical routines in the data mining module. **I am sorry for the inconvenience caused**.
data miningモジュールのチェックに見過ごしがあったようです。**不都合をお詫びします**。

We would like to apologize for the mix-up. We are sorry we couldn't take care of this problem in a more timely way.
この問題よって生じた混乱**をお詫びいたします**。対応が遅れて申し訳ありませんでした。

We are very sorry that we caused this problem and **inconvenienced you**.
この問題を引き起こし、**ご迷惑をおかけしたこと**をお詫び申し上げます。

I am sorry that **I didn't report to you sooner**.
ご報告が遅れて申し訳ありませんでした。

Please accept our sincere apologies for the problem. **It was due to our** shipping error.
今回のトラブルは**こちらの出荷ミスが原因です**。お詫びいたします。

I am sorry that **I sent you the wrong information**.
誤った情報を送ってしまい、申し訳ありませんでした。

Please accept my apologies for having used phrases that may have caused any misunderstanding.
誤解を招くような表現をしてしまい、**お詫びいたします**。

Please forgive our mistake(s).
当方のミスをどうぞ**お許しください**。

結びの表現⑤ ｜ 最後にもうひと言謝意を示す

結びでひと言「〜ありがとう」などと謝意を表すのもよい。単純だが応用範囲は広い。

EXAMPLE

We thank you very much for your help in getting the information we needed to design our new data mining system.

弊社の新しいデータマイニングシステムの設計に必要な資料の収集にご協力いただき、どうもありがとうございました。

VARIATIONS

Thank you for your email of March 8 in which you suggested a project group meeting.
３月８日付けの、プロジェクトグループ会議提案の**メール、ありがとうございました**。

Thank you for your cooperation in setting up a Web server for AquosTech.
AquosTech 社向けWebサーバー立ち上げの件での**ご協力、ありがとうございます**。

It was very thoughtful of you to forward my email to the general manager of the development division at AntiCloseTech Co.
私のメールを、AntiCloseTech社開発部部長に転送**していただき、助かりました**。

I really appreciate all the advice and cooperation you gave me on how to debug our Web service program.
我が社のWebサービスプログラムのデバッグ方法に関する**ご助言およびご協力に深く感謝しております**。

結びの表現⑥ 期待感を示す

「〜を楽しみにしています」などと結びで将来への期待感や願望を示せば、相手との良好な関係づくりに役立つだろう。

EXAMPLE

Thank you very much for your email of March 10 and the attached system design document. We appreciate your cooperation and hope to get your continued support on our development of the ImageEncoder.java program.

3月10日付けのメールと添付の設計仕様書、どうもありがとうございました。ご協力に感謝いたします。また、我々のImageEncoder.javaプログラムの開発についてのご支援、今後ともよろしくお願いします。

VARIATIONS

Thank you for your order of those 3 workstations. We are pleased to hear that our estimate was within your range this time. **We look forward to the possibility of serving you again**.

ワークステーション3台のご注文、ありがとうございました。お見積もりが貴社の許容範囲以内であったと知り、大変うれしく思っております。**今後またご用命いただければ幸いです**。

I wish you every success in your next development project. **It would be our pleasure to be able to** codevelop a large scale system with your company in the near future.

次の開発プロジェクトでのご成功をお祈り申し上げます。近い将来、御社と大規模システムを共同開発できることは、**我々の喜びです**。

I am looking forward to the days when we can work together on the same development project team again. Until then, **I wish you the best of luck with everything**.

また、一緒の開発プロジェクトチームで働けることを楽しみにしています。それまで**どうぞお元気にご活躍ください**。

I am looking forward to seeing you at the project group meeting on June 7 in San Francisco.

6月7日のサンフランシスコでのプロジェクトグループ会議で**お会いできるのを楽しみにしています**。

Thank you for all that you did for us the other day to get our system running. **I will be in touch with you soon**.

先日は、弊社のシステムを稼動させるためにいろいろお世話になり、ありがとうございました。**近いうちにまたご連絡します**。

結びの表現⑦ ｜「よろしく」と伝える

「よろしくお願いします」「よろしくお伝えください」など、日本語で「よろしく」は結びの文句に実によく使用される表現だ。英文には直接「よろしく」に対応する表現はないが、似たニュアンスの言い方で代用できることもある。

EXAMPLE

Thank you for awarding us the new system development contract. We look forward to a long and prosperous business relationship with you.

この度は、新規システム開発契約をいただき、ありがとうございました。今後ともご愛顧いただきますようお願いいたします。

VARIATIONS

It was a great pleasure working with you for the last 2 years. **I look forward to working for** your project in the near future again.

この2年、ご一緒に仕事ができたことは光栄でした。また近い将来、あなたのプロジェクトで**ご一緒できるのを楽しみにしております**。

We appreciate your continued support. Please give my best to Director Yamada.

今後ともご支援のほど、よろしくお願いします。山田部長によろしくお伝えください

Please give my best regards to Mr. Gates, your supervisor.

あなたの上司のゲイツさん**に、どうぞよろしくお伝えください**。

Please convey our congratulations to Vice President Mr. Raymond for successfully completing the search_info project.

search_infoプロジェクトが成功して**おめでとう、**とレイモンド部長に**お伝えください**。

Thank you again for your kind assistance. **Please give my regards to** Mr. Gibson.

ご支援に重ねて感謝いたします。ギブソンさん**に、よろしくお伝えください**。

We appreciate this opportunity to serve you. **My best to** Bill and Paul.

お役に立ててうれしいよ。ビルとポール**によろしく**。

I am scheduled to do a presentation on March 10. When you are ready with the handout file for it, please email a copy of it to Manager Monty Fulghum. **Thank you very much for your help**.

3月10日にプレゼンを行う予定ですが、資料ファイルが準備できたら1部を、モンティ・フルガム課長にメールで送ってください。**よろしくお願いします**。

結びの表現⑧　どうぞご遠慮なく

「今後も協力を惜しまない」というこちらの意向を結びで示すのも、相手との関係づくりに欠かせない表現だ。

EXAMPLE

It is always a pleasure to work with your company in software development. Please feel free to email us if you have questions.

御社と一緒にソフトウェア開発をするのは、我々の喜びとするところですので、今後ともご質問のある場合は、ご遠慮なくメールをください。

VARIATIONS

Regarding the bugs of the Make_Print_Data.c program, if you haven't received the patch program yet, **please do not hesitate to contact us** by email.
Make_Print_Data.cプログラムのバグについてですが、もしパッチプログラムがまだ届いていない場合は、メールで**ご遠慮なくご連絡ください**。

If you have any questions about this bug, please do not hesitate to contact me.
このバグについて**ご質問がありましたら**、ご遠慮なくご連絡ください。

Please feel free to email me if you have questions on the ActionState.java program.
ActionState.javaプログラムについてご質問がある場合は、**ご遠慮なくメールをください**。

Please contact us by email if you need more machines.
マシンがもっと必要な場合は、**メールでご連絡ください**。

Please do not hesitate to send us an email if you have any questions about how the Admin_Auth.c program is designed.
Admin_Auth.cプログラムの設計についてご質問がある場合は、**ご遠慮なくメールを送ってください**。

If you require (need) any (further/additional) information about the BasicApplication.c program, please let us know.
BasicApplication.cプログラムについて、さらなる情報が**必要な場合は**、ご連絡ください。

If we can be of any assistance with this proposal, please do not hesitate to tell us.
このプロポーザルについて**お役に立つことがあれば**、ご遠慮なくお知らせください。

With respect to the development effort of your company, **if there is something we can do for you**, please do not hesitate to tell us.
御社の開発についてですが、**私どもが手助けできることが何かあれば**、どうぞご連絡ください。

3

第 3 章

メール特有の表現

送受信　　　　　　　》P.42 - P.44

レイアウト　　　　　》P.45 - P.48

読み手への配慮　　　》P.49 - P.50

引用と転送の表現　　》P.51 - P.56

メールの作法　　　　》P.57 - P.59

送受信① 添付ファイルで送る／ファイル送信サービスで送る

メールの本文に加え、添付ファイルで追加情報を送るケースは多い。「添付します」という言い方のほか、単に「ファイルを送ります」でも十分通じる。大容量ファイルはファイル送信サービスやオンラインストレージサービスを使う手もある。

EXAMPLE

For your information, I am going to attach a source code file which I have sent to all the members of this project team.

本開発プロジェクトグループのメンバー全員に送ったソースコードファイルを、ご参考までに添付いたします。

VARIATIONS

With reference to the file you requested yesterday, **I am going to attach it to this email**.
昨日ご依頼のあったファイル、**このメールに添付します**。

Attached is our latest product catalogue.
添付しましたのは、当社の商品カタログの最新版です。

I am pleased to send you the data file you requested a week ago.
1週間前にご依頼のありましたデータファイルを**お送りいたします**。

Please find attached a file of the system development contract.
システム開発契約書の**ファイルを添付いたしました**。

Here is the screen dump file **you requested**.
ご依頼のありましたスクリーンダンプファイル**です**。

Attached are some samples of the functions that we plan to use at the demonstration tomorrow.
添付しましたのは、明日のデモで使う予定の関数サンプルです。

Regarding our latest catalogue, I uploaded it on the cloud storage. Please **download it from the link below**. The password is 0312.
当社の最新カタログですが、クラウドストレージにアップロードしました。**下記のリンクからダウンロード**してください。パスワードは0312です。

送受信② ファイルの圧縮／解凍

大きなデータ量のファイルは圧縮して送る。送り先の人が圧縮・解凍形式を承知していない可能性もある。説明するために必要な表現は覚えておきたい。

EXAMPLE

Regarding the source code file you requested by email yesterday, its zip compressed file is attached to this email. If you cannot expand it properly, please let me know.

昨日メールでリクエストいただいたソースコードファイルですが、zip形式で圧縮したものを本メールに添付してあります。もしうまく解凍できないようでしたら、ご連絡ください。

VARIATIONS

I am **going to compress** our latest product catalogue file **and mail it to you**. If you cannot receive it properly, please let me know so that I can resend it as soon as possible.
弊社の商品カタログの最新版ファイルを**圧縮してメール**します。もしうまく受信できないようでしたら、すぐに再送しますので、ご連絡ください。

I **cannot expand** the data file you sent me last week. In what format has it been compressed?
1週間前にいただいたデータファイルが**解凍できません**。圧縮フォーマットは何ですか。

Attached is a file of the system development contract. You **should be able to open it with** WinZip.
添付しましたのは、システム開発に関する契約書のファイルです。WinZipで**解凍できるはずです**。

If you cannot open it with ZipIt, **please try it with** MacLHA.
Macintosh用のZipItで解凍できない場合は、MacLHAを使ってみてください。

Although I have compressed the screen dump you requested, its file size is still too large to send it as one chunk. I will **segment it into 3 files and send them as 3 separate mails**.
ご依頼のありましたスクリーンダンプを圧縮したのですが、容量が大きいので**3回に分けて送ります**。

Thank you for the attached file. Unfortunately, as our system **cannot handle any email attachment whose size exceeds** 5 MB, I would appreciate it if you could send the file by file transfer service.
添付ファイルを送っていただき、ありがとうございました。ただ、弊社では**5MB以上のメール添付はうまく受信できない**ので、ファイル送信サービスで送り直してください。

送受信③ 送付ミスがあったとき

誤って違うファイルを送ったり、ファイルを添付せずに送信ボタンを押したりしてしまうことは少なくない。送付ミスがあったら即座に対処しよう。

EXAMPLE

The file I sent in my previous email is the wrong one. Please use the file attached to this email instead.

直前のメールで送ったファイルは間違いです。このメールに添付してあるファイルを使ってください。

VARIATIONS

I am returning the file which was **apparently forwarded to me by mistake**.
ファイルが**間違って送られてきたと思われます**ので、返送します。

Please excuse me as I made a mistake and sent my previous email **without attaching the file** I wanted you to take a look at. I am going to resend it now.
あなたに目を通していただきたい**ファイルを添付せずに**、直前のメールを送ってしまいました。再送します。

Bill, as **I am not involved** in the development project you are talking about in this email, please send the attached file to our Walnut Creek office.
ビル、このメールの中であなたが話している開発プロジェクトですが、**私は関係していません**ので、添付ファイルは弊社のウォルナットクリーク・オフィスまでお送りください。

I have received the file attached to this email. **It seems that it was intended for you**, please confirm.
私のところに添付のファイルが届きました。**これはあなた宛てと思われます**ので、ご確認ください。

About the file you said you attached to your email of August 12, as I cannot find it on my machine, **can you send it again?**
8月12日付けのメールに添付したとあなたが仰っているファイルを探しているのですが、私のマシン上には見当たりません。**もう一度送ってくださいませんか**。

I have received an email from you on October 15 **without the attached file you were talking about**. Please investigate and give advice.
あなたからのメールを10月15日に受け取りましたが、**言及されているファイルが添付されていませんでした**。ご調査の上、お知らせください。

レイアウト① 箇条書きで情報を整理する

　ビジネスメールでは、情報を整理して伝えるために箇条書きをよく使う。コロンの後で改行し、項目を箇条書き形式で列挙する。

EXAMPLE

Everybody,

As I told you in my mail of July 27, we need to carry out a preliminary analysis of our system. The purpose of performing this analysis is to identify critical areas, evaluate functions, and identify the design concepts. The system should be examined shortly after the analysis effort begins in order to provide a list of points that may require special design emphasis where in-depth analyses need to be done. As a minimum, our analysis should consider the following:

- Functional components
- Design criteria to control critical software commands
- Environmental constraints
- Network standards and specifications

諸君、

すでに7月27日付けのメールで知らせたように、システムの予備分析をする必要がある。この分析を行う目的は、重要ポイントの発見、関数の評価、および設計コンセプトの認定にある。システムの検証は、設計上、さらなる詳細分析が必要とされる箇所をリストアップする目的で、この分析が終了した直後に行わなければならない。予備分析においては最低限、以下の諸点を考慮する必要がある。

・機能コンポーネント
・重要なコマンドを制御する設計上の要点
・環境上の制約
・ネットワーク標準および仕様

レイアウト② ｜ コロンを使って箇条書きにする

　項目名に「：」（コロン）を付けて、その後に説明文を追加する形の箇条書きがある。キーワードが最初に来るので、簡潔でわかりやすい表現になる。

EXAMPLE

John, you can get to our San Jose office from major freeway exits as follows:

From Highway 101 north:
Take the 1st Street/Brokaw exit. Turn left on Brokaw and turn right on Airport Parkway. The San Jose office is on your left.

From Highway 101 south:
Take the Guadalupe Parkway exit south. At the first traffic light, turn right and turn right on Airport Parkway. Continue on Airport Parkway until it changes to McDonnell Road. The San Jose office is on your right.

From Highway 880:
Exit at Coleman Avenue. Go towards the airport and turn left on McDonnell Road. The San Jose office is on your left.

ジョン、幹線高速道路を使って弊社のサンノゼ・オフィスに行く道順は下記の通りです。

101号線を北上してくる場合：
1st Street/Brokaw出口で高速を降り、Brokawの交差点で左折し、Airport Parkwayで右折する。サンノゼ・オフィスはこの通りの左側です。

101号線を南下してくる場合：
Guadalupe Parkway南口出口で高速を降り、最初の信号で右折し、Airport Parkwayで右折し、この道がMcDonnell Roadに変わるまで直進する。サンノゼ・オフィスはこの通りの右側です。

880号線を使ってくる場合：
Coleman Avenueで高速を降り、空港方向に直進し、McDonnell Roadで左折する。サンノゼ・オフィスはこの通りの左側です。

レイアウト③ インデントで区別する

　インデント（字下げ）とは、文章の左側を空けて並べること。インデントを使うと、その部分が視覚的にも分離して区別しやすくなる。視覚的な変化も生まれる。

EXAMPLE

Attached is a monthly review of the system development project that Mr. Taguchi's team has been engaged in since last April.

　　I would appreciate it if you read this report very carefully, as we have noted many typos and misspellings in the past, and advise us of any errors and omissions by email. If the resubmission of the report is necessary, please let us know promptly.

Thank you for your cooperation in advance and we look forward to hearing from you soon.

添付いたしましたのは、田口氏のチームがこの４月から担当しておりますシステム開発の月例レビューです。

　　今までにも誤字脱字がたくさんございましたので、本レポートに注意深く目を通していただき、間違いまたは脱落がございましたら、すぐにメールでご通知いただけると助かります。もし報告書の再提出が必要な場合は、至急ご連絡ください。

ご協力に前もって感謝するとともに、お返事を早くいただけることをお待ちしております。

レイアウト④ 罫線を使う

「-」（ハイフン）や「*」（アスタリスク）を使えば、メール本文中に罫線を引くことができる。重要な情報を視覚的に強調したり、段落を分離したり、表を作ったりといろいろ使えて便利だ。

EXAMPLE

It's good to hear from you, John.
The problem you are reporting is called *mojibake* in Japanese.

****

The application you used takes whatever you give it from the keyboard andstores it in the ODB (object database). The problem comes when you attemptto manipulate that text in a regex. Since the application is not Unicode savvy, it will garble the text which is what you have just experienced. With that application you can store and retrieve text. However, anything interesting, for example, searching, regex, any sort of string manipulation, etc. will not work as far as "Japanese text" is concerned.
****

Cheers,
Naomi

- -

ジョンさん、お久しぶりです。
お知らせをいただいた問題ですが、日本語では＊文字化け＊と呼ばれています。

——（罫線）——
お使いになったアプリケーションは、キーボードからの入力をODB（オブジェクトデータベース）に保存します。このテキストを正規表現マッチングで操作しようとした際に、あなたの経験しているような問題が発生する理由は、アプリケーションがUnicode対応でないため、テキストが文字化けしてしまうからです。このアプリケーションでは、テキストの保存、取出しはできますが、ちょっとでも複雑なこと、例えば、検索、正規表現マッチング、文字列の操作等は、「日本語テキスト」を対象とする限りできません。
——（罫線）——

頑張ってください。ナオミより

読み手への配慮① 宛先複数のメールをわかりやすく

　複数の人に同報で送ったり、メーリングリスト宛てに送ったりするメールは、文面が共通の内容になる。しかし、その中に一部の人にだけ宛てた内容が含まれる場合がある。そのような場合、特定の人に宛てた内容がどこか、すぐわかる書き方をするとよい。

EXAMPLE

To all the staff at Ramblers Software,

I'd like to thank all of you for helping us complete this project without delay.

To Atilla, ──────────────────── アティラさん宛て
Thank you very much for being the best software architect.

To Karen, ──────────────────── カレンさん宛て
Thank you for showing me how to debug that data-mining function. If it wasn't for you, our project wouldn't have been completed on time.

While I was at your lab, I had so much fun that I am considering coming back to see you next Golden Week if my work allows it. Once again, Thank you very much.

Murai (BlueSky Technologies)

Ramblers Software 社の皆様、本プロジェクトが少しの遅れもなく完成したことは、皆様のご協力のおかげです。

アティラさん、最高のソフトウェアアーキテクトとして活躍してくれたことに感謝します。

カレンさん、あのデータアマイニング機能のデバッグ方法を教えてくださり、ありがとうございました。あなたのご協力がなければ、本プロジェクトは予定通りに完了していなかったでしょう。

貴社研究所に滞在中は本当に楽しかったので、もし仕事の都合がつけば、今度の5月の連休にまた皆さんにお会いできたらいいな、と考えております。どうもいろいろありがとうございました。村井（ブルースカイ・テクノロジーズ）

読み手への配慮② ┃ 返信しやすいように本文を書く

　出欠の確認やアンケートのようなメールでは、相手が最小限の労力で返信できるよう配慮したい。空白を埋めるだけとか、選択肢を選んでもらう形式にするなど、いろいろ工夫できる。

EXAMPLE

To whom it may concern:

We will be offering a brainstorm meeting on Friday, June 15 from 10:00 to 17:00. Those wishing to participate are asked to fill in the Reply Form. To assist us in planning the meeting, please return the Reply Form by email at your earliest convenience. The deadline is May 18, 2018.

Thank you.
------------- Reply Form -----------------------------
Please provide us with the following information.
Scope of Interest: Which of the following topics are of particular interest to you? (Check no more than two.)

[ ] IT Education in North America　　[ ] Stanford University and the Silicon Valley
[ ] Grid computing and NCSA　　　　[ ] Open source in Asia

Your contact information:
Name:　　　　　　　　　　　　email Address:
Telephone:　　　　　　　　　　Affiliation:

選択
（[ ] にチェックしてもらう）

連絡先
（：の後に入力してもらう）

各位、

6月15日（金）午前10時から午後5時の予定で、ブレインストーム会議の開催を計画しております。参加を希望される方は、下記、返信フォームに必要な情報をご記入の上、できるだけ早い機会に、お返事くださるようお願いいたします。締め切りは2018年5月18日です。よろしくお願いします。
------------- 返信フォーム ----------------
以下の情報をお知らせください。ご興味のある分野はどれですか？（2つまで）
　［ ］北米のIT教育　　　　　　　　　［ ］スタンフォード大学とシリコンバレー
　［ ］グリッドコンピューティングとNCSA　　［ ］アジアにおけるオープンソース
連絡先：お名前、電子メール、電話番号、住所、所属

引用と転送の表現① | 引用文の間にコメントを書く

ビジネスで一般的な返信メールとして、相手から来たメールの引用文の下に答えやコメントを返信文として書いていくパターンがある。下記は、顧客のメールアドレスを収集する際の要領について、引用文の間にこちらの短いコメントを挟んで返信文を作っている。

EXAMPLE

> The following is my summary of how to gather customers' email
> addresses on our Web page. Since there are things that I cannot
> decide by myself, your comments are appreciated.
>
> Personal information fields:
> Of course, "prefecture", "age", and "sex" attribute fields are
> mandatory to grasp the customer's characteristics, but do
> you think that we need to have "name", "street address", and
> "phone number" attribute fields, too?

We probably don't need them because people don't like to fill in too many fields. ── こちらのコメント

> Permission field:
> Having the customer place a check mark on the check box by
> [latest news from us] is a typical way to find out whether
> he/she prefers to have the [latest news from us] delivered
> automatically from us.

I think it should do it. ── こちらのコメント

> Welcome message:
> I will configure the server so that it will automatically send
> out the welcome message to members when they subscribe
> to our list.

I see. ── こちらのコメント

引用と転送の表現② | 必要のない部分は削除

　長文メールに返信したり、第三者に転送したりする際に必要のない部分を削除する場合、どこを省略したのか相手に明示しよう。下記は、相手の文面を一部削除し、短くして返信した例。

EXAMPLE

Mike,
At 2:16 PM +0900 03.7.15, Mike Stone wrote:
> Bill,
> We have this system development project which has received a
> couple of million dollars in funding from OrbisExpress.

This kind of news makes me feel happy. ────── こちらのコメント

> [sorry deleted] ────── 「中略」
>
> We are looking for an engineer fitting the following description.
> Age: Between 25 and 35 approx.
> Qualifications: BS in Computer Science
> Experience: UML and CAD

I understand what kind of person you are looking for. ────── こちらのコメント

> If you know somebody who may qualify for this position,
> please let me know. Also, please call our San Jose office
> and ... [snipped] ────── 「以下略」

OK, I will try both. ────── こちらのコメント

> If you know somebody who is looking for a job right now, please
> feel free to forward this email to him/her.
> ────── こちらのコメント

Right now, nobody pops into my mind, but I promise I will find someone.

Best regards,
Bill Sunshine

引用と転送の表現③ | 返信文が短いときは冒頭に

　相手が送ってきた長い文面に対し、答えがひと言で済む場合は、全文引用して、冒頭に返信文を付け加えるだけでよい。すぐに返信メールを送れて、手間もかからない。こうした場合に日本語でよく使われる「了解しました」は便利な表現だが、さまざまな意味を持ち得る。英語の場合は、直接目的語をほとんど省略しないので、明示的に「〜についてわかりました」「ご希望に従います」などと書いた方が、コミュニケーションに支障をきたさない。

VARIATIONS

I will do as you said.
仰る通りにいたします。

I will do as you want me to do.
ご希望通りにいたします。

I will follow your instructions.
ご指示に従います。

I will carry out the steps you described.
お示しいただいた手順で実行します。

Thank you for clarifying the confusion. I understand it now.
混乱を正していただいてありがとうございます。理解できました。

OK, I'm fine with the date and place you suggested.
あなたの仰る日時／場所で私も大丈夫です。

This I can agree with.
以下、賛成です。

Thank you for drawing my attention to the problem. Now I see your point.
この問題についてお知らせくださりありがとうございます。仰っていることを理解しました。

Thank you for the information.
情報、ありがとうございました。

On this, I agree with you. (With this I agree.)
下記、了解です。

引用と転送の表現④ | Quote と Unquote で引用して転送

受け取ったメールの一部をさらに別の人に転送する際、"Quote" と "Unquote" でくくって文章を引用する表現も、郵便の時代と同様に使われている。日本語の「記」「以上」に当たる表現といえる。

EXAMPLE

Everyone,

The following text message has been received via email from our Redmond headquarters.

Bill Gatesbox, who has spent 25 years in the industry, was recently appointed managing director of Livermore Cluster Tech Co. Mr. Gatesbox wants us to provide answers to the following questions one by one.

On Mon, Jul 14, 2003 at 12:00:23 PM +0900, Bill Gatesbox wrote:
Quote:
At a very critical time, how do you plan to cope with the situation?

How can you acquire an extra hi-performance computer when you are acutely short of funds?

It is said that excessive political interference has pushed Livermore Cluster Tech Co. to a state of confusion. Do we still face similar pressure now?

If everything goes our way, how long do you think it would take for us to restore the Livermore Cluster Tech Co.'s image?
Unquote.

Please answer directly to Mr. Gatesbox at Gatesbox@LivermoreClusterTech.com.

Best,
Steve Ballfive

引用と転送の表現⑤　転送であることを明記する

　メールを第三者に転送する際には、転送の目的や何のための転送かを明記するのが基本だ。単に参考情報として送る場合であっても、何の断りもなく転送メールを送信することは慎もう。

EXAMPLE

I got the following reply from Richard. Is it possible for you to talk to him and have the router repaired sooner? Hopefully, by the end of this week. I hate to bother you with this, but I really felt I should write...

リチャードから、下記の返事があった。ルーターの故障をもう少し早く直してもらえるように、君から話してもらえないだろうか。希望としては、今週中。この件で君を煩わせたくないのだが、連絡せねばならない、と思ったので…

VARIATIONS

I got this email from PCfront, which **I am forwarding to you for your information**. It looks like they are out of LMPC50025.

PCfront社から以下のようなメールがきました。**ご参考までに転送します**。どうやらLMPC50025は品切れのようです。

COLUMN　フェースマークの意味を知る

　書き手の感情を伝える補助手段として、フェースマークが親しい間柄では使われている。ビジネスの用件を伝えるメールでフェースマークを使う必要はほとんどないだろうが、欧米人からの文面に使われていることもあるので、ニュアンスは理解しておこう。

フェースマーク（smiley）の例とそのニュアンス

　:-) ＝（ニコリ）　　　;-) ＝（ウィンク）
　:-(＝（不満、怒り）　:-o ＝（驚き）
　;-(＝（シクシク）　　:-< ＝（いらだち）
　:-O ＝（大声）　　　　:-P ＝（ベー）

引用と転送の表現⑥ 元の発信者に転送した旨を通知する

社外から来たメールの用件が自分の担当ではないため、社内のしかるべき担当者に転送して処理してもらうことがある。しかし、直接知らない人から問い合わせが入ったりすると、元の発信者はびっくりしてしまう。転送した旨をひと言断っておくべきだろう。担当者に転送する際、CCで元の発信者に同じ文面を送るやり方もある。

EXAMPLE

Dear Mr. Alan Foster,

I received the following email from you but it is Mr. Akira Fujita who is in charge of the System Development Contract 123A in this System Development Group. I took the liberty of forwarding your email of July 27 to him. Is that OK with you?

Best,

Ken Kirishima
System Development Group

At 3:59 PM +0900 03.7.24, FOSTER, Alan wrote:
> Dear Mr. Ken Kirishima,
>
> We would like to request your assistance in producing official report on System
> Development Contract 123A. We should be glad if you would provide us with the
> first draft by not later than Monday 18 August 2003.
> Your cooperation in producing the official report will be very much appreciated.
>
> Sincerely yours,
> Alan Foster (System Sales Division)

アラン・フォスター様、あなたからのメールを受け取りましたが、当システム開発グループ内でシステム開発契約123Aを担当しているのは藤田彰氏ですので、私の裁量で、あなたの7月24日付けのメールを彼に転送いたしましたが、よろしかったでしょうか。
システム開発グループ　桐島健
（引用文の和訳は省略）

メールの作法① 初めてメールを送るときの自己紹介

社外の人に初めてメールを送る場合は、自分がどういう人間で、メールアドレスをどうして知ったかを伝えておこう。いきなり用件を切り出されても、相手は戸惑ってしまう。

EXAMPLE

My name is Takeshi Kitamura. Currently I am working for DigiPoly Co. as an assistant director of the system sales division and I am mainly responsible for generating system development sales. I am writing this email because I was introduced to you by our regional manager in our San Jose office.

北村武と申します。DigiPoly社のシステムセールス部門のアシスタントディレクターで、システム開発セールスの営業を担当しております。弊社サンノゼ・オフィスの地区担当マネジャーの紹介で、このメールを書いております。

VARIATIONS

Hi, I'm Shigeaki. **I got your email address from** John Wordsworth, our chief engineer.
こんにちは、茂明と申します。**あなたのメールアドレスは、**弊社主任エンジニアのジョン・ワーズワースさん**に教えてもらいました**。

My name is Teruya Murakami; I am a system engineer at UI Communications. **I found your email address on** your web page, which I found by following a link from Raibowsoft's web site.
UI Communications社でシステムエンジニアをしております、村上照也と申します。Raibowsoft社のWebページからリンクをたどり、御社のWebページで**あなたのメールアドレスを知りました**。

メールの作法② ｜ ひと言でもよいからすぐ返信

　返事が必要なメールにはすぐ返事を出すよう心がけたい。もし事情があってすぐに正式な返事できないときは、ひと言でもよいから、「とりあえず読んだ」ということは返信メールで相手に伝えておこう。

EXAMPLE

We need at least a couple of days to package it. I am hoping that we can hand it to you by the end of this week.

パッケージ化するのに少なくとも数日必要です。今週末までにはお渡ししたいと思っております。

VARIATIONS

We need time to prepare ourselves. **Please wait for a couple of days**.
準備に時間が必要です。**2、3日、お待ちください**。

Thank you for your information. **I will get on to it right away**.
情報、ありがとうございました。**直ちに取りかかります**。

OK, in that case, I will send Mr. Brown to your office tomorrow.
では、そういうことでしたら、明日、ブラウン氏をあなたのオフィスに派遣します。

It looks like your estimate is slightly over our budget. **We will contact you when we are ready** to award our contract.
貴社の見積もりは、我々の予算を若干オーバーしています。契約発注の**準備が整ったら連絡します**。

Great! Looks like you have finally managed to fix the bug for good.
素晴らしい。ついに、あのバグを完全に解決できた**ようですね**。

I am occupied right now. I will send a mail in about 30 minutes.
いま忙しいので、約30分後にメールを入れます。

About your inquiry, **you can obtain that information at** example.rainbowsoft.com.
お尋ねの件ですが、**その情報は**example.rainbowsoft.com**で入手できます**。

メールの作法③ 感情的な表現には要注意

　売り言葉に買い言葉、という言い方があるが、一時の感情にとらわれて相手を攻撃するメールを送っても、いいことは何もない。今後の仕事がやりにくくなるだけである。また、英語を母国語としない人は、舌足らずなために感情的表現だと相手に誤解されることもあるので、注意したい。

発端のメール（部分）

Why can't we stick to the April 5 deadline plan? I would like to know in detail how they have reached this conclusion.

4月5日締め切りプランがどうしてダメなのでしょうか？ どのようしてこの結論に至ったかを詳しく知りたい、と思います。

冷静さを欠いた返信は送らない！

I understand that **you are still sticking to** the April 5 deadline plan, **which made me laugh.** If you cannot make a compromise under any circumstances, **you had better get out of the project. Your thoughts?**

あなたが4月5日締め切りプランに**依然として執着している**ことを知り、**笑ってしまった**。どうしても妥協できない場合は、**プロジェクトを抜けた方がよいかもしれない。どう？**

I understand that **you are still in support of** the April 5 deadline plan, **which I think is unrealistic.** Isn't it about time for you to come up with a compromise for them if you could, **or to give a thought to start working on a different project? Please let me know what you think.**

あなたが4月5日締め切りプランを**今でも支持している**ことを知り、**非現実的だと思いました**。もしできることならそろそろ**妥協案を提示するとか、別のプロジェクトに移動することを考えてみてはいかがでしょうか**。ご意見をお聞かせください。

4

第4章
定型的な業務連絡

送る・受け取る	≫ P.62 - P.68
通知する	≫ P.69 - P.71
オフィス関係	≫ P.72 - P.74
不在の通知	≫ P.75 - P.77
会議・イベント	≫ P.78 - P.86
社内掲示板	≫ P.87 - P.92

送る・受け取る① 資料や物品を送る

各種の資料や物品を送る機会は、日常的な業務で数多くあるだろう。状況はさまざまなので、いろいろな表現を使い分けよう。

EXAMPLE

This is Mika Suzuki of NasaSoft. I am pleased to inform you that all the programs that we created for the automatic transaction Web system have been tested and no serious problem has been detected. A copy of our test report is attached to this email for your information. If you have any questions regarding this matter, please do not hesitate to contact me at Mika@NasaSoft.com.

NasaSoft社の鈴木美加です。自動決済Webシステム向けに弊社が作成しました全プログラムをテストしましたところ、これといった問題は発見されませんでした。ご参考までに、本テスト報告書のコピーを本メールに添付いたします。この件についてご質問がある場合は、私（Mika@NasaSoft.com）まで、どうぞご遠慮なくご連絡ください。

VARIATIONS

We will ship the CD you requested by email yesterday **today**.
お客さまが昨日メールでリクエストされましたCDは、**本日発送いたします**。

About the server systems that our company is selling, **I am pleased to send you by email** the information you requested.
当社が販売しているサーバーシステムについてですが、ご請求の資料を**メールでお送りいたします**。

In response to your inquiry about the damaged parts you received, **we will immediately reship** the goods at our cost.
損傷部品に関してのお問い合わせですが、当社の負担にて、**直ちに**お客さま宛てに**再発送いたします**。

We are pleased to email you our price list as you requested in your email of March 15.
お客さまが3月15日にメールでご請求されました価格表を**メールでお送りいたします**。

送る・受け取る② ｜ 送付物の内容を伝える

VARIATIONS

I am pleased to send you **a list of samples** as you requested two days ago.
2日前にご請求の**サンプル一覧**をお送りいたします。

I am sending you the five **itineraries** as attached files for your approval.
ご承認いただくために、**出張計画書**5通を添付ファイルでお送りします。

In response to your inquiry about our products, I am pleased to send you **a PDF file of our catalogue** in a separate email.
当社製品に関するお問い合わせの件ですが、**カタログのPDFファイル**を別メールにてお送りいたします。

I am sending my **order** tomorrow. Please acknowledge receipt of it.
明日、**注文書**をお送りいたしますので、受け取りのご確認をお願いいたします。

I am sending you **a set of debug information**. Please compile your program with the debug instructions.
デバッグ情報を送ります。あなたのプログラムをデバッグライン付きでコンパイルしてみてください。

I am attaching for your reference a copy of Mr. Wilson Tayler's email of February 10, 2018, **which should be self-explanatory**.
ご参考までに、ウィルソン・テイラー氏の2018年2月10日付けのメールを添付します。**内容はご覧の通りです**。

I am enclosing **a copy of the quotation from** BullSoft for your retention.
BullSoft社**からの見積もりのコピー**を、あなたの保管用として同封します。

送る・受け取る③ ┃ 送付先を確認する

EXAMPLE

I need to send the draft minutes of our project meeting of September 11 to Bill Kennedy of BitPower Co. If you know his email address, please let me know as soon as possible.

BitPower社のビル・ケネディー氏宛てに、9月11日に開催されたプロジェクト会議の議事録原稿を送る必要があります。彼のメールアドレスをご存じでしたら、できるかぎり早くお知らせください。

VARIATIONS

Thank you for your order for a SmartPro Web service server. As we have it in our stock, we can ship it within this week. **Please indicate your shipping address and phone number by return mail.**

今回はSmartPro Web service serverのご注文ありがとうございました。在庫はございますので、今週中に発送できます。**送付先の住所と電話番号を返信でお知らせください。**

On receipt of this email, **will you please send** your attendance notice for our technical seminar **to the following address** at your earliest convenience**?**

このメールがお手元に届き次第、技術セミナーへの出欠通知を**下記アドレスまで**、都合の良い時にできるだけ早く**送っていただけますか**。

Any project manager who has additional subjects which should be included in next week's brainstorm meeting agenda, **please email them to** Mr. Kawakami at kawakami@SyncCom.co.jp.

来週のブレインストーム会議の議題に追加する問題をお持ちのプロジェクトマネジャーは、できるだけ早く、川上さん（kawakami@SyncCom.co.jp）**までメールしてください**。

Mr. Hasegawa, if you are going to visit our Menlo Park office next month, **please send** your travel itineraries and fare quotations **to this office** at expenses@PlazaSoft.com.

長谷川さん、もし来月、弊社のメンローパーク・オフィスに出張するのであれば、旅程と運賃の見積もりを**当部署**（expenses@PlazaSoft.com）**まで送ってください**。

Those of you who want to get your travel expenses reimbursed **need to send** your account form **to me** (moneyman@ABC123.com). FYI; all claims must be substantiated by receipts.

出張費用の払い戻しを希望する方は、精算伝票を**私**（moneyman@ABC123.com）**までお送りください**。なお、請求できるのは、レシートのあるものだけです。

送る・受け取る④ 送付の目的を述べる

VARIATIONS

The attached file is **for your approval**.
添付したファイルは、**貴社のご承認をいただくため**のものです。

I am sending our Web site address **for your guidance**.
ご案内までに、弊社のWebアドレスをお送りします。

I am attaching our project report **for your information**.
我々のプロジェクト報告書を**ご参考までに**添付いたします。

Regarding the bug report you compiled on July 25, I would be glad if you could provide us with a further copy **for our records**.
貴社が作成した7月25日付けのバグレポートですが、**当方の記録用として、**もう1部コピーをお送りいただければ幸いです。

With reference to your email of November 17, I am going to send a program from now, which is **for your retention**.
あなたの11月17日付けのメールに関してですが、これからお送りするのは**保管用の**プログラムです。

I am emailing this spreadsheet **for your attention**.
あなたのご配慮をいただくために、このスプレッドシートをメールしています。

The reason why we send this information to you is **because we want you to give us some comments**.
この情報をお送りしているのは、**コメントをいただきたいから**です。

I am forwarding this email **for your consideration**.
ご考慮いただくために、このメールを転送しております。

This email is forwarded to you **for your reference**.
本メールをあなたに転送するのは、**ご参考までに参照していただくため**です。

送る・受け取る⑤ | 受け取り確認

相手に何か送ってもらったときは、お礼も兼ねて受け取り確認のメールを出すようにしたい。

EXAMPLE

Thank you very much for your email of July 23. We are really interested in your proposal. I will have my staff review it carefully before I get back to you.

7月23日付けのメール、ありがとうございました。あなたの提案には非常に興味があります。当方のスタッフに内容を慎重に検討させた上で、後日またご連絡いたします。

VARIATIONS

Today, I received the CD-ROM whose shipment I requested on the phone the other day. Thank you for taking care of it right away.

先日電話で発送をお願いしたCD-ROMが**本日、私の元に届きました**。早急にご手配いただきありがとうございます。

Your email which I received yesterday **will help me a lot** because it explains what Manager Smith wants us to do.

昨日、私が受け取ったあなたからのメール、マネジャーのスミス氏が我々に何をさせたいのか説明されているので、**非常に有用です**。

Now that I received your email, I would like to confirm that you plan to stay in Sunnyvale for 3 days. Is this correct?

あなたからのメールを受け取りましたのでお尋ねしたいのですが、サニーベールには3日間、滞在のご予定ですよね？

FYI, **I want to inform you that I have received an email from** Mr. Taro Johnston of NodePeer this morning.

ご参考までに、NodePeer社のタロー・ジョンストン氏からの**メールを今朝受け取りましたので、お知らせいたします**。

I received an email from CoolClik **which confirms that** they can offer us discount prices if we place our order in bulk.

まとめて購入する場合には割引する**との確認メールを**CoolClik社から**受け取りました**。

送る・受け取る⑥ 後日／別便で送る

EXAMPLE

About further details with regard to the system specifications of your new data mining program, I will send you what I have on my hard disk today and will send you the rest in about a week separately.

貴社の新データマイニングプログラムの仕様に関する詳細ですが、今日は私のハードディスク上にある情報を送り、残りについては、1週間ほどのうちに別便で送ります。

VARIATIONS

If you can tell me which program isn't working properly, **I can send you** a new copy of it **at a later date**.
どのプログラムが異常動作しているか教えていただければ、新しいコピーを**後日送ることが できます**。

Please let us know what is happening with your intranet system so that **we can send you** a copy of the collapsed file **at a later time**.
御社のイントラネットで現在何が起こっているかご連絡いただければ、つぶれてしまったファイルのコピーを**後で送ることができます**。

In regard to the project meeting called by Director Yamada, **I will send** the topics **in a separate email** for your consideration.
山田部長が召集したプロジェクト会議ですが、そこで取り上げる項目内容を**別便にて送りますので**、ご検討ください。

I now send you a list of prices and discounts only and a list of shipping and handling costs **will follow**.
今は価格および割引一覧だけとし、発送手数料一覧は**追って送ります**。

I am attaching a technical file and **will send** a sales spreadsheet file **in a separate email tomorrow**.
技術ファイルをこのメールに添付し、営業のスプレッドシートファイルは**明日、別便にて送ります**。

Now that I received a copy of the program that Walter Rosenberg wrote, **I can send** its copy to our Cupertino office **next week**.
ウォルター・ローゼンバーグの書いたプログラムのコピーを受け取りましたので、**来週**、そのコピーを弊社のクパチーノ・オフィスに**送ることができます**。

送る・受け取る⑦ ｜ 情報／資料を提供できない

相手が求めてきた情報や資料が手元にないとき、あるいは何かの理由で提供できないときには、やんわりと断るようにしたい。

EXAMPLE

Regarding how the Database_Connection module is coded, since we are having it developed by LinkPack in San Jose, I am afraid that we don't have the information you requested. If you wish, you can get in touch with them directly. Their email address is info@LinkPack.com.

Database_Connectionモジュールのコーディングについてですが、LinkPacks社にサンノゼで開発させているので、残念ですがお求めの資料は当方にはございません。よろしければ、LinkPack社に直接お問い合わせください。メールアドレスは、info@LinkPack.com です。

VARIATIONS

I regret to say that I am unable to email you the information about the device driver we are developing in Saratoga.

当社がサラトガで開発中のデバイスドライバーに関する資料は、**申し訳ございませんが、そちらにメールできません**。

I am not sure whether the Date_Conversion module is doing memory allocation by itself.

Date_Conversionモジュールがメモリを割り当てているかは、**私ではわかりかねます**。

I am as confused as you are about the specification changes of the Date_Modification module.

Date_Modificationモジュールの仕様変更は、**私にもさっぱりわかりません**。

I wish I could help you, but I don't know anything about what the Export module development group is doing.

お役に立ちたいのはやまやまなのですが、Exportモジュールの開発グループが何を行っているかについては、私は何も知りません。

I am sorry, but I can't tell you anything about the Host_Connection module's test results.

申し訳ございませんが、Host_Connectionモジュールの開発テストの結果は**お知らせできません**。

通知する① 報告する／伝える

状況を正しく伝えることは、業務連絡の基本である。メールの同報性や即時性を活かし、必要な情報を関係者に迅速に周知する。

EXAMPLE

I am sorry that it took a littler longer than we expected to make the new Web service work. However, I am happy to report to you that the new system is up and running without a hitch today.

新規Webサービスを稼動させるのに、予定より少し時間がかかり、申し訳ありませんでした。しかしながら、本日、システムが立ち上がり、滞りなく動作していることを報告でき、うれしく思います。

VARIATIONS

I regret to report to you that the condition of the in-house Web system has not improved.
残念ですが、社内Webシステムの状態はまだもとのままです。

I'm pleased to inform you that if more than 10 people are going to participate in the New York Conference, you may get a substantial discount on the admission fee.
10人以上がニューヨークのカンファレンスに参加なされるのであれば、入場料を大幅に値引きしてもらえると思いますので、**ご連絡いたします**。

I am pleased to inform you that the new Web service is running fine.
新しいWebサービスが正しく動作している**ことをお知らせできるのをうれしく思います**。

I am sorry to inform you that the new Web service just crashed.
残念ですが、新しいWebサービスがクラッシュした**ことをご連絡いたします**。

This is to inform you that Mr. Henry Waldon, the chief engineer, has gone back to the San Jose headquarters.
技術主任ヘンリー・ウォルドンがサンノゼ本社に戻った**ことをお知らせします**。

I would like to inform you of our refund policy on defective products.
欠陥プロダクトに関して、弊社の払い戻し基準**をご連絡いたします**。

通知する② 各種お知らせの表現

EXAMPLE

To Whom It May Concern,

We are pleased to inform you that we will be offering an introductory programming course next month. This course is designed for employees who are approximately in their 30's and preferably have their own PC at home.

関係各位、

来月、プログラミング入門コースを開催することになりました。このコースは、30代の社員の方で自宅にパソコンを所有している方を対象としております。

VARIATIONS

I would like to announce the opening of a new online store at our Web site.

弊社のWebサイトに、オンラインストアが新規**オープンしたことをお知らせします**。

I am pleased to announce that Mr. Brett Grant has been promoted to chief engineer of the Menlo Park office.

ブレット・グラントさんがメンローパーク・オフィスの技術主任に昇進された**ことを発表できるのをうれしく思います**。

This is to announce that the following changes in travel expenses will go into effect at all offices on May 30, 2018.

出張旅費に関して、2018年5月30日より、以下の変更がすべてのオフィスで有効になります**のでお知らせします**。

Please make note of the following changes in reimbursement procedures, effective Monday next week.

払い戻し手続きが来週月曜日から下記のように変更になりますので、**ご注意ください**。

In line with our new policy of streamlining operations, we are letting 3 programers go.

可能なかぎり業務を簡素化するという当社の新しい方針**に沿って**、プログラマーが3人整理されました。

In accordance with the decisions reached at the project meeting last week, **the following changes will be implemented.**

先週のプロジェクト会議の決定に従って、**以下の変更が実施されます**。

通知する③ 知らせてもらう

業務連絡などで、「～について知らせてください」と相手に依頼する際の表現を挙げる。

EXAMPLE

About the system that we have been developing for BullSoft, please inform us if you have tested the automatic transaction program that SpeedStream created. If you haven't, I will have Frank White do it.

BullSoft社向けに当社が開発しているシステムですが、SpeedStream社が作成した自動決済プログラムをあなたがテストしたかどうかお知らせください。もしまだの場合は、フランク・ホワイトにやらせます。

VARIATIONS

Please inform us of your intention of holding the project meeting tomorrow.
明日プロジェクト会議を開催する意図**をお知らせください**。

About the next meeting, **please advise me directly of** suitable dates for you.
次回会議ですが、あなたの都合のよい日を**私に直接知らせてください**。

Will you let me know your comments on my system design **soonest?**
私のシステム設計に関して、あなたのコメントを**すぐに知らせてもらえますか**。

John, **I want you to ensure that** the contents of this email **are brought to the attention of** your project members as soon as possible.
ジョン、このメールの内容をできるだけ早く、君のプロジェクトメンバー全員に**必ず知らせてほしい**。

Please send an email to your people **and explain** what I want them to do immediately so that they will carry out my instructions correctly.
君の部下に**メールを送り**、私が彼らに直ちにやってもらいたいと思っていること**を説明し**、彼らが私の指示を間違いなく実行できるようにしてほしい。

About the schedule delay of your development project, **will you please keep us informed of** what takes place?
あなたの開発プロジェクトの遅れですが、事態を**引き続き知らせてもらえますか**。

About Contract 123A, **will you let us know** RainbowSoft's requirements **as soon as possible?**
契約123Aについてですが、RainbowSoft社の要求を**できるだけ早く連絡いただけますか**。

オフィス関係① 開設や移転を知らせる

オフィスの開設・移転等の連絡の際は、同報で送れるメールが威力を発揮する。

EXAMPLE

I am pleased to inform you that the staff at the Mountain View will be moving to new accommodation on April 12, 2018.

Address: 6855 Sunset Road, San Jose, CA, 95024
Telephone: (408) 980-3232
Fax: (408) 980-3210

Attached is a vicinity map of the Sunset Road area for your reference.

マウンテンビュー・オフィスは、2018年4月12日移転予定です。新オフィスの所在地、電話番号、Fax番号は次の通りです。

住所：6855 Sunset Road, San Jose, CA, 95024
電話番号：(408) 980-3232
Fax番号：(408) 980-3210

ご参考までに、サンセットロード地区の近隣地図を添付します。

VARIATIONS

I would like to advise you that as from 7 o'clock (0700 hours) of Monday, July 22, 2018, the telephone number of the FestaSeven's Tokyo office **will change** from 81-3-5804-1234 to 81-3-7654-3210.
2018年7月22日（月）7時より、FestaSeven社東京オフィスの電話番号が、81-3-5804-1234から81-3-7654-3210に**変更されることをお知らせします**。

Please note that my email address **has been changed to** J_Nagano@SyncCom.com.
私のメールアドレスがJ_Nagano@SyncCom.com に**変更になりました**。

I am pleased to inform you that our California office **has been opened in** Santa Clara.
弊社のカリフォルニア・オフィスがサンタクララに**開設されました**。

Although our office has been moved to a new location, **all the communication details other than** the postal address **remain unchanged.**
弊社のオフィスは移転いたしましたが、住所**以外、連絡先の詳細は変更ありません**。

オフィス関係② ┃ 住所・連絡先の変更

連絡先変更で多いのが、会社や所属が変わったためのメールアドレス変更の通知。この項は個人の連絡先変更の文面である。

EXAMPLE

I will quit EdgePeople as of October 20 and will start working for CoolClick from November. My new email address will be Akiyama@CoolClick.com. I would appreciate it if you would substitute this for the one in your address book. Incidentally, the other contact information is as follows:

1234 Brokaw Road,
Santa Clara, CA 95052
(408) 989-8765

Thank you for your attention.

10月20日をもってEdgePeople社を退社し、11月からCoolClick社で働くことになりました。私のメールアドレスはAkiyama@CoolClick.comに変更になります。アドレス帳の修正をお願いします。ついでながら、その他の連絡先は以下のように変わります。

1234 Brokaw Road,
Santa Clara, CA 95052
(408) 989-8765

よろしくお願いします。

オフィス関係③ 住所・連絡先の変更（応用）

VARIATIONS

Now that I have a new email address (Hashimoto@DynaGrid.com), **I would appreciate it if you would update your address book information.**

Hashimoto@DynaGrid.com が私の新しいメールアドレスですので、**アドレス帳の更新をよろしくお願いいたします。**

Although I am receiving email at my new and old addresses right now, **the old address will no longer be active as of** July 19, 2018.

現在、新旧の両アドレスでメールを受信していますが、**旧アドレスは2018年7月19日をもって使用中止になります。**

Please send your email to my new email address from now on, which is Satoshi@AquosTech.com. I will stop using the old address after July 25, 2018.

今後、メールは新しいアドレスである Satoshi@AquosTech.com **にお送りください。**2018年7月25日以降、旧アドレスは使用を中止いたします。

Please be reminded that **the old email address of mine is no longer in use.**

私の旧アドレスはもう使われていませんのでご注意ください。

I was transferred from the development division **to the sales division** as of June 1. Although **my email address has not changed**, my new phone number is (408) 989-1234.

6月1日付けで、開発部から**営業部に異動になりました。メールアドレスは変わりませんが、**新しい電話番号は（408）989-1234です。

不在の通知① ｜ 出張の連絡

出張で不在する旨の通知。社内宛ての通知のほか、進行中の案件を共有する社外の相手に、「不在するので連絡できなくなる」と断ったり、連絡先を通知したりするケースもある。

EXAMPLE

I just want to inform you that I will be visiting the Sunnyvale office from March 10 through 15 to talk with Mr. Chris Burton, who will soon succeed Ms. Pamela Hedding as senior engineer in charge of the Java application development group. During this period, you can reach me at (phone): (408) 555-1234 and (email): Sugiyama@opensource.PhoneComm.com.

このたびパメラ・ヘディング氏を引き継いでJava開発グループの上級エンジニアになるクリス・バートン氏との打ち合わせのため、3月10日から15日までサニーベール・オフィスに出張します。ご用の節は、電話（408）555-1234、メールSugiyama@opensource.PhoneComm.comにご連絡ください。

VARIATIONS

Manager Yamada **is out of town on a business trip right now**. He **is expected to return** after August 25. Incidentally, his itinerary is as follows:

山田部長は**現在出張中**で、8月25日過ぎには**出社の見込みです**。なお、日程は以下の通りです。

Bryan White will be visiting Richmond, CA from today on a five day business trip and **is not expected to be back for some time**. I will pass your suggestions to him as soon as he returns to the office.

ブライアン・ホワイトは今日から5日間、カリフォルニアのリッチモンドに出張しており、**しばらく出社しません**。本人が戻り次第、ご提案の件を申し伝えます。

My itinerary is as follows: 3/10-15 at the LA office, 3/16-17 at the San Mateo office, 3/20-23 at the Redmond office.

私の出張日程は以下の通り。3/10-15 LAオフィス、3/16-17 サンマテオ・オフィス、3/20-23 レドモンド・オフィス。

I just wanted to let you know that from December 10 through January 10, 2019, I will be out of my Tokyo office on an extended business trip. However, **I can be reached by email anytime**.

12月10日から2019年1月10日まで、私は長期出張で東京オフィスを不在にします。しかし、**メールでの連絡はいつでも可能です**。

不在の通知② ｜ オフィスの休業の通知

　クリスマス休暇や年末年始、夏休みなど、オフィス休業に関する連絡を通知する文面。日本企業は夏休みなど全社一斉休業が多いので、使う機会が多いだろう。

EXAMPLE

Palo Alto office will be closed during the Christmas holiday period. The dates of closure are Dec. 25 - Jan. 1, 2019. The office will reopen Jan. 2, 2019. Standby staff will be available during this period to deal with your urgent needs. You may call (408) 532-2551 and speak to a representative to request our assistance.

パロアルト・オフィスは冬期休暇で、2018年12月25日から2019年1月1日まで閉鎖し、1月2日から再開します。この間、緊急要件を処理するためのスタッフが待機いたします。ご用件のございます方は、（408）532-2551までご連絡ください。

VARIATIONS

Over this period, please use our **24-hour Emergency Services**; the phone number is 81-3-5432-9876.
この間、**24時間緊急サービス**をご利用ください。電話番号は81-3-5432-9876です。

About **the standby staff for the annual summer holidays**, it has been agreed that they will be nominated by managers at their discretion.
夏期休暇中の待機スタッフについてですが、各部長が随意に指名することに合意されました。

If you are placed on standby roster **during the company wide holiday period**, you may take an alternative day off by arrangement with your immediate superior.
全社休暇の間、緊急スタッフになった方は、直属の上司の手配で代休を取れます。

Our Los Gatos office **will be closed** from 18 December of 2018 to 13 April 2019 **for remodeling.**
弊社のロスガトス・オフィスは、2018年12月18日から2019年4月13日まで、**社屋改装のため閉鎖されます。**

While our office **is closed throughout March**, the office will be manned to attend to urgent messages.
弊社オフィスは3月いっぱい**閉鎖されます**が、その間、緊急通信に対処するためオフィスに社員を配置いたします。

不在の通知③ 休暇の連絡

前項の「オフィスの休業の通知」が会社としての通知なのに対し、この項は個人から送る休暇の連絡の文面の例である。

EXAMPLE

During the company wide summer holidays from Tuesday, July 22 to Friday, July 25, I will be on leave for vacation and will not be reading my email. As I don't want my mailbox to overflow, I would appreciate it very much if you refrain from sending email to me as much as possible.

全社夏休みの7月22日（火）から7月25日（金）まで休暇を取り、メールを読みません。その間、メールボックスをあふれさせたくないので、できるかぎり私宛てにメールは送らないでください。よろしくお願いします。

VARIATIONS

This year every member of my project team **will be away from the office on vacation** from Aug. 12 to Aug. 20.

今年、私のプロジェクトチームでは、8月12日から20日までメンバー全員が**休暇を取り、オフィスを留守にします**。

I **will be away for vacation** for 1 week starting the day after tomorrow.

私は明後日から**休暇で**1週間**留守にします**。

Next week I will be going away for the holidays. **My contact information is as follows:**

来週、私は休暇で留守にしますが、**連絡先は以下の通りです**。

While I am away, Tadashi Aomori **is responsible for handling my correspondence.** His email address is Aomori@SilcotSoft.com.

私の不在中は、青森忠が**各種連絡を担当することになっております**。彼のメールアドレスはAomori@SilcotSoft.com です。

If you will be away from September 12 to 18 for vacation, please let me know **your leave contact address and phone number** today.

もし9月12日から18日まで休暇で留守にするのであれば、**休暇中の連絡先の住所と電話番号**を私宛てに今日送ってください。

I will be away from the office next Saturday to attend a Linux user party.

来週の土曜日、私はLinuxユーザーパーティーに出席するため、**オフィスを留守にします**。

会議・イベント① ▎ 開催を通知する

会議やパーティー、製品発表その他のイベントの開催通知の文面を挙げる。

EXAMPLE

We are happy to invite you to the product show that GiantSoft (San Jose, California) will be offering at the Tokyo Big Site on April 22, 2018. The show timetable is as follows:

SHOW TIMETABLE
1.00 p.m. Show opens to guests and special ticket holders.
2.00 p.m. Opening speech (Steve Ballfive, GiantSoft)
2.15 p.m. Guest speech (Mr. Bill Gatesbox, Livermore Cluster Tech Co.)
2.45 p.m. Presentation of new products
3.15 p.m. Q&A
4.00 p.m. Closing speech (Hideki Matsui, GiantSoft)
6:00 p.m. Banquet

We would like to express great appreciation for your support which has made this show possible.

VARIATIONS

You are invited to attend a project meeting **which is going to be held on** Monday, June 9, from 2:00 p.m. to 4:00 p.m.
6月9日（月）午後2時から午後4時まで、プロジェクト会議を**開催いたしますので、あなたもご参加ください**。

We **would like to invite you to present** your development project plan at the director's meeting on Tuesday, July 15, from 7:00 p.m.
7月15日（火）午後7時から開催される部長会に**出席され**、あなたの開発プロジェクト計画の**プレゼンをしていただきたい、と思います**。

You are cordially invited to attend the 10th birthday party of the open source Hello World project in Sunnyvale, California.
カリフォルニア州サニーベールで開催される、オープンソースHello Worldプロジェクト誕生10周年記念パーティー**へのご出席を心よりお待ち申し上げます**。

As the Web service development project group is planning a New Year's party at the home of Mr. Calvin Alman on Friday, Jan 10, from 8:00 p.m., **your team are cordially invited to attend.**
Webサービス開発プロジェクトグループは、1月10日（金）午後8時より、カルビン・アルマン氏宅で新年パーティーを開催いたしますので、**あなたのチームもぜひお越しください**。

会議・イベント② | 出欠を確認する

「出欠をご確認ください」と直接尋ねる表現の他に、「招待状は届いていますか」と間接的に聞く方法もある。

EXAMPLE

When you receive this email, please confirm at your early convenience that you will be able to attend the next project meeting.

このメールがお手元に届きましたら、次回プロジェクト会議への出席を、ご都合のつき次第、ご確認ください。

VARIATIONS

Did you receive my email of March 17 **in which I attached our invitation** to PeerOneCOM's product show?

当方から3月17日にお送りしました、PeerOneCOM社製品発表会への**招待状を添付したメールは届きましたでしょうか**。

Having received no reply to my email of September 11, **I would appreciate it if you confirm your attendance at** the next senior programmer's meeting **with** Ms. Manami Tamori of SyncCom. FYI, her email address is MTamori@SyncCom.com.

9月11日付けのメールに対する返事がありませんので、次回の上級プログラマー会議への**出席の確認を、**SyncCom社の田森真奈美さん**までお願いします**。ちなみに、彼女のアドレスはMTamori@SyncCom.com です。

Would you let us know if the invitation to our business show **reached you**, as it seems that my latest email failed to do so?

前回お送りしたメールがそちらに届かなかったようです。弊社ビジネスショーへの**ご招待券がお手元に届いていましたら、その旨、ご連絡いただけますでしょうか**。

The next project manager's meeting is tentatively scheduled to be on Wed., May 10. As soon as your work schedule allows, **would you please confirm your attendance?**

次のプロジェクトマネジャー会議は今のところ、5月10日（水）に予定されています。仕事の予定がつき次第、**出欠をご確認いただけますか**。

会議・イベント③ 招待を受諾する／断る

招待を受けて出席するときは「喜んで」「必ず」など、進んで参加する意思を伝える。出席できないときは波風が立たないよう丁重に断ろう。

EXAMPLE

Thank you for your invitation to your 5th anniversary party of the Web service development division on Tuesday, August 12. I will definitely attend with my superior.

8月12日（火）、Webサービス開発部門創設5周年記念パーティーへのご招待、ありがとうございます。私の上司ともども、必ず出席させていただきます。

VARIATIONS

We are delighted to accept your invitation to the 10th anniversary party of your company which will be held on Monday, September 10 at the top floor conference room of InfoBank4U Co.

9月10日（月）に（株）InfoBank4U社最上階カンファレンスルームで開催される、御社創立10周年記念パーティーへの**ご招待を喜んでお受けいたします**。

I regret to inform you that I won't be able to make it to the development meeting on Wednesday, April 28, from 3:00.

残念ですが、4月28日（水）午後3時からの開発会議**には出席できません**。

Thank you for your invitation to the "panel discussion on the open source movement" on Wednesday, June 25, from 6:30 p.m. to 9:00 p.m., but **I am afraid I must decline as I have a previous engagement that evening.**

6月25日（水）午後6時30分から午後9時の「オープンソース運動に関する討論会」へご招待いただきありがとうございます。**残念ですが、先約がございますので出席できません**。

Unfortunately, **I will not be able to attend** the project meeting at SouthenNet2Go Co. on June 26, **as I will be visiting** the Seattle office **on business.**

残念ですが、6月26日には**商用**でシアトル・オフィス**に出張しております**ので、（株）SouthenNet2Goでのプロジェクト会議**には出席できません**。

会議・イベント④ 要人の訪問を通知する

高い役職の人が海外に出張したり、逆に来日したりするとき、手配がいろいろ必要となる。

EXAMPLE

General Manager Makoto Takayama will visit Sunnyvale at the time of the December management meeting. His itinerary looks something like this:

12/12-15: San Francisco, 12/16-18: Sunnyvale.

Please arrange accommodation for him from 12th to 16th December at the Castle Rock Hotel.

高山誠部長が12月の経営会議に出席するためにサニーベールに出張いたします。日程は次のようになっています。

12/12〜15：サンフランシスコ、12/16〜18：サニーベール。

12月12日から16日まで、キャッスルロックホテルに宿を手配してください。

VARIATIONS

Mr. Jason Redwood of LuxTech **will be visiting** our Kansai office from June 15-20.
LuxTech社のジェイソン・レッドウッド氏が、6月15日から20日まで関西オフィスを**訪れます**。

Will you please have someone come to the airport **to pick up** Manager Mamoru Akita at 2:00 p.m., August 12?
秋田守部長の**出迎え**を8月12日午後2時に、空港に**寄越してください**。

Chief Engineer Hideki Harada **will visit** Redwood City on November 11 **and stay there for three days** to present his new UML design concept at the UML conference.
原田英樹技術主任は、次回のUMLカンファレンスに出席し、新UML設計概念のプレゼンテーションをするために11月11日にレッドウッドシティを**訪問し、当地に3日間滞在します**。

As **I am attaching** the director's **detailed proposed itinerary**, please proceed with these arrangements.
所長の**詳細旅程を添付**いたしますので、これで手配を進めてください。

President Hideki Seki's visit to your office **has now been postponed** from April 13 to May 16.
関秀樹社長の貴社訪問は、4月13日から5月16日に**延期されました**。

会議・イベント⑤ 議題を通知する

会議の議題は、事前に参加者に周知しておこう。何が目的か、何を決定するのかを簡潔に伝えて、効率的で生産的な会議を開きたい。

EXAMPLE

The next project group meeting will be held at our Saratoga office on May 11 commencing at 1:30 p.m. The proposed agenda is as follows:

Agenda:
a) Manning requirements to September 2018
b) Expenditure to September 2018
c) A farewell party for Mr. Taguchi

It would be appreciated if you would confirm at your early convenience whether you will be able to attend this meeting.

次のプロジェクトグループ会議は5月11日午後1時30分からサラトガ・オフィスで開催いたします。議題は下記のようになっております。

議題、a) 2018年9月までの必要人員／b) 2018年9月までの支出／c) 田口氏の送別会

この会議へのご出席を、ご都合の付き次第ご確認いただければ幸いです。

VARIATIONS

The main purpose of this programmer's meeting **is to review** the position regarding job assignment **and to talk about** the needed addition.
今回のプログラマー会議の**主目的は**、仕事の割り当てについての現状を**再検討し、必要な増員について話すことです**。

The main agenda of the June 24 meeting is how to streamline operations.
6月24日の会議の**主たる議題は**、いかにすれば業務を簡素化できるかです。

I am attaching the draft agenda of the subject meeting.
subject欄に記載されている会議の**議題原案を添付いたします**。

We will discuss the following subjects.
取り上げる議題は次の通りです。

会議・イベント⑥ 議事録を作成する

　会議で何を討議し、何を決定し、何が積み残しか、記録を残して情報を共有するために、議事録を作成することは重要である。箇条書きを使うなどして簡潔に整理する。

EXAMPLE

MINUTES of the Web System Project Group Meeting held on Thursday, January 16 (2018), 16.00 - 19.00 hrs

PARTICIPANTS: ——————————————————— 参加者
Members of the Web System Project Group:
J. Suzuki (Leader), E. Yamada (Sub leader), H. Gross (System Consultant), M. Taguchi (Programmer), J. Bumphead (Programmer).

AGENDA of the MEETING: ———————————————— 議題
1. Agenda of the project group meeting
2. Minutes of the Web system project group meeting held on Wednesday, December 15, 2017
3. Financial situation of the SmartPro project
4. Progress report of the GPS automatic transaction system project
5. Any further matter to be discussed

議題4が3より先に討議されることになった

1. The business meeting is chaired by J. Suzuki. The agenda is changed, point 4 will precede point 3.
2. The minutes of the Web system project group meeting held on Wednesday, December 15 are approved without discussion.
4. The progress report of the GPS automatic transaction system project was presented by E. Yamada. After a lengthy discussion, the chairman proposed and the assembly agreed that the deadline of March 12, 2004 should be extended. Information about the delay will be posted at the project group's web site.
3. The financial situation of the SmartPro project is described by H. Gross. The assembly has looked into the details of the financial report, studied the financial documents and found all material in agreement with the financial report.
5. There are no further questions or remarks.

討議した順に記述する

会議・イベント⑦ ▎議事録を送付する

　できればその日のうちに議事録を作り、記憶が薄れないうちに関係者に送付する。メールの即時性を十分活用したい。

EXAMPLE

I am attaching the minutes of the September meeting. If you note any errors or omissions, please advise me.

9月の会議の議事録を添付いたします。間違いまたは脱落にお気付きの場合は、私までお知らせください。

VARIATIONS

I am sorry to report that **completing the minutes** of the project meeting last week **will take a little longer than I thought.**
申し訳ございません。先週のプロジェクト会議の**議事録の作成には、予定より少し時間がかかりそうです。**

This is to report to you that **the minutes** of the sales manager's meeting **are now completed and attached to this email** for your consideration.
セールスマネジャー会議の**議事録が完成し**、あなたにご検討いただくため、**本メールに添付されている**ことご報告いたします。

The correctly worded minutes are now attached and I would be glad if you would substitute this for the one in your possession.
正しく直した議事録を添付いたしますので、お手元のものと差し替えていただければ幸いです。

When you are done with the meeting, **please email me the minutes within the day.**
打ち合わせが終わったら、**その日のうちに議事録を私にメールしてください。**

会議・イベント⑧ 歓迎会・懇親会を知らせる

EXAMPLE

To Whom It May Concern,

On this occasion of the visit of Mr. John Wisemore of LuxTech to Japan, a reception will be held at the Yamakane Hall, Tokyo on January 17 from 7:00 p.m. to 9:00 p.m. It is hoped that as many senior managers as possible will attend.

関係各位、

LuxTechのジョン・ワイズモア氏の日本訪問に際し、歓迎会が東京の山金ホールで1月17日午後7時から9時まで開催されます。できるだけ多くの上級職が出席することを希望します。

VARIATIONS

This is to announce that **an informal luncheon will be held** to welcome Mr. Akira Kanda of EdgePeople (San Jose, CA). Please confirm your attendance by sending an email to Ms. Yasuko Brown at Y_Brown@CoolClick.com.
EdgePeople（本社、カリフォルニア州サンノゼ）の神田彰氏をお迎えして、**略式歓迎会が開催されます**。ヤスコ・ブラウンさん（Y_Brown@CoolClick.com）にメールを送り、出席を確認してください。

In order to finalize numbers, will you please advise Ms. Patty White prior to October 31 as to your attendance?
人数を把握するため、10月31日までに、パティー・ホワイトさんまで、ご出席の通知をお願いいたします。

I am pleased to inform you that Mr. Ichiro Matsui has been promoted to vice president of marketing and **you are cordially invited to attend a banquet to commemorate the occasion.**
松井一郎氏がマーケティング担当副社長へ昇進されたことをお知らせするとともに、**記念夕食会へご招待できる**ことをうれしく思います。

To commemorate this occasion, we will **have a small party** at Redondo Beach Speedy Joe on November 25 from 7:00 p.m.
これを記念して、11月25日午後7時からレドンドビーチ・スピーディー・ジョーにて、**さやかなパーティーを開催する**ことにいたしました。

会議・イベント⑨ 宿泊を手配する

EXAMPLE

Mr. Masami Tanaka plans to visit your Sunnyvale office on December 10 to attend a business meeting and wants to stay there for three days. I would appreciate it very much if you could arrange accommodation at a hotel near SFO.

田中雅美氏がビジネス会議に出席するために12月10日にサニーベール・オフィスを訪問し、3日間当地に滞在することを希望しています。つきましては、宿の手配をサンフランシスコ空港近くにお願いいたします。

VARIATIONS

I would greatly appreciate **your assistance in arranging hotel accommodation** for me when I visit Seattle in June.

6月にシアトルに滞在する際の、**ホテルの手配のお手伝いをいただける**と助かります。

Please **arrange accommodation at a hotel located** within walking distance from your Santa Monica office.

貴社のサンタモニカ・オフィスに歩いていける距離のところ**にあるホテルに、宿の手配を**お願いします。

I would appreciate it **if you could arrange accommodation at a hotel** in the area from where I can take a train to come to see you at your office.

電車を使ってあなたをオフィスにお訪ねできる場所に**宿を取っていただける**と助かります。

Mr. Masaki Murakami, my immediate superior at BestSonic, will be attending an IT conference in Chicago from January 16 to 20. Please **arrange hotel accommodation for him in the area.**

BestSonic社における私の直属の上司である村上雅基氏が、IT会議参加のため1月16日から20日の予定でシカゴを訪ねますので、**当地での宿の手配**をお願いいたします。

社内掲示板① 共有設備について

厳密にはメールではないが、社内の電子掲示板には共有設備に関する通知などの業務連絡もたくさん掲載されるので、各種の文例を紹介しておく。

VARIATIONS

FYI, **I have placed the latest data on** the project group server.
ご参考までに、**最新のデータをプロジェクトグループのサーバーに****アップしました**。

A new printer **has been added on** our network segment.
我々のネットワークセグメント上に、新しいプリンターが**増設されました**。

The shared file server **will be shut down** from 13:00 to 16:00 tomorrow for maintenance.
明日の午後1時から4時まで、メンテナンスのためファイル共有サーバーが**停止します**。

The customer management system was down for about 3 hours but **it came back a while ago**.
顧客管理システムが3時間ほどダウンしていましたが、**先ほど復旧しました**。

The number 4 meeting room **will be closed permanently starting next month**.
第4会議室は**来月から使用できなくなります**。

A new meeting room has been added on the 4th floor in the area next to the room where the system development group is located. **Those who want to use it need to register themselves** through the Web system.
4階のシステム開発グループの部屋の横のスペースに会議室を新設しました。**使用するにはWebでの****予約が必要です**。

We have purchased a new PC projector. **Those who would like to use it** for their presentation, **please contact us by email at** IT_section5@JugglerNet.com.
PCプロジェクターを新規に1台購入しました。**ご自分のプレゼンでご使用になりたい方は、**IT_section5@JugglerNet.com **まで****メールでご連絡ください**。

社内掲示板② 社内に情報を求める

社内掲示板は、社員同士の情報交換や意見交換にもよく利用される。SNS等でも、この種の表現は使えるだろう。

EXAMPLE

My idea is to increase system development sales volume by lowering our call-out charge for an engineer. If you have any advice or suggestions regarding this, please let me know.

技術者の呼出し派遣料金を下げることによって、システム開発セールスの売り上げを伸ばしたいというのが私のアイデアです。この件に関して、ご意見およびご提案をお聞かせください。

VARIATIONS

Please let me know your comments on this.
この件に関して、**コメントをお聞かせください**。

I am currently trying to find information on grid computing. **I would very much appreciate any information you could send me** regarding where I should look to find books and Web pages about it.
現在、グリッドコンピューティングについて調べています。関係の書籍やWebページを探す場合、どこを探せばよいか**ご存じでしたら教えていただければありがたいです**。

We are interested in obtaining information concerning the latest mobile technology. **Could anyone** who has information about it **let me take a look at it?**
最新のモバイル技術に関する資料を探しています。資料をお持ちの人は**貸していただけませんか**。

Mr. John Newhall, do you know any programmer under your supervision who is familiar with MPEG++? **I would like to get his/her advice ...**
ジョン・ニューホールさん、あなたの部下でMPEG++に詳しいプログラマーをご存じありませんか。**お知恵を拝借したいのですが…**

We have the following inquiry from Mr. Bazil Tronman of SuperLinkPro. **If it rings a bell,** please contact us by email.
下記の問い合わせがSuperLinkPro社のベイジル・トロンマン氏から弊社にありました。**心当たりのある人は**メールで連絡してください。

社内掲示板③ 探し物があるとき

EXAMPLE

Everybody, if you have a printer in your section that you can let us use (we can borrow), please let me know.

皆さん、お貸しいただける（お借りできる）プリンターのある部署がありましたら、ご連絡ください。

VARIATIONS

We have a new temp staff and need a PC for her. Does anybody have a PC that is **not being used right now**?
派遣社員の方が1人増え、彼女のPCが必要です。どなたかのところに、**現在使用中でない**PCが余っていませんか。

If you have an extra monitor **that you can let us use,** please let me know.
もしディスプレイが余っていて、使わせていただけるようでしたら、ご連絡ください。

Anybody who took out the technical materials about the latest mobile technology from the main cabinet last week, **please return them immediately.**
先週、最新モバイル技術関係の資料をメインキャビネットから持ち出した人がいらっしゃいましたら、**至急返却してください。**

I am in trouble because I cannot locate the CD that I sent by in-house mail three days ago. Anybody who knows where it is (Anybody who found it), please contact me by email.
3日前、社内便で送ったCDが**行方不明で困っています**。どこにあるかご存じの人（見つけた人）は、メールでご連絡ください。

I am looking for a postal package **that is missing.** It is addressed to Director Akira Sasaki of OrchidSoft. If you happen to see it among the materials delivered to you, please let me know by email.
行方不明の郵便小包**を探しています**。OrchidSoft社の佐々木章部長宛ての小包です。もし配達物に紛れ込んでいましたら、メールで連絡を。

社内掲示板④ 紛失物があったとき

EXAMPLE

I found a battery pack in the server room. If it belongs to you, please contact me by phone or email.

サーバー室でバッテリーパックの落とし物を見つけました。お心当たりの方は、電話またはメールで連絡してください。

VARIATIONS

Anybody who left a wallet in the cafeteria, please contact me.
カフェテリアに財布を**置き忘れた方**は、私まで連絡を。

I lost my progress report in the No. 3 System Sales building. If you find it, **please let me know by email.**
進捗報告書を第3システムセールスビル内で紛失してしまいました。**見つけた方はメールでご連絡ください。**

I found a USB memory in the No. 2 conference room. It contains 10 Excel files. **It is being kept at the lost/found.**
第2会議室でUSBメモリーを見つけました。Excelファイルが10本入っています。**遺失物室で保管されています。**

I lost an envelope containing the latest progress report from NetSolution4U. Since it is a very important report, **please contact me immediately if you find it.**
NetSolution4U社からの進捗報告書が入っている封筒を紛失してしまいました。非常に重要な報告書なので、**見つけられた方はすぐにご連絡ください。**

社内掲示板⑤ 告知（社内公募）

EXAMPLE

Dear Friends,

At the latest board of directors meeting, it has been decided that we need a new campaign slogan to make our corporate image more attractive.

Although OrbisExpress has received an incredible response to our current slogan "Be a good system consultant", we are now ready to move on to the next stage.

Please give yourself a chance to show your creative spirit and submit attractive slogans of your own.

皆さま、

前回の役員会において、弊社の企業イメージをより魅力的にするために、新しいキャンペーン標語が必要である、と決定されました。

これまでも、OrbisExpress 社の「良きシステムコンサルタントたれ」というキャンペーン標語は絶大な好評を博してまいりましたが、今や弊社が次の段階に一歩を踏み出す時であります。

スタッフ各位、創造的精神を発揮され、魅力的な標語を提案されることをお願いする次第です。

VARIATIONS

We are encouraging every one of you **to submit** new business ideas.
新規事業アイデアを募集しています。各位**奮って応募してください**。

To each of you whose idea we decide to use, we would like to present a small gift **as a token of our appreciation.**
アイデアを採用させていただいた方には、**お礼の印として**記念品が贈呈されます。

The deadline date for this campaign is June 17, 2018.
本キャンペーンの募集締め切りは、2018年6月17日です。

We are planning to **carry out the following activities** company wide.
全社で**以下の活動を展開します**。

社内掲示板⑥ ｜ 告知（研修その他）

EXAMPLE

For your information, we will be offering an early lecture class on UML every Monday from January 10 to February 20. The lecture starts at 7:00 a.m. and ends at 9:00 a.m. Those who wish to attend, please contact us at the secretary's office by email.

UMLの早朝レクチャーのご案内です。1月10日から2月20日まで、毎週月曜日に開催いたします。レクチャーは午前7時から9時までです。参加希望者は事務局までメールでご連絡ください。

VARIATIONS

The system development group is sponsoring an introductory progtamming seminar in August, 2018 and will start accepting applications on July 14, 2018. Staff who are in their 30s **are encouraged to apply.**
システム開発グループは、2018年8月に初級プログラミング研修講座を開催し、2018年7月14日より応募の受付を行います。30代のスタッフは**奮ってご応募ください**。

Those who wish to participate, please contact us at training-seminar@SDGroup.PowerLinkStream.com.
参加希望者は、training-seminar@SDGroup.PowerLinkStream.com までメールで**ご連絡ください**。

Please take your **annual physical examination,** which is scheduled on March 15 this year.
定期健康診断が今年は3月15日に実施されます。必ず受診してください。

The following technical books have newly arrived. They are kept on the usual bookshelf.
下記の新着技術書が入りました。置き場所はいつもの書棚です。

The 2018 **corporate brochure is now ready for distribution.** Those who would like to have a copy, please contact us at the public relations office.
2018年版の**新しい会社案内**ができました。必要な方は広報部まで。

chapter

5

第5章
ビジネスに役立つ表現

情報収集　　　　　》P.94 - P.101

アポイントメント　》P.102 - P.112

スケジュール管理　》P.113 - P.115

各種用件の表現　　》P.116 - P.133

情報収集① 情報を送ってもらう

ビジネスパーソンは、常日ごろから情報収集の努力を怠ってはならない。情報を送ってもらうときの状況はさまざまなので、いろいろな表現を使い分ける必要がある。

EXAMPLE

Regarding the newspaper article you emailed me on March 17, 2018, it was illegible for some reason. Could you please send it again today? Thanks a million in advance.

2018年3月17日にメールしていただいた新聞記事ですが、何らかの理由で判読不能です。今日、もう一度、送っていただけますか。よろしくお願いします。

VARIATIONS

Please send me information concerning your Web services no later than August 12.

御社のWebサービス**に関する資料を**8月12日までに**送ってください**。

Please send us **the details regarding** your Web system advertised in the October issue of Nikkei Linux.

『日経Linux』誌10月号に掲載されていた、御社のWebシステム**に関する詳しい資料を**お送りください。

I would appreciate it if you could inform us as to the specifications of the Data_Display module by tomorrow.

Data_Displayモジュールの仕様**について**、明日までにご**連絡いただけると助かります**。

Is it possible for you to email me information concerning your business catalogue within three days**?**

御社のビジネスカタログ**に関する資料を**、3日以内にメールでお送りいただくことは可能ですか。

Do you have any information regarding the server systems that your company is advertising?

御社が宣伝しているサーバーシステム**に関する資料はありませんか**。

About the e-learning seminar your company has started offering lately, **any information you could provide** at your earliest convenience **would be greatly appreciated.**

御社が最近提供を開始したeラーニングセミナーですが、**どんな資料でも**、都合のつき次第**お送りいただければありがたいです**。

情報収集② こちらの興味を示す

新聞・雑誌などの2次情報でなく、直接の関係者から1次情報を取得することで、人より一歩先んじよう。面識のない相手から情報を引き出すコツは、まずこちらの興味を相手に示すことである。

EXAMPLE

As you may know already, there is great deal of interest in open source software in Japan now. I am really interested in working together with you on the Web service system development which I heard your company has been carrying out as an open source project for about a year. Please let me know what is required for an outsider like me to join.

すでにご存じかもしれませんが、現在、日本では、オープンソースソフトウェアへの関心が非常に高まっています。貴社がここ1年ほど、Webサービスシステムの開発をオープンソースプロジェクトとして展開してきたと聞き及び、私もご一緒できることを楽しみにしております。私のような部外者がプロジェクトに参加するために必要なことをご教示ください。

VARIATIONS

As **I am interested in** object-oriented programming **and want to learn it**, I would be very happy if you could send me a copy of Booch's article published in the June issue of Object-Oriented Review.

オブジェクト指向のプログラミング**に興味があり、それを勉強したいと思っています**ので、『オブジェクト指向レビュー』誌6月号に掲載されたBoochの記事を送っていただけるとうれしいです。

As **I am really interested in the application you developed**, I would be really happy if you would let me know the specs (such as CPU and memory) of the system you are using because I would like to find out whether it can run on my PC.

あなたの開発したアプリケーション**に非常に興味があり**、私のPCでも動作可能か知りたいので、あなたがお使いのシステムのスペック（CPUやメモリなど）を教えていただければうれしいです。

I am very interested in your development project and would like to have a meeting with you to talk about it.

貴社の開発プロジェクト**に大変興味があります**ので、個人的にお目にかかってお話しできればと思っております。

情報収集③ 追加情報を求める

EXAMPLE

Dear Mr. Morris,

Thank you for letting me know the current server configuration. Incidentally, how many requests can this Web system handle concurrently?

モリス様、

現在のサーバー構成をお知らせいただきありがとうございます。ところで、このWebシステムはどれくらいのリクエストを同時に処理できますか。

VARIATIONS

According to your last email, this program is running on a machine located inside a firewall. Could it communicate with a server located outside that firewall?
前回のあなたのメールによると、このプログラムはファイアウォールの内側で動作しているということですが、そのファイアウォールの外側にあるサーバーと通信することはできますか。

I would be grateful if you email me **a little more information about** the topics to be covered at the project group meeting next week.
来週のプロジェクトグループ会議で取り上げる議題**について、もう少し資料を**メールしていただけるとありがたいです。

With great interest I have read the technical information you emailed me and **want to learn more about it.**
あなたがメールしてくださった技術情報、大変興味深く拝見いたしました。**さらに詳しいことを知りたい**と思っております。

About developing the Loadable_Kernel module, please let us know by email about the time framework of it, **in addition to** the cost.
Loadable_Kernelモジュールの開発についてですが、コスト**の他に、**タイムフレームワークについてもメールで教えてください。

With regard to the system requirements for the server software that your company developed last year, **could you be more specific?**
御社が昨年開発したサーバーソフトウェアのシステム条件について、**もう少し詳しくご説明願えませんでしょうか。**

情報収集④ 紹介してもらう

情報収集をする上で欠かせないのは、人脈を広げる努力だ。興味のある分野に詳しい人をどんどん紹介してもらい、自分の知識の引き出しを増やしていきたい。

EXAMPLE

Could you introduce me to someone who is familiar with peripherals that are compatible with devices that we have in our office?

本オフィス所有の機器と互換性のある周辺機器について詳しくご存じの方をご紹介いただけますでしょうか。

VARIATIONS

If you know someone who is familiar with PDF security issues, I would appreciate it very much if you could introduce him/her to me. I would like to meet the person to get some advice.
もしPDFのセキュリティ関係に**詳しい方**をご存じでしたら、紹介していただけるとありがたいです。お目にかかって助言をいただきたいと考えています。

Please let me know **who is in charge of** this contract.
本契約の**ご担当**をご紹介ください。

If you know somebody who can program in C++, **can you let me know?**
もしC++でプログラミングができる人をご存じでしたら、**教えていただけますか**。

If you know Mr. James Nelson of JSE Co., **please let me know his contact information.**
JSE社のジェームズ・ネルソンさんをご存じでしたら、**連絡先を教えてください**。

If you know a reliable Web design production company, please introduce it to us.
信頼できるWebデザイン専門の制作会社**をご存じでしたら、ぜひ紹介してください**。

I am sorry to bother you but **can you introduce me to** Mr. James Nelson of JSE Co.?
お手数ですが、JSE社のジェームズ・ネルソンさん**に私を紹介していただけないでしょうか**。

As I have been asked to give a lecture on Web business for the next in-house IT seminar, **I would appreciate it very much if you could introduce me to someone** who has been to the 2018 Web Business Conference in New York.
次回の社内IT研修セミナーでWebビジネスについての講議を依頼されましたので、ニューヨークの2018ウェブビジネス・カンファレンスに参加された**どなたかにご紹介いただければありがたいです**。

情報収集⑤ 情報源を尋ねる

情報源には、人、会社、刊行物、Webサイト、メーリングリストなどいろいろなものがある。詳しい人に尋ねて、自分の知識を深める努力を重ねよう。

VARIATIONS

If it is OK with you, can you tell me **who you got this news from**?
もしよろしければ、**このニュースの情報源の方**を教えていただけますか。

Is it possible for you to **reveal the source of this information**?
情報源を明らかにしていただくことは可能ですか。

Can you let me know **the source of this information and who I should contact to get it**?
情報源と、その方の連絡先を教えていただくことは可能ですか。

Can you tell us **who we should ask regarding** this matter?
この件についてはどなたに質問すればよいか、ご教示いただけますか。

I would appreciate it very much if you could let me know **where to send my inquiry about** the memory products listed below.
以下のメモリ製品**についての問い合わせ先**を教えていただけますでしょうか。

Do you know **any good information sources** about MPEG++?
MPEG++について、**何か良い情報源**をご存じないでしょうか。

Can you tell me **which information sources we should look into**?
どんな情報源に当たればよいか、教えていただけますか。

情報収集⑥ 紹介元を説明する

VARIATIONS

I learned the name of the sub-directory **from** the senior programmer of AnnexInfo Co. in Hayward, CA.
そのサブディレクトリ名は、カリフォルニア州ヘイワードにある（株）AnnexInfoの上席プログラマーから伺いました。

Your company's name was given to us by the chief editor of Nikkei Linux.
御社のことは、『日経Linux』誌の編集長にご紹介いただきました。

I got your name from Mr. Suzuki of CondorVersa Co.
あなたのことは、（株）CondorVersa社の鈴木さんから教えていただきました。

I got your email address from Mr. Henry Matsumoto of ClusterShell, whom I met at the Internet Conference in San Jose last month.
あなたのメールアドレスは、先月サンノゼで開催されたインターネットカンファレンスで会った、ClusterShell社のヘンリー松本さんから教えていただきました。

I found the telephone number of your company **in the Web page** of BayTech Co.
御社の電話番号は、（株）BayTechの**Web**ページで見つけました。

I got your email address **from the database** of your company.
あなたのメールアドレスは、御社の**データベースで知りました**。

Regarding the server software that your company has been developing, **I heard about it from** President Stanley of LexusWebCom Co. in Tokyo.
御社が開発中のサーバーソフトウェアですが、**それについては**東京の（株）LexusWebComのスタンレー社長**から伺いました**。

情報収集⑦ 適任者を紹介する

　何か情報や助言を求められたとき、自分が適任でないと思ったら、誰か知り合いを紹介する。紹介した相手も人脈が広がるので、相互の利益につながるだろう。

EXAMPLE

I think that Mr. Lester Grant, who heads the Marketing division, is more qualified than I am to answer your questions because he has an excellent background in the field of biocomputers.

マーケティング部門責任者のレスター・グラントさんは、バイオコンピューターの分野に精通しているので、あなたの質問に答えるのに私より適任だと思います。

VARIATIONS

Why don't you email your question to Dr. Hiramatsu because he is our specialist in grid computing?
我が社におけるグリッドコンピューティングのスペシャリストは平松博士なので、彼に**質問をメールしてみてはいかがですか**。

Regarding your question of where the latest bug report file is saved, it seems that Mr. Lucas Fremont, the chief engineer of the Development division, **is more qualified to answer it than I am.**
最新のバグレポートファイルがどこに保存されているかとのご質問ですが、開発部の技術主任ルーカス・フレモントさん**の方が私よりも答えるのに適任**だろうと思います。

I think that Mr. Luke Silversteen, our chief programmer, is more knowledgeable than I. So, I forwarded your email to him and **asked him to answer it.**
主任プログラマーのルーク・シルバースティーンさんの方が私より物知りだと思ったので、あなたのメールを彼に転送して、あなたの**質問に答えるように頼んでおきました**。

I passed the program you are developing to Mr. Matthew Hawkins. **I think he will be able to help you on that matter.**
あなたが開発しているプログラムをマシュー・ホーキンスさんに渡しておきました。**きっと助けてもらえると思います**。

I recommend you to ask Mr. Nicholas Wright, our project leader, **about your questions by email** because I can't answer them.
あなたの質問は私には答えられないので、プロジェクトリーダーのニコラス・ライトさん**にメールで尋ねてみることを勧めます**。

情報収集⑧ 使用許諾を求める

取得した情報や資料を使うとき、注意しなければならないのが著作権の問題だ。使用するに当たって許諾が必要か確認する必要がある。もらった情報の著作権者は、送ってくれた人や会社とは限らないので注意が必要だ。

EXAMPLE

About that technical article; if we want to post it on our in-house magazine, do we need to get written consent from its copyright holder (author)? Where should we inquire about it? Who has the copyrights?

その技術記事ですが、社内報に掲載するには、著作権者（著者）からの使用許諾の書面が必要でしょうか。どこに問い合わせればよいでしょうか。どなたが著作権を持っているのでしょうか。

VARIATIONS

I **would like to get your permission**, if I may, **to use** your graphical content on our Web site.
もしよろしければ、あなたの図版を弊社のWebに掲載するための**使用許諾をいただきたい**のですが。

With your permission, we **would like to** translate parts of your technical document into Japanese and **reproduce it** as our reference material.
ご許可をいただければ、御社がWebに掲載している技術解説のテキストの一部を日本語に翻訳して、弊社の資料に**転載使用したい**と考えています。

We would like to use the image file of your memory products for our pamphlet. **Would that be all right with you?**
御社のメモリ製品の画像ファイルを弊社のパンフレットに使用したいのですが、**問題ないでしょうか。**

Would it be copyright infringement for us to duplicate the image content of your product brochure in order to use with our materials for the Japanese market?
御社の製品パンフレットに掲載されている画像を複製して、弊社の日本向け資料と一緒に使うのは、**著作権上、問題があるでしょうか。**

I would appreciate it very much **if you allow me to use** a part of the program **to which your company holds the copyrights**.
御社が**著作権を持つ**プログラムの一部の**使用を許可していただければ**感謝します。

アポイントメント① 面会を申し込む

　メールで多くの用件が済ませられる時代とはいえ、直接会って話をすることの重要性は、昔も今も変わらない。他社や外部の組織の人に面会することは、人脈を広げるという意味でも、ビジネスパーソンにとって重要な仕事の1つだ。積極的にアポイントメントをとって人に会い、仕事の幅を広げたい。

EXAMPLE

If it is possible, I would like to see you in person to hear your opinion on this new technology. Please let me know when is convenient for you so that I can come see you at that time.

できましたら、一度お会いしてこの新しい技術について直接お話を伺いたいのですが、いかがでしょうか。ご都合のよい日時を指定していただければ、いつでも御社に伺います。

VARIATIONS

I wonder if it would be convenient for you to see me in the early part of next week.
来週の前半にお会いしたいのですが、**ご都合はいかがですか**。

Could you spare about 30 minutes **with me?** I would like to talk with you.
お話をしたいのですが、**30分ほどお時間をいただけますでしょうか**。

Is it **possible for me to see** you?
お会いすることは可能でしょうか。

Would it be possible to set up an appointment with you on March 10 **and discuss** the next version upgrade?
3月10日に**お会いして**、次のバージョンアップグレードについて**話し合うことは可能**でしょうか。

I plan to be in San Jose from February 5 to March 7 and **would like to consult with you about** the problems of the server project. I am prepared to accommodate my schedule to yours.
2月5日から3月7日までサンノゼに滞在する予定ですので、サーバープロジェクトの問題**についてご相談したいと思います**。お時間はそちらの都合に合わせます。

Is it possible to **set up an appointment with you** early next week to discuss the progress report of this project? If your schedule is full next week, how about the week after next?
来週早々お会いして、このプロジェクトの進捗レポートについてお話しする**アポイントメントを取る**ことは可能でしょうか。来週はすでにご予定があるようでしたら、再来週はいかがでしょうか。

アポイントメント② | 来社してもらう

EXAMPLE

It looks difficult for me to get to your place, but if you can come to see me at my office, I can probably spare you about one hour from 6:00 p.m. (I can make myself available for about one hour after 6:00 p.m.)

時間的にそちらに伺うのは難しそうですが、もし弊社にいらしていただくことが可能でしたら、午後6時から1時間くらい時間が取れます。

VARIATIONS

Since I am available on Monday, November 17, **it would help me a lot if you could come to our place.**
11月17日（月）は時間が空いていますので、**弊社にお越しくだされば大変助かります**。

As I will reserve a meeting (conference) room for tomorrow, **please come to our office.**
こちらで会議室を手配しておきますので、明日、**弊社にお越しください**。

It seems that it is convenient for all parties to get together at our office. **I am really sorry to bother you, but can I ask everybody to come here?**
弊社に集まっていただくのが一番好都合のようなので、**大変恐縮ですが、皆様にご足労いただけますでしょうか**。

On Monday, June 23, **you are invited to come to our office for a job interview with** our chief engineer.
6月23日（月）、**弊社にお越しいただき、弊社技術主任との面談をお願いいたします**。

We are wondering if you and your project manager **would like to come to our office to discuss** this development contract with us on Monday, May 19.
5月19日（月）、あなたとあなたのプロジェクトマネジャーに**弊社にお越しいただいて、**この開発契約について**ご相談できないか**、と思案しております。

アポイントメント③ 面会の目的を述べる

VARIATIONS

I would like to set up an appointment with you **so that I can explain** the new service of our company to you.
弊社の提供する新しいサービスについて**ご説明するために**、お目にかかりたいのですが。

I would really appreciate it if I could visit you and **hear your view on** the P2P market in Japan.
あなたを訪問し、日本におけるP2P市場について**教えていただければ**大変ありがたいです。

About the new development project for CrossWay, how about getting together, if you could, next Tuesday **to exchange our opinions** on it?
CrossWay社向けの新規開発プロジェクトですが、できましたら、来週の火曜日にお会いして**意見を交換する**のはいかがでしょうか。

I would like to hear how you view the US IT market in the near future.
近い将来の米国のIT市場について**どうお考えか、お聞きしたいと思います**。

I would appreciate it **if I could have an interview with you on the subject of** how the US IT market will grow from now on.
米国のIT市場が今後どのように成長するか**というテーマでインタビューさせていただければ**ありがたいです。

Is it possible to hear about the recent trend of the US market?
最近の米国市場のトレンドについて、**お話を聞かせていただけますでしょうか**。

I would like to come see you to discuss possible solutions for the bugs that have been reported to us lately.
そちらに伺って、最近報告されたバグの解決方法を**ご相談したい**のですが。

I would like to see you **to examine** what kind of business models your company can develop in the future.
将来、御社がどのようなビジネスモデルを開発できるか**検討するために**、お目にかかりたいのです。

I would like to see you **so that I can introduce you to** our new person in charge of the business who has succeeded me.
私の後任の新担当者を**紹介するために**お目にかかりたいです。

アポイントメント④ 他人を紹介する

EXAMPLE

Mr. Yoshida works for the archives section of my company and wishes to see you if he can. Since he is responsible for constructing an archive server, I would appreciate it if you could listen to him and give some advice about it.

弊社文書管理室の吉田が、ぜひお会いしたいと申しております。文書サーバーの構築を担当していますので、相談に乗っていただければありがたいです。

VARIATIONS

This is to introduce Mr. Takehiko Yamamoto, who worked for me at Open UML Technologies Co. for five years.

（株）Open UML Technologies社で5年間、私の部下として働いていた山本武彦氏を**ご紹介いたします**。

Within the next few weeks, our engineer **will visit your company** and set up a Web server.
ここ数週間のうちに、弊社のエンジニアがWebサーバーの立ち上げに、**御社に伺います**。

Dear Mr. Paul Jenkins, Iwate Masanori of my development team will be in San Jose next month and **would enjoy meeting you very much**.
ポール・ジェンキンス様、私の開発チームの岩手正典が来月サンノゼに行きますので、**ご面会いただければ大変喜ぶと思います**。

Taguchi, who works for me, wishes to listen to your opinions on this matter. I would appreciate it if you could see him and if so **I will instruct him to get in touch with you**.
私の部下の田口がこの件についてあなたからご意見を伺いたいそうです。彼にお会いいただければ大変ありがたいです。もしお会いいただけるのであれば、**本人から直接連絡させます**。

アポイントメント⑤ ｜ 面会を承諾する／辞退する

面会の可能性を打診されたら、あまり時間をおかずに返事する。辞退する場合には角が立たないように。

VARIATIONS

OK, **I will be happy to meet with** you as you requested.
お申し込みいただいた面会の件ですが、了解いたしました。**喜んでお会いいたします。**

Surely, I can meet with you. **When do you prefer?** (When is a good time for you? / When would you like to meet me? / What time is convenient for you?)
もちろん、お会いすることは可能です。**いつがよろしいですか。**

Yes, I can meet you at that time because **I will be free**.
はい、その時間なら**空いています**ので、お目にかかれます。

I think I can spare about one hour to meet with you if it is all right with you.
1時間**程度なら時間を割くことができます**。それでよろしければお会いいたしましょう。

As Mr. Hasegawa is a junior fellow who is working in that field in our company, **I would like to bring him with me to the meeting** with you. Would that be all right with you?
弊社でその分野を担当している若手社員の長谷川**も同席させたい**のですが、よろしいでしょうか。

I am very sorry but I will be occupied that week. **I hope that I can see you some other time.**
残念ですが、その週はふさがっております。**また別の機会にお会いできればと思います。**

Thank you for asking me to meet you, but **I am afraid I must decline** as I don't think I can be of much help.
せっかくのお申し出ですが、私ではあまりお役に立てそうにありませんので、面会の件は**辞退させていただきます**。

アポイントメント⑥ 会合場所を調整する

　面会について基本的に合意が取れた後、会合の場所や時間を別途調整しなければならない場合がある。どうしてもらいたいか、遠慮なく相手に伝えよう。

VARIATIONS

We can get together for the meeting either at your place or mine. **Which will be convenient for you?** (Please let me know which place you prefer to get together for the meeting, at your place or mine.)
打ち合わせの場所は貴社と弊社の**どちらがご都合よろしいでしょうか**。

Please name **the place where you want to meet**? (Please let me know where we will be meeting?)
お会いする場所をご指定ください。

I will be **coming to your place**.
こちらから**御社に伺います**。

Is it possible **for you to come to our place**?
こちらにお越しいただくことは可能ですか。

It helps me a lot **if you could come to our place**.
こちらにお越しいただければ助かります。

Then, **why don't we meet at** the lobby of the Hirakawa Hotel on September 11**?**
それでは、9月11日に平河ホテルのロビー**でお目にかかりましょう**。

I would appreciate it if you could visit us at the following address (location):
ご来社いただければ幸いです。住所は下記の通りです。

アポイントメント⑦ 別の日時を打診する

EXAMPLE

Dear Peter Sharrock,

I understand that August 12 is very convenient for you, but unfortunately I am afraid I will be occupied for the whole day. Can you think of a different date that will be convenient for you?

ピーター・シャーロック様、

8月12日がご都合が良いとのことですが、残念ながら、その日は都合がつきません。別の日時ではいかがでしょうか。

VARIATIONS

How about sometime in the afternoon on September 22?
9月22日の午後**ではいかがでしょうか**。

Can you name **a couple of dates that will be convenient for you?**
ご都合のよい日時の候補をいくつかお知らせください。

I have an opening on Monday, July 24 from 2:00 p.m. to 4:00 p.m.
7月24日（月）の午後2時から午後4時なら**空いています**。

I am afraid I am **occupied and have no opening** this week.
今週は**すべてふさがっていて、空いているところがありません**。

I **will be free anytime** next week. Can you come to our San Francisco office?
来週は**どの時間帯も**空いています。弊社のサンフランシスコ・オフィスにおいでになれますか。

I will be available **except for the following hours**.
以下の時間帯以外ならいつでも大丈夫です。

Are you free next Wednesday, February 17, at 3:00?
来週の水曜日、2月17日の3時は**空いていますか**。

I will be available next Thursday, February 18, at 4:00, if it would be convenient for you.
あなたの都合がよろしければ、来週の木曜日、2月18日の4時が**空いています**。

アポイントメント⑧ 当日の面会手順

大きなビルなどでは、セキュリティの問題もあるので、面会に手順がいる場合がある。当日戸惑わないよう、必要なら当日の面会手順を確認しておく。

EXAMPLE

OK then, I will come visit your place to listen to your view on this project on March 14. Should I come to the 3F office directly on that day?

では、3月14日に、本プロジェクトに関するあなたのご意見を聞きに、御社に伺います。当日は3階オフィスに直接行けばよいでしょうか。

VARIATIONS

Who should I visit on that day**?**
当日は**どなたを訪ねれば**よろしいでしょうか。

Please dial extension 123 at the reception desk. I will come to meet you at the lobby.
受付で**内線123番をお呼び出しください**。ロビーまでお迎えに上がります。

Please **tell the receptionist that you have an appointment with** Yamashita at the system development department.
システム開発部の山下と**約束がある**と、**受付で仰ってください**。

I will make an arrangement so that the receptionist can show you the way when you tell her/him your name.
受付で名前を言っていただければ案内させる**ように手配しておきます**。

Please come directly to the system sales department located on the 5th floor of the building.
5階のシステム営業部に**直接お越しください**。

アポイントメント⑨ 約束を変更する

約束した日時に都合がつかなくなってしまうこともある。約束を変更するときは、まずこちらから、できるだけ近い別の日時の候補を打診した方がよいだろう。

EXAMPLE

I was going to visit you at your Shinjuku office tomorrow night, but I'm afraid I cannot make it. How about the following Tuesday at 4:00?

明日の晩、新宿オフィスにあなたをお訪ねする予定でしたが、できなくなってしまいましたので、翌週の火曜日4時、ということではいかがでしょうか。

VARIATIONS

I am very sorry that I am **placing my convenience ahead of yours** and asking you to make a change. (I am very sorry for any inconvenience in asking you to make a change.)
こちらの都合で変更をお願いすることになり、大変恐縮です。

Could you tell me **when you would like to meet** next week because I think I can do something with my schedule?
来週でしたら何とかなりますので、**ご希望の日時**をご指定くださいますか。

Please be kind and allow me **to suggest an alternative date**. (Let me **come up with a different date** and inform you of it later.)
改めて**別の日時を提案**させてください。

I'm afraid that something came up and I won't be able to meet you next Tuesday. **Is it possible to reschedule our appointment for** Monday, April 16, at 10:00?
申し訳ありませんが、来週の火曜日は都合が悪くなりました。お約束を4月16日（月）の10時に**スケジュール変更できますか**。

アポイントメント⑩ 約束を取り消す

やむにやまれぬ事情で、約束をキャンセルしなければならない事態に陥ったときは、後々の関係に悪影響を与えないよう、理由を説明するなどして、きちんとその旨を伝える必要がある。

EXAMPLE

I'm afraid that I must cancel our appointment for Friday, April 20, at 10:00 because I have to meet Manager Russell Franklin of the Development division and explain the bug report of the Data_Input module.

開発部のラッセル・フランクリン課長にData_Inputモジュールのバグレポートについて説明しなければならなくなったので、4月20日（金）10時の約束をキャンセルしなければならなくなりました。

VARIATIONS

I am very sorry to inform you that **I cannot make it to** the project group meeting next Tuesday **due to circumstances beyond my control.**
大変申し訳ございませんが、**不測の事態のため、**来週の火曜日のプロジェクトグループ会議**に出席できなくなりました。**

I am sorry but **I won't be able to keep our appointment** for Friday, February 16, at 3:00.
申し訳ありませんが、2月16日（金）3時に**お会いできなくなりました。**

Something urgent came up and I am sorry that **I will be unable to attend** the meeting at San Jose next week.
急用ができたので、申し訳ありませんが、来週参加を予定していたサンノゼでの会議に**出席できなくなりました。**

I was going to meet Mr. Ed Gibson, our senior programmer, on February 14, at 2:00 to discuss the development schedule of the CheckDataType.java program, but **I am afraid that I have to cancel the appointment** for that meeting because I am going to have to visit President Stanley of SigUsrOne Co. on that day at 1:00.
2月14日2時に上席コンサルタント、エド・ギブソン氏と会って、CheckDataType.javaプログラムの開発スケジュールについて話すことになっていましたが、その日の1時に（株）SigUsrOneのスタンレー社長を訪問しなければならなくなったので、その会議の**約束を取り消さなければならなくなりました。**

アポイントメント⑪ 面会のお礼を述べる

初めての人に面会を申し込んで話をしたら、その日のうちにお礼のメールを送ろう。今後の長期的な関係づくりの第一歩である。

EXAMPLE

Thank you very much for your time today. Your talk on case studies in email marketing was really informative and educational to us. We hope to make good use of what we learned from you today for the benefit of our project(s).

本日はお時間をいただきましてありがとうございました。教えていただいたメールマーケティングの導入事例は大変参考になり、勉強になりました。本日伺ったことは、弊社のプロジェクトにぜひ役立てたいと思います。

VARIATIONS

Thank you very much for **taking your busy time to come to our office** today.
本日は、**お忙しい中わざわざご来社いただき**、ありがとうございました。

Thank you very much for meeting with us today. **Your talk was really informative.**
本日はご面会いただきありがとうございます。**お話を伺って大変参考になりました。**

Thank you very much for **having a productive** (useful) **discussion** with me today. I plan to use what you pointed out as guiding principles in my future work.
今回はとても**有意義な議論ができ**、感謝しております。ご指摘いただいた点は、今後の私の仕事の指針にさせていただきます。

I am really grateful to be able to meet you today, and **am looking forward to a good working relationship with you.**
本日お目にかかる機会を得て、大変うれしく思っております。**今後ともよろしくお付き合いくださいませ。**

スケジュール管理① 日程を伝える

グループで仕事をする際は、メンバーにスケジュールを正しく伝える必要がある。メールの同報性と、メールボックスに保存されるという記録性が、スケジュール管理に大いに役立つ。

EXAMPLE

The next month's schedule for the production group looks something like this: first week: group meetings, second week: designing, and third and forth weeks: programming.

プロダクショングループの来月の予定は、おおむね次のようになっています。第1週：グループ会議、第2週：設計、第3週と第4週：プログラミング。

VARIATIONS

The rough schedule for the project is as follows:
プロジェクトの**今後の概略スケジュール**は以下の通りです。

Now that we **plan to go forward with the project in line with** the following schedule, your cooperation will be appreciated.
以下のスケジュール**に沿って仕事を進めます**ので、ご協力ください。

This week's schedule for the A2ZLink project group **is as follows:** Monday through Wednesday, at the San Jose office; Thursday and Friday, at the LA office; Saturday, at the Redmond office.
A2ZLinkプロジェクトグループの**今週のスケジュールは以下の通り**。月曜日から水曜日：サンノゼ・オフィス、木曜日と金曜日：LAオフィス、土曜日：レッドモンド・オフィス。

The Suzuki group's **schedule over the next few weeks includes** taking part in the project group meetings, brain storming with the prototyping group, and visiting the San Jose office.
鈴木グループの**今後数週間のスケジュールは**、プロジェクトグループ会議への参加、プロトタイピンググループとのブレインストーミング、そしてサンノゼ・オフィス訪問です。

スケジュール管理② | 進捗状況を確認する

プロジェクトのリーダーは、進捗状況を正しく把握していなければならない。定期的に問い合わせのメールを送り、日程に問題がないか確かめるようにしたい。

EXAMPLE

I want you to keep me informed by email about how this development project is going. Please CC the email of your status report to my boss, too.

この開発プロジェクトの進捗具合については、メールで常時お知らせください。その際、私の上司にも進捗報告のメールをCCしてください。

VARIATIONS

How is everything coming on (with your project, plan, etc.) lately**?**
その後、（プロジェクト、計画などの）**進展はいかがでしょうか**。

Please inform me how this development project **is coming on.** (Please inform me about the status quo of this development project.)
この開発プロジェクトについて、**現在の進捗状況をお知らせください**。

Our work is **progressing without a hitch**.
作業は**問題なく進んでいます**。

It is **going a little behind schedule**, but I promise we will make the March 16 deadline.
予定より若干遅れ気味ですが、3月16日の締め切りには間に合わせます。

Up to now, we **haven't encountered any big problems**.
今のところ、**大きな問題はありません**。

Fortunately, we are **a little ahead of schedule**.
幸い、**予定よりも少し早いペース**で進んでいます。

We **have encountered** the following **problem(s)**.
以下のような**問題が出てきました**。

Please **try to identify** the current problems.
現状での問題点を**洗い出してみて**ください。

スケジュール管理③ 進捗に問題があるとき

スケジュールに遅れは付き物だ。進捗に問題があるとわかったら、メンバーの尻をたたくだけでなく、原因を明らかにして有効な解決策を講じなければならない。

EXAMPLE

This is the 3rd time I have attempted to contact you in regard to our system development project for XacBit. Have you taken a look at my email of May 17? As you know, the project is behind schedule. I would appreciate it if you go ahead and reexamine the development process (to make the project go faster).

XacBit社向けシステム開発プロジェクトに関して連絡をとるのはこれで3回目です。5月17日付けの私のメールは読みましたか。ご存じのように、開発プロジェクトの進捗が遅れています。作業工程を再検討して（早めて）ください。

VARIATIONS

We need to **add more people** to the project. (We need to **bring in more people**.)
そのプロジェクトには**追加で人員をつける**必要があります。

As it stands now, **we cannot make it to the deadline.**
このままでは**期限に間に合いそうもありません**。

Now we are at a crucial point. Although the going may get tougher, please hang on and try your best.
今が山場です。大変でしょうが、頑張ってください。

Please **report a summary of your analysis** (identify the cause of the problem and report it to me) by June 27.
6月27日までに**検討結果をまとめて報告**（問題の原因を究明して報告）してください。

About adding more programmers to the project, **could I have more time** before I come up with the decision? I need time to adjust the conflicts of interest between the different sections.
プログラマーを追加する件ですが、決定までに、**もう少し時間をいだけませんか**。部門間の意見調整にかなりの時間がかかりそうです。

各種用件の表現① | 注文／予約する

EXAMPLE

I would like to order three PCs and two monitors and want to ask you to email me your price list, estimate, and delivery date today.

PCを3台、モニタを2台注文したいと思っていますので、本日、価格表、見積もり、納期をメールしてください。

VARIATIONS

Could you reserve a meeting room for ten system consultants under the name Greg Fairbanks for Wednesday, June 20, at 11:00 a.m.**?**

6月20日（水）午前11時に、グレッグ・フェアバンクスの名前で、システムコンサルタント10人のために会議室を**予約してくださいますか**。

Please reserve a PC and a projector for the chief engineer for Wednesday, July 18, at 1:00 p.m. for his presentation of a new development project.

7月18日（水）午後1時に、技術主任が新規開発プロジェクトのプレゼンを行いますので、パソコン1台とプロジェクター1台を**予約してください**。

This is our order sheet for workstations that the chief engineer wants.

技術主任が要望しているワークステーション**の注文書です**。

I plan to stay for 5 nights from October 10 to 15. **Can I make a reservation for** a single room**?**

10月10日から15日の日程で5泊したいのですが、シングルルーム**の予約はできますか**。

As I would like to stay at your place on the night of May 30, **do you have** a twin room **available?**

5月30日に一晩宿泊したいのですが、ツインの部屋は**空いていますか**。

各種用件の表現② ｜ 各種の問い合わせ

VARIATIONS

I am interested in the server that your company is selling. Do you **have any detailed information (material) regarding it**?
御社が販売しているサーバーに興味があるのですが、**何か詳しい資料はあります**でしょうか。

Who is the developer of the software product that your company is selling**?**
御社の販売されているソフトウェアの**開発元はどこ**でしょうか。

Is this product **available for delivery** now?
現在、この製品は**入手可能**でしょうか。

Could you give us your rough estimate of the cost and delivery date**?**
おおまかなコストと納期を見積もってもらえますか。

Are you still **accepting applicants**? (Are there still openings for applicants?)
定員にまだ空きはありますか。

Supposing I place my order right away, what is your **rough estimate for the delivery date**?
いますぐ発注したとして、**納期はどれくらい**になりますか。

Do you have this part **in your stock** right now**?** If so, I would like you to send it to me.
現在、この部品の**在庫はあるでしょうか**。もしあれば送っていただきたいのですが。

I am writing to ask you about the sample I ordered the other day, which I haven't received yet. Has it **been shipped already**?
先日注文したサンプルがまだ届いていないのですが、**もう出荷されて**いますでしょうか。

各種用件の表現③ ┃ 問い合わせに答える

EXAMPLE

In response to your inquiry about the software that we are selling, we are developing it in our headquarters in Mountain View.

当社が販売しているソフトウェアについてのお問い合わせですが、それは当社のマウンテンビュー本社で開発しています。

VARIATIONS

The names of the programs **you inquired about** by email yesterday are listed below.
昨日、メールで**お問い合わせいただいた**プログラムの名前を以下に列挙します。

In response to your inquiry about the damaged parts you received, we will immediately reship the goods at our cost.
損傷部品**に関してのお問い合わせですが**、当社の負担にて、直ちにお客さま宛てに再発送いたします。

About the server systems that our company is selling, I am pleased to send you by email **the information you requested**.
当社が販売しているサーバーシステムについてですが、**ご請求の資料**をメールでお送りいたします。

With regard to PlazaSoft Co. helping us financially with this development project, their answer was "no".
（株）PlazaSoft社がこの開発プロジェクトを資金的に援助**する件についてですが**、彼らの回答は「ノー」でした。

About your proposal for development in Tokyo, you need first to hire 3 competent programmers.
東京で開発作業を行う**提案ですが**、まず有能なプログラマーを３人雇う必要があります。

各種用件の表現④ ｜ 中止／取り消し／変更

EXAMPLE

As for this development project, we have been experiencing a great number of unexpected problems. Consequently, we have regretfully decided to cancel it.

この開発プロジェクトですが、予期せぬ問題があまりにも多く発生しています。つきましては、残念ながら、中止することに決定いたしました。

VARIATIONS

This is to inform you that we will not be needing a meeting room on Tuesday, September 4, at 3:30 p.m. as the project meeting **has been called off**.
ご連絡いたします。プロジェクト会議が**中止になりました**ので、9月4日（火）午後3時30分の会議室の使用は必要なくなりました。

Something unexpected has come up and **I would like to cancel** the project meeting that I have called to discuss our future plan.
急用ができましたので、今後の計画を話し合うために私が召集したプロジェクト会議は**キャンセルしたいと思います**。

About the order of 10 workstations I placed yesterday, **please cancel it and confirm this** by email.
私が昨日出した10台のワークステーションの注文ですが、**キャンセルして**、メールで**確認の連絡をしてください**。

We have no choice but to **pull ourselves out of** the co-development project with your company due to problems beyond our control.
やむを得ない事情のため、弊社は御社との共同開発プロジェクト**から手を引く**ことになりました。

We have been **forced to withdraw ourselves from** this project due to financial difficulties.
財政難のため、当プロジェクト**から弊社は撤退する**ことになりました。

It is with great reluctance that I send this email to you to inform you that we **have been forced to close** our Dallas branch.
残念なことですが、ダラス支社を**閉鎖せざるを得なくなった**ことをご連絡いたします。

各種用件の表現⑤ ｜ 原稿／投稿を依頼する

　社内出版やPR活動、業界団体の刊行物などで原稿／投稿を依頼する機会もあるだろう。依頼する際には、締め切り、語数、テーマを明確に相手に伝えよう。

EXAMPLE

We would really appreciate it if you would provide us with an article for the October issue of "TOPICS", our in-house newspaper. It can be anything about good news or an event that happened around you at your workplace. We look forward to hearing from you.

10月の社内報の「TOPICS」に原稿を書いていただきたいので、ぜひご協力ください。テーマは、最近職場に起こった明るいニュースや出来事に関するものなら何でもかまいません。原稿を楽しみにお待ちしています。

VARIATIONS

Would you be so kind as to **provide a short explanatory article** for our magazine and discuss the recent trends in digital copyrights?

私どもの雑誌に、デジタル著作権の最近の動向ついて、**簡単な解説記事をご寄稿**いただけないでしょうか。

We would really appreciate it if you would **write an article for us with a title like** "Software testing techniques for Web applications."

「Webアプリケーションのソフトウェアテスト技法」**というテーマで原稿を執筆**していただければ幸いです。

Please be reminded that your deadline is September 30.

締め切りは9月30日ですので、厳守してください。

Could you please **send your article by** Tuesday, September 11?

9月11日（火）**までに原稿を送って**いただけますか。

Please email your article as a Word file or a plain text file. Please keep **the number of words of your article around 2000**.

原稿はWord形式、またはテキスト形式のファイルで、メールで送ってください。**語数は2000語前後で**お願いします。

It would be great if you could **draw graphs using** Excel, but hand-drawn graphs are acceptable, too.

グラフはExcel**で作成**していただければ助かりますが、手書きでも構いません。

各種用件の表現⑥ 関係者の協力を請う

「目標達成のために皆様よろしくお願いします」という儀礼的な連絡の他、役割分担をきちんと説明して仕事を円滑に進める、という要素を含める場合もある。

EXAMPLE

Now that the Web marketing project has been approved, we would appreciate it if we could have your cooperation in carrying it out. I will inform you of the details of it in a separate email for your consideration.

Webマーケティングプロジェクトが承認されましたので、今後の遂行に当たっては関係者のご協力をお願いします。詳しくは別のメールでご連絡します。

VARIATIONS

Since **your unanimous cooperation is absolutely needed** to solve this problem, we appreciate your help from all parties concerned.
今回の問題の解決には関係各部署が**一致協力して臨む必要があります**ので、ご協力のほどよろしくお願いします。

We appreciate **your cooperation** to shorten the delivery time.
納期短縮のため、**皆さんのお力添え**をお願いします。

The new **job assignment** has been decided as follows. We appreciate your cooperation.
新しい**役割分担（仕事のアサイン）**は以下のように決まりました。ご協力ください。

We would appreciate it if the 1st sales division could **steer visitors to show them** the way and if the 2nd sales division could **take care of the reception**.
販売第1課は**入場者の誘導**、第2課は**受付を受け持ってください**。

Please provide us with at least two people who can work as exhibition guides at the product show next month. **Your cooperation will be really appreciated.**
来月の製品展示会では説明員を最低2人は出していただきたいです。**ぜひともご協力ください。**

Could I request your help for the success of the project**?**
プロジェクトの成功のため、**ひとつ力を貸してはくれないだろうか**。

OK (Very well), **I will help you out.**
よろしい、**一肌脱ぐことにしましょう**。

各種用件の表現⑦　連絡先を知らせる

EXAMPLE

In his email, Mr. John Smith of AquosTech Co. has inquired about the technical details of the document system that we announced the other day. According to him, he has some questions that he would like to ask to the developer directly. Please contact him by email. His email address is as follows:

AquosTech社のジョン・スミスさんから、先日発表したドキュメントシステムの技術面での詳細について、メールで問い合わせがありました。開発者に直接尋ねたい項目があるとのことなので、メールで連絡してください。メールアドレスは下記の通りです。

VARIATIONS

Concerning your inquiry, Mr. Mamoru Akita of the technical support division **would like to contact you** later, as he knows about it in detail.

お問い合わせの件は、技術サポート部門の秋田守が詳細を理解していますので、後ほど**こちらから連絡を差し上げたい**とのことです。

How about getting in touch with Mr. Masanori Iwate of JSE **who is "Person to Contact"** in regard to this?

この件に関しては、JSE社の岩手正典さん**が窓口になっています**ので、一度連絡を取ってみてはいかがでしょうか。

Please get in touch with Mr. Hiroaki Yamate of the International Business Development Department **who is in charge of** distributor license agreements.

代理店契約についての**担当者は**国際業務開発部の山手宏明ですので、連絡を取っていただけますか。

The contact information in regard to this matter is as follows:

本件に関する**問い合わせ先**は以下の通りです。

Please forward all the complaints and claims that you receive regarding this matter to Shigeru Fukushima as the customer service division is going to handle them.

今回のクレームはすべて顧客サービス室が対応しますので、問い合わせが入ったら、すべて福島茂**に回してください**。

In case of emergency, please be reminded **to get in touch with** the director-level manager.

何か緊急の用件があった場合は、すぐ部長に**連絡するよう**留意してほしい。

各種用件の表現⑧ 申し出を断る

相手の申し出を断るのは難しいし、なかなか勇気がいる。状況に応じて、正当な理由を説明したり、婉曲的に断ったりするなど、角が立たないように注意しよう。

EXAMPLE

We regret that our company cannot give the green light to this development project immediately. We will be happy to reconsider it at a later time when our current difficulties will have been resolved.

残念ですが、弊社はこの開発プロジェクトにはゴーサインをすぐ出せません。後日、弊社の一時的問題を克服した段階で、改めて検討させていただきますので、よろしくお願いします。

VARIATIONS

Thank you for your offer, but **we are afraid we must decline it.** Your understanding of the circumstances that we are facing is greatly appreciated.

せっかくのお申し出で**心苦しいのですが、お断りせざるを得ません**。弊社の事情をご理解いただければ幸いです。

Unfortunately, we cannot agree with the conditions that you suggested. We would like you to **come up with an alternative plan**.

残念ながら、お知らせいただいた契約条件には合意できません。**別の案をご提示**いただきたく思います。

About the maintenance contract with BareSoft Co., **we are sorry to tell you that we cannot grant** a six-month extension.

(株)BareSoftとの保守契約に関してですが、**申し訳ありませんが**、6ヵ月の延長**を差し上げることはできません**。

About the development plan that the marketing division submitted; **after careful consideration of it,** we have decided that we cannot go ahead with it next month.

マーケティング部門が提出した開発計画ですが、**よくよく検討してみた結果**、来月の開始は無理だ、ということになりました。

Unfortunately, I **am unable to help you** with debugging this time.

残念ながら、今回はデバッギングの**お手伝いはできません**。

各種用件の表現⑨ ｜ 申し出を承知する

　依頼を受ける場合の表現は、断る場合よりも簡単である。「喜んで」「光栄です」などといったフレーズを入れた定型的な文面を使えば、だいたいにおいて事足りる。

EXAMPLE

About your kind offer of providing us with software CD samples, we have considered it with other sections in our company and are glad to inform you that our section has been put in charge of it.

先日お話をいただいたソフトウェアCDサンプル提供の件について、社内で検討いたしました。今回は私どもの部署で、ご親切なお申し出をありがたく受けさせていただきます。

VARIATIONS

We are **happy to accept** your offer this time.
今回のお申し出、**喜んでお受け**いたします。

We are **honored and pleased** to be able to join your project.
プロジェクトに参加できて**非常に光栄でうれしく**思います。

Thank you very much **for asking**.
わざわざ私に**声をかけていただき**、ありがとうございます。

Let me **give you a hand**, please.
ぜひ私に**お手伝い**させください。

We appreciate your asking us and are willing to **comply with your request**.
お問い合わせいただき感謝します。喜んで**ご依頼にお応え**する所存です。

With regard to the changes in specifications, we understand them now and **foresee no particular problems** with them.
仕様の変更の件、了解しました。**特に問題はありません**。

I will be **delighted to meet you** at the time you suggested.
お申し出の日時で、**喜んでお目にかかりたい**と思います。

各種用件の表現⑩　指示を求める

具体的にこちらにどうして欲しいのか、相手に指示してもらうときの表現。ストレートに聞くのが基本だ。

EXAMPLE

In regard to setting up a Web server, we would like to have our engineer visit your place and would appreciate it if you let us know the date that would be convenient for you.

Webサーバー設定の件ですが、こちらから技術者を伺わせたいと思います。ご都合のよい日時のご指定をお願いします。

VARIATIONS

I would like to **have your instructions about** how to proceed with the new sales contract.
新しい販売契約の手順**について、ご指示をいただきたく**存じます。

Please instruct us on how you would like us to proceed with this development project.
この開発プロジェクトをどのように進行させるのをお望みか、**ご教示いただきたい**と思います。

Please email us as soon as you have made a decision on how you want to fix this bug.
このバグをどのように修正したいか、**決定次第、メールをいただきたい**のですが。

Regarding the development contract with BestSonic Co., **please let me know whether** you want to extend it because I would like to discuss it with the chief engineer.
（株）BestSonic社との開発契約に関して、それを延長したい**かどうかをご連絡ください**。技術主任と話し合いたいので。

We await your instruction regarding hiring programmers.
プログラマー採用の件について、**あなたの指示をお待ちしております**。

We would like you to **make your decision as soon as possible** so that my development team can get on with designing a prototype next month.
私の開発チームがプロトタイプの設計に来月とりかかれるように、**結論を早急に出していただきたい**、と思います。

What do you want me to do about this project?
このプロジェクトを**どうしてほしいのですか**。

各種用件の表現⑪ 指示を知らせる

EXAMPLE

Thank you for your email of July 10. With regard to the estimate, please visit Mr. Hiromitsu Miyagi at our purchase department on July 28, at 15:00. If you have any questions, please let me know.

7月10日付けのメール、ありがとうございました。見積もりの件につきましては、7月28日15時に弊社購買部門の宮城浩光をお訪ねください。ご不明の点がありましたら、ご遠慮なくお尋ねください。

VARIATIONS

When you attempt to implement this function, **please follow the following instructions** carefully.
この関数の実装に当たっては、**以下の指示に注意して従ってほしい**。

Regarding how to fix this bug, **my instructions are as follows:**
このバグの修正に関して、**私の指示は次の通りです**。

My instructions to you, Chiba, **are to** meet with the chief engineer of this development project in the San Jose office and discuss foreseeable problems with him.
千葉、**私の指示は**、サンノゼ・オフィスでこの開発プロジェクトの技術主任と会って、予知できる問題について話し合う**ことだ**。

After due consideration **I have decided to** appoint Mr. Sheldon Tomas as the supervisor of this development project.
熟慮の末、シェルダン・トーマス氏をこの開発プロジェクトの統括責任者に指名する**ことに決定しました**。

It is my decision that all future changes to the programs involved in this application must first be approved by me.
今後、このアプリケーションに含まれるプログラムの変更に際しては、あらかじめ私の承認を得なければならない**ことに決めました**。

It has been decided that a developer's meeting will be held on Friday, June 8, at 5:00.
6月8日(金)5時に開発者会議を開催する**ことになりました**。

I have decided to ask PhoneComm to help us with this development project.
PhoneComm社に本開発プロジェクトのお手伝いを**していただくことにしました**。

各種用件の表現⑫ | 誤解がないか確認を求める

「こちらはこういうふうに理解していますが、それでよいですね」と相手に確認するときに使う表現である。

EXAMPLE

To confirm our recent email exchange, am I correct in assuming that your PC freezes as soon as you try to run your IE?

先日のメールのやりとりの内容を確認させていただくと、インターネット・エクスプローラーを起動しようとするとすぐにパソコンの画面が固まる、と考えてよろしいですか。

VARIATIONS

I just want to make sure; are you saying that the development group would like to be involved at every phase of this project?
確認したいのですが、開発グループは、このプロジェクトの全フェーズに積極的にかかわりたい、**と仰っているのですか。**

I understand from our telephone conversation yesterday that the first phase of this project will start on March 15. **Is my understanding correct?**
昨日の電話でのお話では、このプロジェクトは3月15日に第1フェーズが始まる**との理解でよろしいですね。**

About the maintenance contract of the product division's Web service, **am I correct in assuming that** it has already been awarded to NasaSoft Co.?
プロダクト部門のWebサービスの保守契約の件ですが、すでに(株)NasaSoft社**と契約されたと推測してよろしいのでしょうか。**

Let me make sure that **we have the same understanding about** the significance of this project.
このプロジェクトの重要性**に関して、理解が同じであることを確認させてください。**

It is my understanding that the development group will send 3 programmers to Mr. Takeru Akasaka's team. Would that be OK with you?
開発グループが赤坂猛さんのチームに3人のプログラマーを送る、**と理解しました**が、それでよろしいですか。

This is to confirm the main points of the email of May 29 in which you explained this project.
このプロジェクトについてご説明くださった、5月29日付けメールの**要点を確認します。**

各種用件の表現⑬ | 念を押す

相手は承知しているはずだが、念のためにお知らせする、というときに使う。

EXAMPLE

I suppose that you have taken care of it already, but let me remind you that it is the due day to deliver a bulk of product B333 to LinkPack tomorrow.

すでに手配済みのこととは思いますが、B333製品のLinkPack社への納期は明日ですので、ご確認のほどよろしくお願いします。

VARIATIONS

Please be reminded that the expiration date of the maintenance contract is the end of this year.
保守契約書の有効期間は本年末日までとなっています**ことをご確認ください**。

This is just to remind you that this project team will be moving to the 3rd floor next month.
本開発チームは来月から3階に移動する**ことをどうぞお忘れなく**。

I hope the minutes of the March 15 meeting **will help you understand** my position.
3月15日の会議の議事録が私の立場を**理解していただくのに役立つ**と思います。

This is just a reminder that the project meeting will be held at the meeting room on the 4th floor.
プロジェクト会議の場所が4階の会議室になったこと**の確認のお知らせです**。

I would like to remind you that all programmers who are involved with this development project have been asked to attend tomorrow's meeting.
この開発プロジェクトに参加しているプログラマーは、全員、明日の会議への出席を要請されている**ことをお忘れなく**。

I would like to take this opportunity to inform you of the problems I want us to discuss at the meeting tomorrow.
明日の会議で検討したい問題について、**ついでですがご連絡しておきます**。

Can you recall that Spiky Rogers, our current chief engineer, is scheduled to go back to the Walnut Creek office next month? We need an engineer for his replacement.
現在の技術主任であるスパイキー・ロジャーズが来月にウォルナットクリーク・オフィスに戻るので、彼に代わる技術者が必要なことはご記憶でしょうか。

各種用件の表現⑭ 相手の理解を確認する

相手が大筋は理解しているはずだが、少しあやふやなことがあった場合、「実際にはどうか」を確認するときに使える表現を挙げる。

EXAMPLE

I suppose that you already know that we will have a project meeting with MoveOn's development group. However, has anybody informed you that the meeting date has been changed from October 10 to Monday, October 15?

MoveOn社の開発グループとプロジェクト会議を持つことは多分ご存じのことと思いますが、会議の日付が10月10日から10月15日（月）に変更になったとの連絡は入りましたでしょうか。

VARIATIONS

This is to inform you again that we have made reservations for you at the Atlantic Hotel Yokohama (phone: 045-765-2222) in Minatomirai, Yokohama from March 5 to 10.

3月5日から10日まで、横浜みなとみらいのアトランティックホテル横浜（電話番号045-765-2222）に部屋を予約しました旨を、**再度ご連絡いたします**。

This is to report that we have checked our log data and found out that the bug hasn't been fixed yet.

ログデータを調べてみたところ、そのバグはまだ修正されてないことが判明しましたので、**ご報告いたします**。

Am I correct in assuming that you would like to make a brief presentation at the project group meeting next week?

来週のプロジェクトグループの会議で、簡単なプレゼンを行いたいとお考えである、**と思ってよろしいでしょうか**。

I would like to make sure, if I may, that our staff will support the server development project as explained in the email of March 29, 2018. Won't we?

確認させていただきますと、2018年3月29日付けメールでご説明したように、我々のスタッフがサーバー開発プロジェクトを支援する、**ということですね**。

To confirm the main points of what we discussed in the San Jose office on March 20, Mr. Eisaku Kanda's group of the Tokyo office will take part in the server development project, won't they?

サンノゼ・オフィスで3月20日に行った話し合いの**主要点を確認させていただきますと**、サーバー開発プロジェクトには東京オフィスの神田栄作さんのグループが参加する、**ということですね**。

各種用件の表現⑮ 伝言する

EXAMPLE

I have a message from Director Michel Jackson at the Cupertino office that you need to inform all staff on your project team of the content of Bug Report 123.

クパチーノ・オフィスのミシェル・ジャクソン部長からの伝言で、あなたのプロジェクトチームのメンバー全員に、バグレポート123の内容を周知してくださいとのことです。

VARIATIONS

Please inform Mr. Brown that I won't be able to be back in the San Jose office tomorrow at all.

結局、私は明日サンノゼ・オフィスには戻れない、とブラウン氏に**お伝えください**。

In an email I received from Mr. White, **he wrote that** he has been having difficulty contacting your company.

ホワイト氏**からのメールに**、貴社と連絡が取れない、**と書いてありました**。

In the email I received from the senior programmer of SyncCom Co., **he was saying that** he wants you to get started developing the Web service right away.

（株）SyncCom社の上席プログラマー**からのメールに**、そのWebサービスの開発をすぐ始めてほしい、**とありました**。

Mr. Terry Raymond **asked me to tell you that** he is planning to leave San Jose on June 15 and return to Tokyo on June 18.

サンノゼを6月15日に発って、6月18日に東京に戻る予定だ**とあなたに伝えるように**、テリー・レイモンドさんに**頼まれました**。

Mr. Barry Porter, the chief engineer, **asked me to communicate to you that** he will be attending the meeting in Tokyo next week and looks forward to seeing you there.

技術主任バリー・ポーター氏**からの伝言で**、来週、東京での会議に出席するつもりなので、あなたにお会いできるのを楽しみにしている、**とのことでした**。

各種用件の表現⑯ 希望や期待を伝える

単に自分の願望や期待を示すときのほか、「〜だろう」と予想を伝えるときにも使える。

EXAMPLE

Regarding Bug Report 123, if I can have my PC repaired by tomorrow, I have every hope that I can fix the bug in three days.

バグレポート123についてですが、もし私のPCを明日までに修理してもらえれば、そのバグはきっと3日で修正できると思います。

VARIATIONS

About joining the Web service development project, **I hope you like** this assignment.
あなたがWebサービス開発プロジェクトに参加する件ですが、このアサインメントが**気に入ってくれるといいのですが**。

I hope and pray that you will get your PC back as soon as possible.
あなたがご自分のPCをできるだけ早く取り戻される**ことを祈っています**。

I think that there is some hope that ClusterShell Co. will reverse its decision and wants to continue this development plan.
（株）ClusterShell社が決定を覆し、この開発計画を継続する**希望はある、と思います**。

We can only hope that FestaSeven Co. will continue the development contract with us.
FestaSeven社が我々との開発契約を継続してくれる**ことを望むだけです**。

As for the automatic transaction system development project, **it is our sincere hope that** we can establish a lasting partnership with NodePeer Co.
自動決済システム開発プロジェクトに関してですが、（株）NodePeer社と継続性のあるパートナーシップを結べる**ことを心より願っています**。

It is our hope that someday we will be moving our office to San Mateo, California.
いつかオフィスをカリフォルニア州サンマテオに移転できるようになる**ことが、我々の希望です**。

I hope to improve my programming skills.
プログラミングの腕をもっと上げ**たい、と思っています**。

各種用件の表現⑰ 返事を催促する

　返事を忘れているかもしれない相手に対する軽い催促から、いつまでも返事をよこさない相手に抗議する強い催促まで、いろいろな状況が考えられる。「〜日付けのメールは届いていますか」と間接的に催促するのも1つの方法である。

EXAMPLE

I sent you an email on August 12 concerning the possibility of us using portions of the program your company developed lately. As we haven't heard from you yet, I would appreciate it very much if you would be kind enough to contact us as soon as possible.

8月12日に、御社が最近開発されましたプログラムからの引用の可能性についてメールしました。まだお返事がございませんので、至急ご一報いただけるとありがたく存じます。

VARIATIONS

Regarding when to start testing, I wonder if the email I sent on November 4 ever reached you. If you have already received it, **please respond right away.**

テストをいつ始めるかについてですが、11月4日に出したメールは届いていますか。もし届いていましたら、**早急に返信してください。**

About the Import module, we can't start testing it yet because we haven't received your reply to the email I sent on July 10. **Please let us know by return mail.**

Importモジュールについてですが、7月10日に出したメールに対する御社からの回答がまだなので、テスト作業を始めることができません。**折り返しご連絡ください。**

This is the third time that I have emailed you about this problem. **Please let us know your solution within three days.**

この問題に関しまして、私が御社にメールを出すのはこれで3回目です。**解決策を3日以内にお知らせください。**

Because it seems that you didn't receive the first email I sent you, could you let us know by return email **if this email reaches you**?

最初に出したメールがそちらで受信されなかったようですので、**このメールが届きましたら、**その旨、折り返しメールでご連絡ください。

That can't be right. **Did you receive my email** of July 4?

そんなはずはない。**私が7月4日に出したメールは受け取りましたか。**

各種用件の表現⑱ クレーム対応

顧客から来たクレームに対する初期対応の例を示す。迅速な対応を顧客は期待している。

EXAMPLE

Thank you for taking time to let us know about your recent unfortunate experience with one of our products. I am Hiroshi Tajima of the user support division. We are having our specialists look into the problem you reported and will get back to you as soon as we find a solution to it.

弊社製品の不具合につきお知らせいただき、ありがとうございます。私はユーザーサポート部の田島裕司と申します。ご指摘いただいた件ですが、現在、専門家に調査させております。対処法がわかりましたら、すぐにご連絡を差し上げます。

VARIATIONS

John, we have received the following complaint/request/comment. **Please take appropriate action.**
ジョン、ユーザーから次のようなクレーム／要望／意見が来ました。**適切な対応をしてください。**

James, I am attaching a complaint that we got from one of our customers. **Please respond right away.**
ジェームズ、お客さまからの苦情をこのメールに添付しました。**早急な対応をお願いします。**

About the complaint we received by email today, please **look into the matter** and think about a solution to it.
本日、メールで寄せられた苦情ですが、**事実関係を確認して、**対応策を検討してください。

To find out **what to do to deal with the problem** you are experiencing, please visit our Web page at the following URL.
ご指摘の**問題に対する対処法**は、弊社のWebページに掲載されておりますので、ご参照ください。URLは下記の通りです。

When you try to contact the customer, **please include me in the CC.**
そちらの部署からお客さまに連絡するときは、**私にもCCで知らせてください。**

Please be reminded that **we will deal with this claim through** the customer service division.
今回の**クレーム対応は、**すべてお客さま相談室**経由**で行います。

6

第 6 章

人事や社交の表現

異動や転職	▶▶ P.136 - P.138
人材採用	▶▶ P.139 - P.140
病気や訃報	▶▶ P.141 - P.143
個人的なお見舞い	▶▶ P.144 - P.146
好意を伝える	▶▶ P.147 - P.150

異動や転職① | 転職／転勤／帰国の挨拶

ここに挙げたのは一般的な挨拶状の表現各種。職場や任地が変わることの、やや事務的な通知が中心である。

EXAMPLE

Due to the recent company-wide organizational changes, I will be going back to Japan. Thank you very much for everything you did for me during my stay. Mr. Shinden will be coming from Japan to take my place. He is young but is a very competent engineer. Incidentally, I will be taking up the following position next.

今回の全社的組織変更の結果、日本に帰国することになりました。滞在中はいろいろお世話になり、本当にありがとうございました。日本から新田さんが来て、私の後任となります。彼は若いですが、優秀なエンジニアです。なお、私の新しい所属は下記の通りです。

VARIATIONS

As a result of the March 10 personnel changes, **I will be transferred to** the San Jose office.
3月10日付けの人事異動で、サンノゼ・オフィス**に転勤することになりました。**

I will quit LuxTech on October 20 and will start working for SilcotSoft from November. **My new contact information is as follows:**
10月20日をもってLuxTech社を退社し、11月からSilcotSoft社で働くことになりました。**新しい連絡先は以下の通りです。**

Thank you for everything you have done for me during my stay (tenure) with this company.
在任中は**いろいろとお世話になりました。**

I will write **once I am settled**.
落ち着き先が決まりましたら、また連絡いたします。

I will try to keep in touch by email and so forth whenever possible.
今後も可能な限りメール等で**ご連絡させていただきたいと思います。**

異動や転職② 送別会開催の通知

EXAMPLE

As you may probably know already, Manager Adam Larsen will be transferred to the Tokyo headquarters as of April 1, 2018. To commemorate this occasion we are planning to have a farewell party with his friends and acquaintances and are happy to invite you to attend. As we would like to know how many people want to attend, may we hear from you by March 16 to Mogami at the following email address?

ご存じのように、アダム・ラーセン部長は2018年4月1日付けで東京本部に転勤になります。ご栄転を祝して、身内だけで送別会を開きますので、ご招待いたします。参加希望者の人数を知りたいので、出席をご希望の方は、3月16日までに最上まで、下記のメールアドレス宛てに連絡してください。

VARIATIONS

You are **invited to attend a farewell party for** Mr. Alex Bertland, who will be going back to the U.S.A. due to this month's personnel changes.
今月の異動で米国に帰国するアレックス・バートランドさんの**送別会にご招待いたします**。

Please advice Yamada **if you will attend.**
出欠を山田まで**ご連絡ください**。

If you are not attending, please respond by replying to this email to indicate your absence.
欠席される方のみ、このメールの返信でお知らせください。

About the farewell party for Mr. Anton Montague, **I am looking for a good place** now.
アントン・モンタギューさんの送別会ですが、今、**適当な場所を探しています**。

We are planning a farewell party for Manager Bill Hansen. If you are interested, please sign up and pay 10,000 yen to Masato Ueno by March 16. It covers food and drinks and a farewell gift to him.
ビル・ハンセン部長**の送別会を行います**。出席される方は3月16日までに、上野雅人に連絡し、会費1万円をお支払いください。この中には、食事、飲み物、部長に送る記念品代が含まれます。

異動や転職③ 転勤者からのお礼

新任地に着いた後、送別してもらったことや、世話になったことに感謝の意を込めて、親しい間柄の人に送るお礼メール。新住所や連絡先の告知を含めてもよい。

EXAMPLE

Thank you very much for having a heartwarming farewell party for me the other day. And the wonderful present you gave me will serve as the lasting memory of my happy times I shared with all of you in the Silicon Valley. I wish to say thank you to every one of you for your friendship and hospitality. When you have a chance to come to Japan, please let me know as I surely would like to see you again.

先日は心温まる送別会を開いていただき、ありがとうございます。また、素敵な記念品は、シリコンバレーでのよい思い出になります。皆様のご親切と友情に、心から感謝いたします。日本にいらっしゃる際にはぜひお会いしたいと思いますので、どうぞご遠慮なく連絡してください。

VARIATIONS

Thank you very much for all your help (both officially and privately) during my stay in U.S.A.
在米中は公私にわたって**本当にお世話になり、ありがとうございました。**

I would like to thank you for all that you have done for me during those 3 years I stayed in Menlo Park. **I am wishing you the very best of health.**
3年間のメンローパーク滞在中はいろいろお世話になり、ありがとうございました。**ご健康を心からお祈りいたしております。**

We are finally done moving in and are settled. **Our new address is as follows:**
引っ越しも終わり、ようやく身の周りも片付いてきました。**新しい住所は以下の通りです。**

My new contact information is as follows:
私の新しい連絡先は以下の通りです。

人材採用① 人を推薦する

EXAMPLE

I have the pleasure to inform you that Mr. Walter Watson worked for our Web service project for three years during which his performance was superb. He is an excellent engineer and knows the C programming language very well. I think that he would be a great asset to the automatic transaction system project that you are heading. Therefore, I have no hesitation in recommending him.

ウォルター・ワトソン氏は弊社のWebサービスプロジェクトで3年間働いており、その間、氏の仕事ぶりは大変素晴らしいものでした。彼は優れたエンジニアであり、Cプログラミング言語の知識が豊富ですので、あなたが総括責任者である自動決済システムプロジェクトにとって有能な人材となると思います。彼を推薦するにあたり、何の躊躇も覚えません。

VARIATIONS

This letter recommends Mr. Francis Brown, who worked with me at EdgePeople Co. for a few years.
これは、(株) EdgePeople社で数年間私と一緒に働いていたフランシス・ブラウン氏**を推薦する書状**です。

This is to introduce Mr. Yoshinori Kawasaki, a close acquaintance of mine, who is also a competent engineer.
私の近しい知り合いで、有能なエンジニアである、川崎好則氏を**ご紹介いたします**。

I am happy to have this opportunity to recommend Mr. Casper Goldstein to you as a possible candidate for the network administrator position at your company.
御社のネットワーク管理者の候補として、カスパー・ゴールドスタイン氏**を推薦**いたします。

I am happy to recommend Mr. Andres Shipway. He is a good programmer and is dependable.
アンドレス・シップウェイ氏**を推薦いたします**。彼は優秀なプログラマーであり、信頼が置けます。

I am sure he/she would be a great asset to the Web service project of your company.
御社のWebサービスプロジェクト**にとって有能な人材となる**ことを確信しています。

I would like to recommend Mr. Dennis Homestead **without reservations for the position of** the collaboration manager at your company.
デニス・ホームステッド氏を、御社のコラボレーションマネジャーに**自信をもって推薦したい**、と思います。

人材採用② | 採用／不採用を通知する

採用の通知は一言でも済むが、不採用を通知する場合は相手の能力や人格を否定するような表現にならないよう、気を遣う必要がある。

EXAMPLE

Thank you for your application for the position of Web designer we advertized. There is no question that your qualifications are impressive, but unfortunately, in your resume, we did not find any mention of work in Web designing. We thank you for considering our company and wish you well.

このたびはWebデザイナー職にご応募いただき、ありがとうございました。ご経歴が素晴らしいことには感心いたしましたものの、残念ながら、履歴書を拝見した限り、Webデザインのご経験がございません。就職先として当社を考慮してくださり、ありがとうございました。今後のご活躍をお祈り申し上げます。

VARIATIONS

We are **very pleased to offer you the position of** programmer at SmartPro Co.
（株）SmartPro社のプログラマー**として、あなたを採用したい**と思います。

We would like to hire Mr. Dexter Harris as manager of the development division.
開発部のマネジャーとして、デクスター・ハリスさん**を採用したいと思います**。

We regret to inform you that **although your qualifications are excellent,** we would like to hire someone with more programming experience this time.
あなたの資格は非常に素晴らしいのですが、当社としては、今回はよりプログラミング経験の豊富な方を採用したいので、残念ながら、不採用のご連絡をさせていただきます。

I am afraid **the position has already been filled.**
残念ですが、**すでに採用が決定しております。**

There is no question that your qualifications are excellent, but at this moment, the development division **has no plan to hire** interns.
あなたの資格が素晴らしいことに疑問の余地はございませんが、現在、開発部はインターン**を採用する予定はございません。**

Unfortunately, your Japanese proficiency **is not quite enough for us to offer you the position of** chief engineer at SuperLinkPro Co.
残念ながら、あなたの日本語能力は、（株）SuperLinkPro社の技術主任**として採用するには不十分**です。

病気や訃報① | 病欠の連絡

VARIATIONS

Manager Brown, as I have a really bad headache, **could I stay home from work today?**
ブラウン課長、とてもひどい頭痛がしますので、**本日はお休みさせていただいてもよろしいでしょうか。**

I would like to report that **I will take a day off today** as I have a high fever.
高熱が出てしまったので、**今日1日休みを取る**ことを連絡します。

I would like to take a day off, if I could, because I feel like I am coming down with the flu.
インフルエンザのようなので、**できれば休ませてください。**

Everybody, Mr. Taguchi called and left a message that he **won't be coming to work today because he has a severe headache** (stomachache, hangover).
皆さん、田口さんから電話があり、**頭痛（腹痛、二日酔い）がひどいので今日は休む**、という伝言を残されました。

As I **need to undergo a thorough medical examination** on November 10, I would like to take a day off on that day.
11月10日は**病院で精密検査がある**ので、休みを取らせていただきます。

If you have to be absent from work for a long period, you need to **present your doctor's report**.
長期の欠勤の場合は、**医師の診断書を提出する**必要があります。

As I will be operated on for a stomach ulcer, I **will be off from work for some time** starting next week. I will send my doctor's report in a separate mail.
胃潰瘍の手術のため、来週から**当分の間、欠勤**いたします。医師の診断書は別途送ります。

As I broke my ribs in a traffic accident, **I will stay home and take it easy** for a while.
交通事故で肋骨を骨折したため、しばらく**自宅で療養します。**

As Mr. Takagi **was injured in a traffic accident**, he is taking a few days off now (he will be taking days off for an undetermined period of time).
高木さんは**交通事故で怪我を負ってしまった**ので、現在、会社を休んでいます（しばらくお休みします）。

It seems that Mr. Fred Bascom **needs to be hospitalized** for about three weeks for treatment.
フレッド・バスコムさんは治療のため、3週間ほど**入院する必要**がありそうです。

I was hospitalized for a while but got better enough to be released yesterday. It looks like I **can get back to work on** June 15.
長らく病気療養中でしたが、昨日退院することができました。職場には**6月15日から復帰**できます。

病気や訃報② | **社員／元社員の訃報**

　訃報の形式はその国の文化により異なる。日本では、亡くなった人の氏名や元の所属、葬儀の日時や場所などを列挙した、あえて感情を交えない形式が多い。英語圏では、儀礼的ではあっても、「悲しいことですが〜」といった書き出しで知らせるのが一般的だ。

EXAMPLE

With great sadness and sorrow we regretfully announce the sudden passing away of Mr. Fredrik Copeland on March 15, formerly Vice President at San Jose. We express our greatest condolences.

大変悲しいことですが、弊社のサンノゼ支社元副社長フレドリック・コープランドさんが3月15日に急逝されました。謹んでお悔やみを申し上げます。

VARIATIONS

I am very sorry to have to report that Mr. George Wolfe, deputy director at the Legal Affairs Department, **suddenly passed away with** a stroke on October 21. Funeral details will be given later.

残念ながら、法務部副部長のジョージ・ウルフさんが10月21日、脳卒中で**突然お亡くなりになった**ことをお知らせしなければなりません。葬儀の詳細については、後ほどお知らせします。

Mr. Henry Miller's **funeral will take place at** 2:00 p.m. on Wednesday, March 14 at the Berkeley Memorial Hall.

ヘンリー・ミラー氏の**葬儀は**、3月14日（水）の午後2時から、バークレー・メモリアルホール**で執り行われます。**

We have been told that **there will be a private funeral service attended by the family and relatives only.** The family requested no flowers or donations.

葬儀は親族の方だけで行われるそうです。献花や香典は辞退されるとのことでした。

病気や訃報③ 葬儀の献花／寄付

EXAMPLE

The chief mourner said that in lieu of flowers, contributions may be sent to Dr. Haward Chen memorial fund at Good Samantha Hospital, 2425 Samantha Drive, San Jose, CA 95124.

喪主の方は、お花は辞退されるそうですが、寄付はカリフォルニア州サンノゼ、サマンサドライブ2425番地にあるグッドサマンサ病院のハワード・チェン博士記念基金宛てにしていただきたい、と仰っています。

VARIATIONS

There is a specific request from the family that **no flowers should be sent.**

ご家族から、**花は送らないようにと**、特にお願いがありました。

Family flowers only have been requested. Instead, **donations can be sent to** the scholarship foundation at University of Sunnyvale as a lasting memorial to him.

身内のお花だけにとのお願いがありました。しかし**寄付は**、氏の思い出として、サニーベール大学の奨学金基金**に送ることができる**そうです。

Ms. Louise Weisenberger has said that **the family will accept flowers** but **wishes no donations to be sent**.

ルイーズ・ワイゼンバーガーさんは、**お花は受け取りたい**と仰っておられますが、**香典は絶対に送らないように**とのことです。

個人的なお見舞い① お悔やみ

　知人の訃報に接した場合、お悔やみを親族等にメールで送ってよいかどうかは、その国の文化にもよるだろう。とはいえ、会社の要人の訃報を聞いたとき、社交儀礼の一環としてその会社の知り合いにお悔やみを送ることは少なくない。

EXAMPLE

We at the Japan branch of PowerLinkStream Co. are saddened to learn of the sudden death of your president, Bill Bellkeeper. He will be long remembered for what he leaves behind him in the IT industry. My associates and I want to extend our heartfelt sympathy.

（株）PowerLinkStream社日本支社社員一同、御社社長ビル・ベルキーパー氏の突然の訃報に接し、悲しみの念を禁じ得ません。氏はIT業界に残した業績により、いつまでも私たちの心に残ることでしょう。同僚ともども、慎んで哀悼の意を表します。

VARIATIONS

All of us at the system development group **want to express our heartfelt sympathy.**
システム開発グループのメンバー一同、**謹んでお悔やみ申し上げます**。

We were saddened to learn of the passing of Walter Watson, Los Angeles district manager of your company. All of us here **would like to express our condolences.**
貴社LA支局マネジャーでおられたウォルター・ワトソン氏の訃報に接し、一同悲しんでおります。**謹んでお悔やみ申し上げます**。

We are distressed to learn from the TV news this morning that your president has passed away. **We would like to extend our deepest sympathy.**
御社社長の死を今朝のテレビのニュースで知り、悲しみの念を禁じ得ません。**お悔やみ申し上げます**。

I was very sorry to hear that Mr. Donald Norman passed away. **I had the privilege of knowing him** for the past decade. Please know that I share your sorrow at this sad time.
ドナルド・ノーマン氏の訃報に接し、悲しみの気持ちでいっぱいです。ここ10年程、**お付き合いさせていた**だいていただけに、謹んでお悔やみ申し上げます。

個人的なお見舞い② | 元気づける

状況はさまざまだろうが、親しい人が大変な境遇に陥っていることを知ったら、その人を元気づける心のこもった励ましメールを送るのも良い考えである。

EXAMPLE

I heard about the big network trouble and wanted to let you and your team know that our thoughts and prayers are with you all in this most difficult time. Take it easy.

ネットワークシステムの大障害について聞きました。さぞかし大変でしょう。皆様のお気持ちをお察し申し上げるともに、この非常に大変な時期を乗り切られるよう、お祈り申し上げます。無理をなさらないでください。

VARIATIONS

My staff and I **are saddened to learn that** CoolClick Co. is going to close their Dallas branch.
（株）CoolClick社がダラス支社を閉鎖する**と知り**、スタッフともども**大変残念に思っております**。

I am just writing this email to **let you know how sorry I am** that your development project has been canceled.
あなたの開発プロジェクトが中止になったと聞き、**ご同情に耐えません**。

Upon hearing that your maintenance team is experiencing network trouble, my project members and I just **want to wish you a speedy recovery.**
あなたの保守チームがネットワーク障害を経験していると聞き、プロジェクト部隊の部下ともども、**素早い復旧を願っております**。

I am so sorry to hear that they are making you work overtime every night, and **I am praying that** you will find a different job soon.
残業を毎晩させられていることを聞きました。早く別の仕事が見つかる**ようお祈りしております**。

I am sorry to hear the news of your PC being stolen and I just want to say I hope that you will get a new machine soon.
あなたのPCが盗難にあった**と聞き**、**お気の毒に思っています**。早く、新しいマシンを入手できますよう願っております。

個人的なお見舞い③ **お悔やみ／励ましへの返信**

お悔やみや励ましのメールをもらったら、下記のような返信を送るとよい。例文のうち、上の2つは「お悔やみ」、中の4つは「励まし」や「お見舞い」向け。下の2つは「お悔やみ」と「励まし」の両方に使える。

VARIATIONS

On behalf of the members of my system development group, I thank you for your email **in which you expressed kind words of sympathy** on the death of our system architect, Mr. Calvin Alman.
弊社のシステムアーキテクト、カルビン・アルマンの逝去に際しまして、**心のこもったメールをいただきましたこと**に、システム開発グループのメンバーを代表してお礼申し上げます。

Your email with expressions of sympathy upon the death of our CEO, Steve Stewart, was greatly appreciated.
弊社CEOスティーブ・スチュワート逝去**に対し、丁重なご弔詞をメールでいただき**、ありがとう存じます。

Everybody, I am now back at work. I want to thank all of you **for the encouragement** you gave me while I was in the hospital with a broken leg. Thank you very much again.
皆さん、仕事に復帰しました。脚の骨折で入院中は**励ましのお言葉をいただき**ありがとうございました。本当にありがとうございました。

Thank you for your kind email. **It cheered me up** a lot.
親切なメールをありがとうございました。大変**元気づけられました**。

Thank you for sending me a kind email, and the beautiful flowers, too. They **really made my day.**
お心遣いの伝わるメールと、きれいな花を送っていただき、ありがとうございました。**その日は本当に元気が出ました**。

Thank you for coming the other day **to see how I was doing at the hospital**. The beautiful flowers really brightened up my room.
先日は私の様子を案じて**お見舞いに来ていただき**、ありがとうございました。頂戴したお花で病室が明るくなりました。

Your kind email was greatly appreciated.
ご親切なメールを本当にありがとうございました。

Your email of encouragement **meant a lot to me.**
あなたからの激励のメールで**励まされました**。

好意を伝える① クリスマスや新年の挨拶

VARIATIONS

We wish you a **Merry Christmas and a Happy New Year.**
楽しいクリスマスと新年をどうぞお迎えください。

We wish you **Happy Holidays.**
楽しい休暇をお過ごしください。※非キリスト教徒向けのニュートラルな表現

We wish you **a wonderful new year.**
皆様が**素晴らしい新年を**お迎えになるようお祈りします。

Have a Happy New Year!
明けましておめでとうございます。

We wish you **a very wonderful year** next year!
来年が皆様にとって**幸多い1年**であることを期待しております。

Our best wishes to every one of you for a Merry Christmas and **a Happy and Prosperous New Year**.
皆様の**ますますのご発展を**お祈りいたします。

John, **have a wonderful vacation** and don't worry about us none!
ジョン、我々のことはご心配なさらずに、**素晴らしい休日をお過ごしください！**

As the new year is nearly upon us, we would like to thank you **for your patronage this year**.
年末にあたり、**この1年のご愛顧に**厚くお礼申し上げます。

Providing great services to meet our customer expectations is again our goal this year. **All of us here** at the system development division **will try our bes**t to achieve this goal.
本年も素晴らしいサービスでお客さまのご期待に応えられるよう、システム開発部スタッフ**一同頑張りたい**と思います。

This year, BayTech Co. plans to **expand** its product line-up more **than we did in the past**.
本年、我々（株）BayTech社は、製品のラインナップを**これまで以上に充実させていく**つもりです。

好意を伝える② | **好意／尽力に感謝する**

何か世話になったことがあった場合、簡単なものでよいから、時間をおかずに感謝のメールを出そう。

EXAMPLE

I came back to Tokyo two days ago and am back at work today. Thank you for everything that you did for me while I was staying in San Jose. If you do visit Japan in the future, please make sure to let me know because I will always be very pleased to see every one of you.

2日前に東京に戻り、今日から出社しております。サンノゼ滞在中はいろいろお世話になりました。改めてお礼申し上げます。将来、日本にお越しになる際には、いつでも喜んでお会いしたいと思いますので、ぜひご連絡ください。

VARIATIONS

Thank you very much **for arranging** a job interview with the chief engineer.
技術主任との面接を**セットしていただいて**、本当にありがとうございました。

Thank you very much for arranging a visit to Prof. Chris Trent's cognitive science lab. I **look forward to repaying** you for this in the near future.
クリス・トレント教授の認知科学研究室を訪問する段取りをつけていただき、ありがとうございました。近い将来、**お返しができれば**と存じます。

It was **very thoughtful of you to** have someone come to the San Francisco airport to meet me. Thank you very much again.
サンフランシスコ空港に出迎えを寄越**していただき**、**大変助かりました**。本当にありがとうございました。

Nancy, **many thanks for booking** me a flight to San Jose on August 7.
ナンシー、8月7日のサンノゼ行きのフライトを**予約してくれてありがとう**。

I really appreciate **all the advice you gave me** for fixing this bug.
このバグを修正するに当たり、**さまざまな助言をいただき**、感謝しております。

I am very grateful **for all the help you gave me** while we were trying to set up the system.
システム立ち上げ作業の間、**いろいろお世話になり**、感謝しております。

I am greatly indebted to you for all the time you spent to debug the system.
システムをデバッグするために多くの時間を割いていただき、**大変意義を感じております**。

好意を伝える③ | 賞賛する

人を賞賛するのは簡単そうで難しい。自分と相手との関係によって、いろいろなニュアンスの表現を使い分ける必要がある。

EXAMPLE

We all at the development division of BitPower have been extremely impressed with the productivity and efficiency of your company and are pleased to say that we have found your company excellent. We are satisfied that we have awarded this development contract to you.

BitPower社開発部社員一同、貴社の優秀さ、開発チームの生産性と効率の良さにはこれまでも感服しておりました。今回、貴社に対して本開発契約を発注できたことに、大いに満足しております。

VARIATIONS

Mr. John Newhall, about this project, **I think** your design **is excellent.**
ジョン・ニューホールさん、このプロジェクトですが、あなたの設計は**素晴らしい、と思います**。

Mr. Morris, you will be very pleased to know that the Redmond office people **were very impressed with** your presentation last night.
モリスさん、喜んでください。レッドモンド・オフィスの面々は、昨晩のあなたのプレゼンに**非常に感心していました**。

John, don't worry about what the San Jose office people think of you. **I have heard nothing but praise for you** from them.
ジョン、サンノゼ・オフィスの人々が君のことをどう思っているか、気にする必要はない。彼らは**君のことをいつも褒めている**。

We have been impressed by how user-friendly the Web system is, which your company developed for us.
貴社に開発していただいたWebシステムがユーザーフレンドリーなので、**感心しました**。

We couldn't be more pleased with the performance of the automatic transaction system you developed.
御社が開発した自動決済システムの性能に**非常に満足しております**。

I want to commend you for your leadership while you were supervising the Web service development project.
Webサービス開発プロジェクトの監理における、あなたのリーダーシップ**を褒めたいと思います**。

好意を伝える④ 祝い状

昇進、栄転、プロジェクトの成功など、おめでたいことがあったときに親しい人に送るお祝いの表現である。

EXAMPLE

I am delighted to learn of your promotion to Director of the development division. There isn't a better man for the important job as far as I am concerned. Please accept my congratulations on your promotion.

開発部長にご就任と伺い、大いに喜んでおります。この重職に就けるのは、あなたを置いて他にないと思っております。ご栄進おめでとうございます。

VARIATIONS

Mr. Lester Grant, **I was delighted to hear that** you will be joining my development team.
レスター・グラントさん、あなたが私の開発チームに参加すると**聞いて喜んでいます**。

As for this Web copyright management system development project, **I want to congratulate you** for succeeding in convincing your immediate superior to go ahead with it.
このWeb著作権管理システム開発プロジェクトですが、直属の上司の説得に成功して、プロジェクトが進められるようになったそうで、**おめでとうございます**。

It was with great pleasure that I learned of you being transferred to the Tokyo office to join this project team.
あなたが東京オフィスに転勤してこられ、このプロジェクトチームに参加すると**聞いて、大変喜んでおります**。

Dear Mr. Fremont, **I was overjoyed at the news that** you have been promoted to senior executive vice president.
フレモント様、あなたが副社長に昇進なされた**と伺って、大いに喜んでおります**。

Allow me to congratulate you on your recent success with the Web content delivery system development project.
Webコンテンツ配信システム開発プロジェクトでの、貴社の最近のご成功に**お祝いを述べさせてください**。

Let me congratulate you on your recent promotion to chief engineer, on behalf of everyone here at the development division of JugglerNet.
JugglerNet社開発部門を代表いたしまして、技術主任への昇進に**お祝いを述べさせてください**。

第7章

説得・交渉の表現

相手に何かを求める	P.152 - P.155
助言	P.156 - P.159
意向を伝える	P.160 - P.169
意見を交換する	P.170 - P.181
同意する表現	P.182 - P.185
反対する表現	P.186 - P.192
妥協の表現	P.193 - P.195
問題が生じたとき	P.196 - P.203

相手に何かを求める① | 援助を求める

EXAMPLE

Mr. M. Hawkins, I hate to trouble you, but you can help me a lot if you give me some advice on which language I should use for the development of the Data_Selection program. Is it possible?

M・ホーキンスさん、ご面倒をおかけしたくありませんが、Data_Selectionプログラムの開発に使用する言語についてご相談に乗っていただけると非常に助かります。いかがでしょうか。

VARIATIONS

We **would like to have the benefit of** your experience, skills, and suggestions in fixing this bug.
このバグの修正に当たって、あなたの経験、スキル、そしてお知恵**を拝借できれば**、と思っております。

I hate to put you to the trouble of emailing the bug report to me, **but** I would be most grateful if you could.
お手数ですが、そのバグレポートを私宛てにメールしていただけるとありがたいのですが。

Would you **be so kind as to have** someone come to the server room at 1:00 a.m. tomorrow?
明日、午前1時に、誰かをサーバールームに寄越**していただけると助かる**のですが。

Could I ask you to help me out with nailing down this bug**?**
このバグを解決する仕事**を手伝ってもらえませんか**。

We would greatly appreciate your assistance in obtaining the necessary information concerning the Web picture delivery system of LinkPack Co.
(株) LinkPack社のWeb映像配信システムに関して、必要な資料を入手する上での、**あなたのご協力に深く感謝します**。

I would be most grateful if you would email the name and telephone number of the chief engineer of your department.
あなたの部署の技術主任のお名前と電話番号をメール**していただければ感謝いたします**。

Could you help us find the itinerary of Mr. Luke Silversteen, who is scheduled to go to California next week**?**
ルーク・シルバースティーンさんが来週、カリフォルニアに行く予定です。彼の出張日程**を調べていただけませんか**。

相手に何かを求める② | 婉曲に許可を求める

単純に「許可してください」ではなく、「もし〜なら」と条件を付けるなどして、やや婉曲に許可を求めるようにした表現である。

EXAMPLE

I have been told to explain the bug report on the Transaction module at the project manager meeting scheduled on March 15. If I can get your permission, I would like to email this bug report to all the project managers. Would that be all right with you?

3月15日に予定されているプロジェクトマネジャー会議でTransactionモジュールのバグレポートについて説明するように言われました。もしご許可がいただけるのであれば、このバグレポートをプロジェクトマネジャー全員にメールしたいのですが、よろしいでしょうか。

VARIATIONS

Would it be all right with you if I go to San Francisco to attend an IT conference?
ITカンファレンスに出席するためにサンフランシスコに出向いて**よろしいでしょうか**。

May I ask your permission to hire at least 3 new programmers for this project?
このプロジェクトのためにプログラマーを最低3人採用したいので、**許可をいただきたいのですが、いかがでしょうか**。

Director Adam Cowman, **if it is all right with you,** I would like to award the contract to PeerOneCOM Co.
アダム・カウマン部長、**もしご異存がなければ、**（株）PeerOneCOM社と契約を結びたいと思います。

Manager Brown, **I would like to get your permission to** set up a firewall to shut off unauthorized access into our system from outside.
ブラウン課長、**もし許可がいただければ、**外部からシステムへの不法侵入をシャットアウトするために、ファイアウォールを設置したいと思います。

Please allow me to show the design of this system to Mr. Oscar Lawrence of PlazaSoft Co.
（株）PlazaSoft社のオスカー・ローレンス氏に、本システムの設計を見せる**許可をいただきたいと存じます**。

相手に何かを求める③ 何かの行動を依頼する

相手に何かしてほしい旨を伝える際の表現。wouldを使うと丁寧な印象になる。

EXAMPLE

I seem to have misplaced the email address of Manager Paul Jenkins of OrbisExpress Co. I hate to put you to the trouble of emailing me his address, but I would be most grateful if you could do so as quickly as possible.

（株）OrbisExpress 社のポール・ジェンキンス課長のメールアドレスをどこかにやってしまったようです。お手数ではございますが、課長のメールアドレスをできるだけ早くメールしていただけると感謝します。

VARIATIONS

Mr. Bruce Rupert of the Tokyo office came down with appendicitis last night and was hospitalized at St. Luke Hospital at Tsukiji. **Would one of you be so kind as to** go visit him today**?**

東京オフィスのブルース・ルパートさんが昨晩、盲腸で築地の聖路加病院に入院しました。**皆さん方のうちのどなたかが**今日、お見舞いに行っ**ていただけませんか**。

It would be helpful if you would introduce the chief engineer of our company to the president of PowerLinkStream Co. while he will be in San Jose.

弊社の技術主任がサンノゼに滞在中に、（株）PowerLinkStream社の社長に紹介**していただけると助かります**。

We would like you to email an estimate on fixing this bug.

このバグ修正の見積もりをメール**してください**。

Manager Franklin, **would you** forward Michinori Shibuya's email to me**?**

フランクリン課長、渋谷道典からのメールを転送**していただけませんか**。

I would be grateful if you could email the technical document because it is not available in the Tokyo office.

あの技術文書は東京オフィスでは入手できないので、メール**していただけるとありがたいのですが**。

A new bug came up and **we request that** you send 3 programmers right away.

新たなバグが発生しましたので、プログラマーを3人、直ちに派遣**してください**。

Would you please email me the information for the development plan**?**

その開発計画についての資料を私にメール**していただけますでしょうか**。

相手に何かを求める④ 催促する

急を要することであるから、こちらの切迫感をストレートに伝え、早い対応を期待する。

EXAMPLE

About fixing this bug, as it is one of those cases that requires a very urgent response, please look into the matter right away and let us know what you find out.

このバグ修正ですが、非常に緊急な対応が必要なケースですので、直ちに調査し、結果がわかり次第知らせてください。

VARIATIONS

This is extremely urgent. **I want you to** take care of this bug **right away.**
非常に急いでいます。**直ちにこのバグを修正してください**。

We are in urgent need of three programmers and **would appreciate having** two of them **right away.**
緊急にプログラマーが3人必要になりました。**直ちに2人派遣していただければ感謝します**。

About the specification change that LuxTech Co. requested, I **require your immediate action on it**.
（株）LuxTech社が要請してきた仕様変更ですが、**直ちに対応するように要請します**。

If there is any reason why you cannot set up a Web server **right away,** please email me.
即時にWebサーバーを立ち上げ**られない理由が**あれば、メールで知らせてください。

It is urgent to complete this project by August 5.
このプロジェクトを8月5日までに完了する**ことは急務を要します**。

About fixing this bug, please treat it **as one of the special urgency cases**.
このバグを修正する件ですが、**特別な緊急事態として**対応してください。

Please email your resume **without delay**.
あなたの経歴書を**即刻**メールしてください。

Please **waste no time in** emailing me the information for the development plan.
その開発計画についての資料を、**間髪を入れず**、私にメールしてください。

助言① | アドバイスを請う

助言を求める際は、自分より知識・経験のある人にお願いするのであるから、もちろん丁寧な表現を心がける。

EXAMPLE

A company in Tokyo has ported our translation system onto the PC platform and has been marketing it without our permission. We would be very grateful for your advice about what action we should take.

東京のある会社が弊社の翻訳システムを、弊社の許可を得ずにPCに移植し、日本で販売しています。どういう方法に訴えればよいかについて、何かアドバイスをいただければ、大変ありがたく存じます。

VARIATIONS

I am wondering **if you could suggest some idea(s)** on how to respond to the bug report from NetSolutions4U Co.

(株)NetSolutions4U社からのバグレポートにどのように対応すべきかに関して、**何かいいアイデアを提案していただければ**と存じます。

I would like to ask your advice on how to debug the Get_Application_data.c program.

Get_Application_data.cプログラムのデバッグについて、**アドバイスをいただきたいです**。

I would be greatly indebted to you if I could get any advice on the design of our Web service program.

Webサービスプログラムの設計に関して、**何かアドバイスをいただけたら、恩義に感じます**。

If you have any advice or suggestions regarding Chris Byrd's proposal, please let me know.

クリス・バードのプロポーザルに関して、**何かいい案がありましたら教えてください**。

Your advice on the Web search program modification **would be greatly appreciated.**

Web検索プログラムの修正に**関して、助言をいただければ幸いです**。

Please advise me on this matter by return email.

この件に関して、折り返しメールで**ご助言ください**。

Could you advise me by email about how to shrink the development budget**?**

開発予算を縮小させる方法について、メールで**ご助言いただけますか**。

助言② アドバイスする

アドバイスは指示とは違う。一般には「～してはどうでしょう」など、あまり押し付けがましくない表現を使うとよいだろう。

EXAMPLE

Regarding what action you should take, our advice would be to take immediate legal action against that company in Tokyo.

どういう方法に訴えればよいかについてですが、我々のご助言を申し上げると、直ちに法的手段を講じ、その東京の会社を訴える、ということでしょう。

VARIATIONS

I would get in touch with a good system consultant **if I were you**.
もし私だったら、優秀なシステムコンサルタント**に連絡を取ります**。

I think that it would be in the best interest of your company to save all the log files.
すべてのログファイルを保存しておくのが御社**のためになる**、と思います。

It seems to me that you should call SilcotSoft Co. before you visit them.
訪問する前に、（株）SilcotSoft 社に電話を入れておいた**方がいいように思われます**。

I suggest that we add another programmer.
もう1人、別のプログラマーを加える**ことを提案します**。

Why don't you email the program tomorrow**?**
明日、そのプログラムをメール**してみてはいかがですか**。

My advice would be to call the main office and discuss it with Manager Bob Young.
本社に電話してボブ・ヤング部長と話す、**というのが私のアドバイスです**。

I advise you to wait and see if you get a better offer from JugglerNet Co.
JugglerNet 社からもっと良い引き合いがあるまで様子を見**てみたらいかがでしょうか**。

I recommend that you start planning a new development project immediately.
新しい開発プロジェクトの計画を直ちに開始する**ことを勧めます**。

The best thing for you to do is to have them email you all the information concerning the new project.
一番いいのは、彼らに新プロジェクトに関する情報をすべてメールしてもらう**ことです**。

助言③ 強く勧める

前項のような控えめな表現の助言とは別に、「ぜひこうするべきです」と強く勧めなければならないときもある。婉曲な表現は使わず、ズバリ言い切る必要がある。

EXAMPLE

Regarding the bug that disables our automatic transaction function, if LexusWebCom is unable to fix it by March 15, 2018, I strongly advise you to consult with our corporate attorney immediately.

弊社の自動決済機能を不能にするバグですが、LexusWebCom社が2018年3月15日までに修正できない場合は、社の顧問弁護士と相談することを強く勧めます。

VARIATIONS

I strongly advise you to consult with the general manager before reprimanding Paul Longman.
ポール・ロングマンを譴責する前に、部長に相談することを**強く勧めます**。

I suggest strongly that we should get a better workstation.
もう少し性能の良いワークステーションを購入することを**強く提案します**。

I am convinced that it is about time to replace this server machine because we have been using it for the past three years.
このサーバー機は3年目なので、そろそろ交換する時期だ**と確信しています**。

In my view, it is about time that we update the top page design of our company's Web site.
私の考えでは、そろそろ会社のWebサイトのトップページのデザインを更新する時期だと思います。

In the view of the development team, **the only viable solution** to this problem is to hire an American programmer.
開発チーム**の考えでは、**この問題に対する**唯一の有効なソリューション**は、米国人のプログラマーを1人雇うことです。

Unless we update our existing legacy system, **we will surely** lose at least one of our important clients.
既存のレガシーシステムをアップデートしなければ、大切な顧客を少なくとも1つ失うことになる**のは確かでしょう**。

助言④ アドバイスを採用する

EXAMPLE

Thank you for your advice with regard to the development schedule change. We plan to follow it because your advice is quite right.

開発計画変更に関するアドバイス、ありがとうございました。あなたのアドバイスはまったく正しいので、我々はそれに従う予定です。

VARIATIONS

My development team has decided to **take the advice of** your company's chief engineer and is going to change the design of the Web mining system.

私の開発チームは、御社の技術主任**のアドバイスを受け入れて**、Webマイニングシステムの設計を変更することにしました。

We have decided not to change our development schedule **by following the suggestions from** the senior consultant of CondorVersa Co.

（株）CondorVersa社の上席コンサルタント**の意見を取り入れて**、開発スケジュールを変更しないことにしました。

The development project group **has decided to carry out** the San Jose office's proposal.

開発プロジェクトグループは、サンノゼ・オフィスの提案を**実行することにしました**。

Manager Keita Aoyama's group **has made an excellent point** with respect to how to fix this bug. Why don't we use it?

このバグをどのように修正するかに関して、青山慶太課長のグループが**素晴らしい意見を出してくれましたので、それを採用するのはどうでしょうか**。

We have decided to put a temporary freeze on the development plan **as you suggested**.

あなたの提案に従って、我々は開発計画を一時中止することにしました。

I can't tell you how much **I really appreciate** your group's **suggestions** on overseas development.

海外での開発に関するあなたのグループの**提案には**、言葉に表せないほど、**本当に感謝しています**。

I appreciate the chief engineer's **advice** regarding the method of how to implement this function.

この機能を実装する方法に関する技術主任の**アドバイスには感謝しています**。

意向を伝える① ｜ 要望を婉曲に伝える

　ストレートに言いにくい要望は、婉曲的な表現を使うことで、遠回しに伝えることができる。

EXAMPLE

As for this development project for SpeedNet2U Co., it seems to me that we are using too many programmers on it.

このSpeedNet2U社向け開発プロジェクトですが、プログラマーを雇い過ぎているように私には思えます。

VARIATIONS

Wouldn't it be preferable to hire three programmers rather than two**?**
プログラマーは2人採用するより、3人採用した方がいいのではないでしょうか。

As far as this project is concerned, **I prefer** working with ClusterShell Co.
このプロジェクトでは、（株）ClusterShell社と一緒に仕事を**したいと思っております**。

Out of these prototypes that your company submitted, **I like** number 2 **the best**.
貴社が提出した、これらのプロトタイプの中では、2番目が**一番いいと思います**。

I would rather visit the San Jose office next week, **if I could.**
サンノゼ・オフィスには、**もしできれば**、来週出張したいのですが。

Mr. Raymond, **would it be possible** for you to work overtime today and finish this program rather than leave the office on time**?**
レイモンドさん、今日は、定時に退社するのではなく、残業してこのプログラムを完成させていただきたいのですが、**可能でしょうか**。

As I don't like system consultants, please let me hire programmers instead, **if I may**.
私はシステムコンサルタントは好きではありませんので、**もしできることなら**、プログラマーを雇わせてください。

As for this development project, **I would prefer that** you report any problem to me as soon as it occurs. **How about it?**
この開発プロジェクトに関しては、問題はどんなものでも発生次第すぐに私に報告**してほしいのですが、どうでしょうか**。

意向を伝える② | 売り込む

EXAMPLE

We specialize mainly in system development. With this Web house loan application system development project, we would be interested in working together with your company on it from the basic design phase. We look forward to hearing from you.

弊社は主にシステム開発を手掛けております。今回のWeb住宅ローン出願システム開発プロジェクトには、基本設計の段階から御社と一緒に携わりたいと思っております。お返事をお待ち申し上げます。

VARIATIONS

We at BullSoft **have developed an innovative** customer management system.
弊社はBullSoftと申しまして、**画期的な顧客管理システム**を**開発しました**。

With its very high cost performance advantages, it is a very useful sales support tool for Web marketing that **we can certainly recommend with confidence.**
本システムは、Webマーケティングにおいて非常に有用なコスト効果の高い販売支援ツールであり、**自信を持ってお勧めできます**。

This new technology **is superb in that** it not only has a very high compression ratio of animation data but also has a very simple decompression algorithm.
この新技術は、動画の圧縮効率が高く、しかも復号化のアルゴリズムが単純だという点で、**特に優れています**。

We are contacting you **to inquire whether you would be interested in using** a WebMailExpress as your in-house mailing system server.
御社の社内メールシステムにWebMailExpressを**採用いただきたく**、ご連絡いたしました。

If you are interested, please do not hesitate to ask me by email at Ken@CrossWay.com.
もしご**興味がおありでしたら**、何なりとメールで私宛て（Ken@CrossWay.com）にお問い合わせください。

Please visit our Web site as **we have posted detailed information** about this new technology there.
この新技術の**詳細**が弊社のWebサイトに**掲載されています**ので、ぜひご参照ください。

As we are **very familiar with** Linux, we are really interested in joining this embedded system development project with your company.
弊社は、Linuxに関することには**熟知しております**ので、今回の組み込みシステム開発プロジェクトに御社と一緒に参加したいと存じます。

意向を伝える③ 計画／目標を伝える

「目的は〜です」「我々はこう考えています」とストレートに表現して印象付けるのがポイントである。

EXAMPLE

The purpose of this development plan is to release a new server software on May 15 of this year as shown in the gantt chart below.

本開発計画は、下記ガントチャートに示す通り、今年の５月15日に、新しいサーバーソフトウェアをリリースするのが目的です。

VARIATIONS

What we must do is to regain trust from A2ZLink Co. for our development project group.
我々がすべきことは、当社の開発プロジェクトグループに対する（株）A2ZLink 社の信頼を取り戻すことです。

By offering a better service, **we are hoping to** increase sales volume and grasp a bigger share in the server software market.
より良質なサービスを提供することによって、売り上げを増加させ、サーバーソフトウェアの市場シェアを拡大させたい、**と考えています。**

The message I want to get across to Ms. Karen Lafayette, the chief engineer, is that improving the processing speed of this server software **is our first priority.**
技術主任カレン・ラファイエットに伝えたいメッセージは、このサーバーソフトウェアの処理速度を向上させることが**我々の最優先課題だ、**ということです。

Everybody! **The primary goal** of this product team **is to** increase the market share of the cluster server software of our company.
皆さん、当プロダクトチームの**第一の目的は、**当社のクラスターサーバーソフトウェアの市場シェアを拡大する**ことにあります。**

We aim to close the deal with AquosTech Co. within the following two weeks.
ここ２週間以内に、（株）AquosTech 社との商談を成立させる**ことが我々の目標**です。

The purpose of our activities **is to** improve the processing speed of this email server.
我々の活動の目的は、このメールサーバーの処理速度を向上させる**ことです。**

I am concerned with improving the image of the development project group.
私の関心は、開発プロジェクトグループのイメージアップ**にあります。**

意向を伝える④ | 援助を申し出る

EXAMPLE

I don't usually give unsolicited help, but this seems to be a special case so I am writing this email. As I have a free software that can solve your problem, please let me know if you are interested.

余計なおせっかいはしないたちなのですが、今回は例外的だと思い、このメールを書いております。当方に、あなたの問題を解決できるフリーウェアがありますので、ご興味があるようでしたら、お知らせください。

VARIATIONS

If you need some helping hands in setting up a Web server, just get in touch with me.
Web サーバーをセットアップするのに**人手が必要であれば、**ご連絡ください。

If you need anything that you want me to bring back from the San Jose office, just email me a list of items while I am still here.
サンノゼ・オフィスから持って帰ってきて**ほしいものがあれば、**私がここにいるうちに、その項目リストをメールしてください。

I would be happy **to assist you in any way I can** in hiring programmers.
プログラマーを雇う件で、**私にお役に立てることがあれば、**喜んでお手伝いします。

If there is anything I can do for the development project that you are managing, please let me know.
あなたがマネジメントしている開発プロジェクト**に関して、何か私にできることがあれば、**ご連絡ください。

It will be a pleasure for me **to help you in any way I can** in completing this development project.
この開発計画を完成させる上で、**あなたのお役に立てれば光栄です。**

If you think it would be helpful, let me email a letter of recommendation to Alex Bertland at the San Jose office.
お役に立つとお思いでしたら、私からサンノゼ・オフィスのアレックス・バートランド宛てに推薦状をメールさせてください。

If you want me to vouch for you, **I would be happy to do so.**
あなたの身元を保証してほしければ、**喜んでそうします。**

意向を伝える⑤ ┃ 懸念／不安があることを伝える

ストレートに反対意見を唱えるだけの材料がなかったり、それができる状況ではなかったりするとき、「懸念がある」という言い方で、間接的に反対の意を表明する方法がある。

EXAMPLE

Regarding the plan that the Web system development project group has submitted, I think I am very much in agreement with it, but I have certain reservations about those matters that we haven't dealt with.

Webシステム開発プロジェクトグループが提出した計画ですが、全体としては賛成ですが、まだ検討していない点について多少疑問があります。

VARIATIONS

It concerns us that the Web service development project is 2 months behind schedule.
Webサービス開発プロジェクトが予定より2カ月遅れているので**心配しています**。

My team **are concerned** about the delay of the Web service development project.
Webサービス開発プロジェクトが遅れていることを、私のチームは**懸念しています**。

It seems to me that **we should take time to think** about what to do with this project.
このプロジェクトをどうするかは、**時間をかけて考えた方がいい**と思います。

My concern is whether the collaboration business manger is someone who really understands the software industry.
私の心配は、そのコラボレーションビジネスマネジャーが本当にソフトウェア業界のことをわかっている人間**かということです**。

It is cause for my concern that many clients of ours have complained about our user support service division.
多くの顧客が当社のユーザーサポートサービス部門について、同じ苦情を訴えてきている**のは問題だと思います**。

We shouldn't draw a hasty conclusion on his proposal of adding three server machines.
サーバーを3台追加する彼の提案**に関しては**、**軽率な結論を下してはなりません**。

I am not 100% confident that we will be able to complete the development project by the end of January as we originally agreed with WiFiPlus Co.
(株)WiFiPlusと当初合意した1月末までに、この開発プロジェクトが完了できるか、**100%の自信はありません**。

意向を伝える⑥ 婉曲に疑問や質問を提示する

相手に疑問を提示したり、質問したりするとき、ストレートに聞くのではなく、和らげて問う表現がある。

EXAMPLE

About whether or not we should get some help from the network management team, it seems to me you ought to take a little more time to consider it before you draw a conclusion.

ネットワーク管理チームの支援を受けるべきかどうかですが、結論を出す前に、もう少し時間をかけて検討した方がいい、と思います。

VARIATIONS

I am wondering if you could tell me where XacBit Co. has moved to.
（株）XacBit社の移転先は**ご存じでしょうか**。

Of course, we would like to get rid of all bugs, but **do you have any idea about** how long it will take to fix this kind of bug**?**
もちろんバグはすべて修正したいのですが、この種のバグをフィックスするのにどのくらい時間がかかるか**ご存じですか**。

Could you tell me who is heading the Web service development project group**?**
Webサービス開発プロジェクトグループを率いているのは**誰か、教えていただけるでしょうか**。

My only question is when I should come to the meeting room next Tuesday.
1つだけ質問があるのですが、来週の火曜日、会議室には何時に行けばいいでしょうか。

There is some question as to whether Mr. Bill Gateskeeper would be of any help to the server development project team.
ビル・ゲイツキーパー氏がサーバー開発プロジェクトチームの役に立つか、**少々疑問です**。

I would like to know if you will be attending the project meeting this Wednesday.
あなたが、今週の水曜日のプロジェクト会議に出席するの**か知りたいのですが**。

I wonder whether we could complete the development project by the end of January as we originally agreed with WiFiPlus Co.
（株）WiFiPlus社と当初合意した1月末までに、この開発プロジェクトを完了**することができるのでしょうか**。

意向を伝える⑦ 約束する／請け合う

相手に「必ず～するので、ご安心ください」と太鼓判を押したいときに、こうした表現を使う。

EXAMPLE

Regarding hiring programmers, I will await your instruction, and I assure you that I will not hire any additional programmers without your approval.

プログラマー採用の件についてですが、あなたの指示をお待ちし、あなたの承認なしに新規採用はしないことを請け合います。

VARIATIONS

Please rest assured that we will take care of the bug immediately.
そのバグにはすぐに対応します**ので、ご安心ください**。

As for the development project, **you don't have to worry about it at all** as everything is going well with it.
開発プロジェクトについてですが、すべて順調に進んでいますので、**心配する必要はまったくありません**。

You have my word that we will not go over budget on the Web service development project.
Webサービス開発プロジェクトでは、絶対に予算超過にならない**ことをお約束します**。

About the function you wanted, **we will be done** testing it by July 14 **for sure**.
あなたが要求した関数は、**確実に**7月14日までにテストを**終了します**。

I assure you that we will complete the Web service development project by May 20.
Webサービス開発プロジェクトを5月20日までに完了する**ことを保証します**。

Let me assure you that we will never again get behind schedule in shipping.
二度と発送スケジュールに遅れを出さない**ことを請け合います**。

I guarantee that the work will be done exactly according to the specifications that the development team created.
開発チームが作成した仕様書通りに仕事が行われる**ことを保証します**。

I promise you that we will not hire new programmers without the San Jose office's approval.
サンノゼ・オフィスの承認なしにプログラマーの採用はしない**ことを約束します**。

意向を伝える⑧ 承認／許可する

EXAMPLE

We have decided to grant GiantSoft Co. the two-month extension of the original deadline that they requested, although we sincerely hope that this will never be needed in the future again.

（株）GiantSoft社から依頼のあった最初の締め切り期限の2カ月延長を承認することにしましたが、今後二度とこのようなことが絶対にないようにお願いします。

VARIATIONS

I grant you permission to use the server room on August 12.
サーバールームを8月12日に使用する**許可を与えます**。

I have decided to grant your request to work overtime.
あなたの残業の依頼を**許可することにしました**。

After careful consideration, **I have decided to let** Jeff Walker **be removed from** this development project.
熟慮の上、ジェフ・ウォーカーをこの開発プロジェクト**から外すことを許可することにしました**。

I approve of the plan to co-develop a Web automatic transaction system with NetSolutions4U Co.
（株）NetSolutions4U社とWeb自動決済システムを共同開発する**計画を承認します**。

We grant that programmers be allowed to take a 15 minute break every 2 hours.
プログラマーは2時間おきに15分の休憩を取る**ことができます**。

I hereby give my approval to you to let Kiyota go.
あなたが清田を解雇すること**をここに承認します**。

I entirely approve of Koga's decision to quit this job and go back to Saga prefecture to take care of his aging parents.
この仕事を辞め、佐賀県に戻って年老いた両親の世話をするという古賀の決断に**全面的に賛成します**。

I approve of the plan that we will complete the development project by the end of January as we originally agreed with WiFiPlus Co.
（株）WiFiPlus社と当初合意した1月末までに、この開発プロジェクトを完了させる**計画を承認します**。

意向を伝える⑨ 承認しない

承認する意を伝える表現がどちらかというと単純なのに対し、承認しないときは必要に応じて理由を述べたり、遺憾の意を伝えたりすることも多い。

EXAMPLE

Mr. Brett Grant, about your assessment that you need to add 3 more programmers to your system development project, I am afraid I don't share your assessment. As it seems to be too costly, I cannot give my approval to it either.

ブレット・グラントさん、あなたのシステム開発プロジェクトにプログラマーを新たに３人追加する必要があるとのご判断ですが、あなたのご判断には賛成しかねます。また、費用がかかりすぎそうに思えますので、承認することもできません。

VARIATIONS

I cannot grant your company the two-month extension of the original deadline that you requested because it is simply too long.
御社から要請のあった、当初の締め切り期限の２カ月延長**は認められません**。長過ぎます。

You do not have my permission to attend the Java conference next month in San Francisco.
来月、あなたがサンフランシスコのJavaカンファレンスに出席する**ことを認めません**。

I am sorry to say that your development plan **was not approved** by the board of directors last week.
残念ですが、あなたの開発計画は先週の役員会で**承認されませんでした**。

I am strongly against letting CrossWay Co. join the development team because I think they are totally incompetent.
私は（株）CrossWay社が無能だと思うので、同社を開発チームに参加させることには**大反対**です。

Due to budget constraints, **I cannot give the green light to** your plan to hire new programmers.
予算の問題で、プログラマーを新たに雇用するあなたの計画には**ゴーサインを出せません**。

I am sorry to inform you that we cannot approve of any changes in the original deadline that we agreed with your company last April.
申し訳ありませんが、この４月に御社と合意した締め切り期限の変更は**承認できませんので**、お知らせいたします。

意向を伝える⑩ 必要性を訴える

「どうしても必要だ」という意向を伝えるために、直接的で強い表現を使う。

EXAMPLE

It is both necessary and important for you to get Mr. Drake Finch's approval before you go ahead and hire 5 programmers.

プログラマーを新規に5人雇う前に、ドレイク・フィンチ氏の承認を得るのは、必要かつ重要なことです。

VARIATIONS

We need to hire 5 more programmers.
プログラマーをさらに5人雇う**必要があります**。

We absolutely must succeed in this project.
どうしてもこのプロジェクトは成功させ**なければなりません**。

Don't ever forget that you will send us an email and let us know the outcome of the system development meeting at least 24 hours before you leave the San Jose office.
サンノゼ・オフィスを発つ少なくとも24時間前にメールを入れて、システム開発会議の結果を知らせることを**絶対に忘れないようにしてくれ**。

Just make sure to fill out the attached application form and send it back by email to me.
添付した申請書に**必ず**記入し、それをメールで私に送り返す**ように**。

It is necessary for you to use some charts and graphs if you are going to do a presentation on the server development project.
サーバー開発プロジェクトについてプレゼンするのなら、表やグラフを使う**必要がある**。

There is no question that we must think about getting into the server software market.
サーバーソフトウェア市場への参入について、我々も考えなければならない**のは間違いありません**。

What is necessary for you is to get a letter of recommendation from Mr. Calvin Alman, the chief engineer.
必要なのは、技術主任のカルビン・アルマン氏から推薦状をもらう**ことです**。

I would like to inform you that President Casper Goldstein of BareSoft Co. is asking payment in advance, as **I think we should not overlook** that fact.
（株）BareSoft社のカスパー・ゴールドスタイン社長が前金での支払いを要求していることは**見逃すべきでないと思う**ので、お知らせします。

意見を交換する① 相手の意見を求める

「〜についてどう思うか」と質問を投げかけることは、意見交換の出発点だ。

VARIATIONS

Regarding the next development project, we would like to proceed along the line described above. **Please let me know what you think**.
次期開発プロジェクトですが、上のような構想で進めたいのですが、**いかがでしょうか**。

I would be interested to find out your opinion about the attached bug report.
添付したバグリポート**について、あなたの意見を伺いたいと思います**。

I would like to hear your opinion on whether or not your company intends to make the development group stay in Tokyo a littler longer.
御社が、あとしばらく開発グループを東京に駐在させるつもりなのかどうか、**あなたの意見を伺いたいと思います**。

I would appreciate your honest opinion about how the development group is doing these days.
最近の開発グループの仕事ぶりについて、**君の正直な意見を知りたい**。

I am interested in hearing the San Jose office's views on the program we developed.
我々が開発したプログラムについて、サンノゼ・オフィスの**意見を聞きたいです**。

I hesitate to trouble you with this when you are busy, but **I need to have your opinion** on the program I emailed yesterday.
お忙しいところ申し訳ありませんが、昨日メールしたプログラムについて、**あなたの意見をぜひとも知りたい**のですが。

I am curious to hear your opinion on how our new senior consultant, Carl Beckett is doing.
我が社の新任のシニアコンサルタント、カール・ベケットの仕事ぶりについて、**あなたのご意見を聞かせてください**。

I would like to hear your company's view on the potential for our server software in the US market. Please let us know **your honest opinion about it.**
当社のサーバーソフトウェアについて、アメリカ市場での可能性を御社から伺いたいと思っております。**率直なご意見**をお聞かせください。

I would be **interested to know what you think** about the shrinking employment market in Japan.
日本の縮小する雇用市場について、**あなたがどのようにお考えかを知りたい**と思います。

意見を交換する ② | こちらの意見を述べる

　意見を尋ねられたら、「私の意見はこうだ」と自分の考えをはっきり述べるのが第一の選択肢。相手もそれを求めている。

EXAMPLE

My feelings on the matter are that we should not be making exceptions, even for the server development group. And I am convinced that we should tell them to get started immediately.

その件に関する私の考えは、サーバー開発グループといえども例外扱いすべきではない、ということです。彼らに命じて、直ちに作業を開始させるべきだ、というのが私の意見です。

VARIATIONS

From my point of view, we should send an email of apology to DigiPoly Co. for not being able to have completed the Web service program on schedule.
私の意見としては、Webサービスプログラムをスケジュール通りに完成できなかったことに対する謝罪のメールを、（株）DigiPoly社に送るべきだと思います。

It is the opinion of Mr. Malcom Billington that the Saratoga office should send 3 programmers to Tokyo to support us.
サラトガ・オフィスは3人のプログラマーを東京に派遣して我々をサポートすべきというのが、マルコム・ビリントン氏**の意見です**。

As far as I am concerned, the addition of 3 programmers is unnecessary.
私としては、3人のプログラマーの追加は不必要**と考えます**。

In my opinion it is a very good programming method.
私の考えでは、それは非常に良いプログラミング方法です。

I would like to meet you and talk about the solution that the sever development group proposed.
サーバー開発グループが提案したソリューションについては、**直接お会いして、話し合いたいと思います**。

意見を交換する③ 断定的／曖昧に意見を述べる

「こうである」と断定したいとき、あるいは逆に、単純に言い切れないときは、それにふさわしい表現を状況に応じて使い分ける。

EXAMPLE

I understand that you wish us to allow an extension on the system development project whose initial deadline is March 12, 2018. We regret to inform you that we ourselves are in the position that we must work against that deadline and have no authority to do anything with it.

システム開発プロジェクトの当初の締め切り、2018年3月12日を延期してほしいというご希望ですが、当方もその締め切り期限に間に合わなければならぬ立場にあり、それをどうこうできる権限を持ち合わせておりません。

VARIATIONS

I am convinced that the change the server development group suggested is most effective to fix the bug.
サーバー開発グループが提案した変更がバグを修正するのに最も効果的だ**と私は確信しています**。

I am absolutely certain that the Web service of our company will start within two weeks.
我が社のWebサービスが2週間以内にスタートする**のは確実だと私は思います**。

There is no doubt that this project is going to be a success.
このプロジェクトが成功する**ことに疑いの余地はありません**。

It seems to me that the Web service project group is spending too much time to fix the bug.
Webサービスプロジェクトグループは、そのバグをフィックスするのに時間をかけすぎている、**と私は思います**。

I could be mistaken, but Mr. Hammond's method seems to me very crude.
間違っているかもしれませんが、ハモンドさんの方法は非常に粗雑な方法に思えます。

It could be that President Robert Hopkins of DataZone Co. prefers the method because it has been suggested by the development group.
(株)DataZone社のロバート・ホプキンス社長がこの方法を好むのは、開発グループが提案した方法だから**かもしれません**。

As far as I am able to observe, the project group is doing a good job these days.
私が観察できる限りでは、プロジェクトグループは最近よくやっているようです。

意見を交換する④ 意見を述べるのを控えたい

何か理由があって、こちらの意見を相手に伝えたくない場合もある。こうしたケースでの表現は官僚の答弁のようになってしまうかもしれないが、最低限こちらの立場を相手に伝えることはできる。

EXAMPLE

Regarding the design change of the Web system for PhoneComm, the project group hasn't had a chance to form an opinion on it yet and we are so pressed for time that we are afraid we cannot give you a constructive opinion.

PhoneComm社向けWebシステムの設計変更に関してですが、まだプロジェクトグループの意見がまとまっておらず、あいにくいろいろ忙しく時間がとれず、建設的な意見を申し上げることができません。

VARIATIONS

Not having read the white paper, **I don't think that** our team **is in a position to comment.**
ホワイトペーパー（技術文書）を読んでいないので、私のチームは**意見を述べる立場にはない**と思います。

About the chief engineer's proposal, I haven't had enough time **to consider it to form an opinion.**
技術主任の提案ですが、考える時間が十分なくて、まだ**考えがまとまっていません**。

I don't have an opinion on Mr. Daisuke Tabata's proposal one way or the other.
田端大輔さんの提案に対して、**特に意見はありません**。

Concerning OrchidSoft Co.'s claim, **I would like to think more about it before giving an opinion.**
（株）OrchidSoft社のクレームについては、**意見を述べる前にもっと考えたいと思います**。

I don't have enough information to give a constructive opinion about this bug report.
このバグリポートに関しては、**資料が不十分なので建設的な意見が言えません**。

I am **not in a position to give an opinion** on the Web server construction.
Webシステムの構築について、私は**意見を述べる立場にはおりません**。

It is difficult for us to comment on the multimedia program change.
当方がマルチメディアプログラムの変更について**コメントするのは困難です**。

意見を交換する⑤ ｜ 注意を喚起する

自分が述べたいテーマに相手の注意を引きつけ、議論をこちらが意図している方向に誘導する。

EXAMPLE

I understand that you people are debating whether or not the deadline of March 12, 2018 should be extended. It must be noted that DataZone Co. is one of the trouble makers and gets behind schedule every so often.

2018年3月12日の締め切りを延長するかしないかで議論をしているようですが、（株）DataZone社はトラブルメーカーの1つで、スケジュールに遅れを出すことがよくあることに注意する必要があります。

VARIATIONS

Let me remind you that we have over twenty years of experience in system consultation.
我々がシステムコンサルテーションの分野で20年以上の経験がある**ことをお忘れなく**。

I would like to draw your attention to some of the advantages of our plan over those of other development teams.
他の開発チームの計画に比べて、我々の計画の方がいくつかの点において優れていることに**注目していただきたい**。

The important point is that more and more companies are using open source software to cut down their development cost.
重要な点は、開発コスト削減のためにオープンソースソフトウェアを利用する企業が増えて**いるということです**。

We should not forget that the RPA market is growing fast although it is still relatively small.
RPA市場はまだ比較的小さいけれど、急成長している**ことを忘れてはならない**。

We should not overlook the fact that the vast majority of our clients have very little knowledge about programming.
我々の顧客の大多数はプログラミングについてほとんど知らない**という事実を見過ごしてはなりません**。

Allow me to point out that this is not the first time LinkPack Co. has failed to complete the project on schedule.
（株）LinkPack社がプロジェクトをスケジュール通りに終了できなかったのは、今回が初めてではない**ことを指摘させていただきたい**。

意見を交換する⑥ | 理由を示す

自分の考えや立場の論拠をはっきり相手に伝えることは、説得・交渉テクニックの基本だ。「理由は〜です」と明示的に伝えるのがよい。

EXAMPLE

Since one would not expect any problems with a company of your caliber as far as system development contracts are concerned, the main reason we at SpeedStream Co. decided to discontinue this project is that you refuse to abide by the original terms of the contract that we agreed upon with you on November 4, 2016.

システム開発契約に関して、御社のような企業にこのようなことは申し上げにくいのですが、我々SpeedStream社がこのプロジェクトを継続しないことに決定した主な理由は、2016年11月4日に合意した契約書の条項に御社が従おうとしないからです。

VARIATIONS

One reason why we are developing the program is the growing demand for open source software.
弊社がそのプログラムを開発している**理由の1つは**、オープンソースソフトウェアに対する需要の拡大です。

MoveOn Co. is going to suspend the Web server development project **for the following reason.**
(株) MoveOn社は**以下の理由で**Webサーバー開発プロジェクトを中止することにします。

We have been unable to process the budget for the Web server development project group **because of** this new policy.
この新しい方針**が原因で**、Webサーバー開発プロジェクトグループの予算を処理できずにいます。

The steady development budget cut **is the reason why** we have decided to focus on the server software market.
このところ開発予算が削減され続けている**ので**、サーバーソフトウェア市場に的を絞ることにしました。

There are a number of reasons for discontinuing this development project.
この開発プロジェクトを中止する**理由はたくさんあります**。

意見を交換する⑦ | 重要性を指摘する

一方的に「〜すべきです」と主張するより、ことの重要性を指摘したうえで、相手に正しい判断を求める方がうまくいくケースは多い。

EXAMPLE

When you try to convince the Sunnyvale office on this development plan, it could prove important to go through the proper channels.

この開発計画に関してサニーベール・オフィスを説得しようとする場合、適切な人的チャンネルをたどることが重要かもしれません。

VARIATIONS

As for the development plan that David Johnston created, **I believe that it is important for us to** discuss it further.

デビッド・ジョンストンが作成した開発計画ですが、さらに話し合う**ことが重要だと私は思います**。

It is important to release this product on schedule and expand our market share.

この製品をスケジュール通りにリリースし、マーケットシェアを拡大する**ことは重要です**。

What is important about this development project is to get it done by the end of this month.

この開発プロジェクト**に関して重要なのは**、今月末までにそれを完了させることだ。

We should not overlook the fact that Kerry Marshall stays in the office late in the evening everyday and works overtime.

ケリー・マーシャルが毎晩夜遅くまでオフィスに残って残業している**という事実を見逃してはなりません**。

It is your important duty to email your progress report daily.

進捗報告を毎日メールするのは**あなたの大切な義務です**。

It is a good idea for you to read over any email you write before you send it.

メールを書いたとき、送る前に読み返す**ことは良いアイデアです**。

意見を交換する⑧ 重要性を強調する

「不可欠だ」「絶対に必要だ」というニュアンスで、ことの重要性を、前項よりもさらに強く相手に訴える表現。

EXAMPLE

As we cannot stress enough the importance of fixing this bug, it is absolutely necessary that we respond to the claim from the Los Altos office immediately.

このバグを修正することの重要性は、強調してもしすぎることはないので、ロスアルトス・オフィスからのクレームに直ちに対応することが絶対に必要です。

VARIATIONS

I cannot stress enough how important it is to email your progress report to the chief engineer everyday.
技術主任に自分の進捗報告を毎日メールすることがいかに大切か、**強調してもしすぎることはない**。

Regarding this project, **I consider it most important** for us to meet our delivery deadline.
このプロジェクトに関しては、納期に間に合うことが**最も重要だと私は思います**。

I would like to emphasize that the goal of this development meeting is to come up with a solution.
何らかのソリューションを考え出すことが、この開発会議の目的である、**ということを強調したい**。

We would like to lay special emphasis on the importance of listening to what SyncCom Co. wants to tell us.
（株）SyncCom社の言い分に耳を傾けること**の重要性を、我々は特に強調したい**。

The issue of overtime pay **is very significant** if we are going to hire new programmers.
新しくプログラマーを雇うのであれば、残業手当**の問題が非常に重要です**。

I feel that placing limits on what Kiyota demands **is a vital issue**.
清田からの要求に限度を設ける**ことは不可欠**だと、私は思います。

意見を交換する⑨ | それほど重要でないと言いたいとき

何かの案件が、相手が考えているほど重要だとは自分には思えない、と言いたいときに使う。

EXAMPLE

Although George Wolfe is against adding more programmers to the project, when we consider the size of the overall budget of the project, the cost of adding 3 programmers is a very minor issue.

ジョージ・ウルフはプログラマーの増員に反対しているが、プロジェクト全体の予算規模を考えると、プログラマーを3人追加するコストなど、非常に些末な問題だ。

VARIATIONS

Who will be fixing this bug **is of secondary importance.**
誰がこのバグを修正するかは**二次的な問題です**。

Assigning Stephen Rendel to Tabata's team is **a relatively minor** personnel change.
スティーブン・レンデルを田畑のチームに割り当てることは、**比較的小さな**人事異動だ。

I'm afraid I'm not convinced of the importance of you having a UML certification unless you plan to do object-oriented programming.
オブジェクト指向でプログラミングするのでない限り、UML認定資格を持っていることが**重要だとは、私には思えません**。

It is not so important at which office we will be doing development, since we will be all connected through the network.
どこにいてもネットワークでつながっているので、どのオフィスで開発作業をしているかは**さほど重要ではない**。

I don't see the importance of keeping paper documents since all the information is saved on our file server.
すべての情報がファイルサーバー上に保存されているのだから、紙の書類を取っておく**重要性が私にはわかりません**。

I really do not think Tanaka, who is in charge of the Web division, **is all that important.**
Web担当の田中がそれほど重要だとは思いません。

I don't think collaboration **is as important as you think it is** in this project.
このプロジェクトでは、**あなたが考えるほど**コラボレーションが**重要だとは思いません**。

意見を交換する⑩ | 確実性が高いとき

「確実だ」「自信がある」「絶対だ」というニュアンスで、確信があることを述べる表現。

EXAMPLE

Although we will need to introduce 3 new workstations into the development environment, I am certain that this project is going to be a success.

開発環境にワークステーションを新規に3台導入する必要はあるが、私はこのプロジェクトの成功を確信している。

VARIATIONS

Regarding Joe Weisenberger, who heads the development division now, **I have every confidence that** he will do an excellent job in his new assignment.
現在、開発部門を率いているジョー・ワイゼンバーガーですが、彼が今度の仕事で素晴らしい働きをする**ことは確実だ、と私は思います**。

We are confident that we will be able to meet our delivery deadline.
我々には、納期に間に合う**という自信があります**。

I hate to say it, but **it is obvious that** Kiyota is having a negative impact on this development project.
言いたくはないが、清田がこの開発プロジェクトに悪影響を及ぼしている**のは明白**だ。

It is beyond question that we have to pay some extra expense to PlazaSoft Co. because their programmers worked overtime last week.
(株)PlazaSoft社のプログラマーが先週残業したので、同社に所定外費用を払わなければならない**ことは確実**だ。

It is self-evident that something has to be done about this delay.
この遅れについて、何かがなされなければならない**のは自明**だ。

There is no doubt that the product we developed will continue to sell in the US market.
米国市場で、我々が開発したプロダクトが売れ続ける**ことは間違いない**。

We have every reason to believe that this software will be a bestseller throughout the world.
このソフトウェアが世界中でベストセラーになる**のは確実**だ。

179

意見を交換する⑪ | 可能性が高いとき

確実とまでは言えないが、可能性が大いにある、というときの表現。

EXAMPLE

Since I consider it most important to meet the delivery deadline in any project, if you cannot complete the system construction by the promised date, it is highly likely that we will start looking for another developer.

いかなるプロジェクトにおいても納期に間に合うことが最も重要だと私は考えますので、もし約束の期日までにシステム構築が終えられない場合は、開発先を変更する**可能性が大いにあります**。

VARIATIONS

We can be fairly certain that most of the information needed in this project is saved on FestaSeven Co.'s file server.
このプロジェクトで必要とされる情報の大部分は、（株）FestaSeven社のファイルサーバー上に保存されている、**と考えていいでしょう**。

It could very well be that your email has been sent to a wrong address.
あなたのメールが違う宛先に送られた**可能性が大いにあります**。

I am almost positive that Manager Makoto Takayama can attend the meeting in Menlo Park next week.
高山誠課長が来週、メンローパークでの会議に出席できる**のはほぼ確実だろう、と私は思います**。

As far as this development project is concerned, **it is very likely that** we have to let 3 programmers go.
この開発プロジェクトについては、**おそらく**プログラマーを３人削減しなければならない**でしょう**。

It is quite likely that you will have a chance to meet Ralph Paxton when you are visiting the Tokyo office.
あなたが東京オフィスを訪問なさっている間に、ラルフ・パクストンに会う機会が**きっとあるでしょう**。

There is a good chance that our company will be moving to the Shiodome area next year.
我が社は来年、汐留エリアに引っ越す**可能性が高いです**。

There is every possibility that John Smith will be promoted to a chief engineer.
ジョン・スミスが技術主任に昇進する**可能性は十分にある**。

意見を交換する⑫ 可能性がほとんどないとき

「〜は無理でしょう」（＝可能性はほとんどありません）というニュアンスで、相手の希望的観測をやんわりと否定するときの表現。

EXAMPLE

Regarding the bug that disables the automatic transaction function, it looks difficult to fix in a day because it is a very complex problem.

自動決済機能を不能にするバグですが、非常に複雑な問題なので、1日で修正するのは難しそうです。

VARIATIONS

There is very little likelihood of us meeting the delivery deadline within this year.
今年中に納期に間に合わせる**のは無理でしょう**。

Between you and me, **it is very unlikely that** Kiyota of NodePeer Co. would be able to fix this bug within this week.
ここだけの話ですが、（株）NodePeer社の清田が今週中にこのバグを修正できる**可能性は少ないです**。

It is not likely that this development plan will be canceled this year.
この開発計画が今年、キャンセルされる**可能性は少ないです**。

The chances of hiring a programmer with all those qualifications and skills **are extremely remote.**
それだけの資格とスキルを持ったプログラマーを雇用できる**可能性はほとんどありません**。

I think it will be difficult to find an ultimate solution for this bug.
このバグに対して究極の解決策を見つける**ことは困難**だと思います。

It is very unlikely that we will be able to launch this development project this year as I hoped because the financial status of our company isn't that great.
この開発プロジェクトを今年スタートしようと思っていましたが、会社の経済状態がそれほど思わしくないので、今年は**無理のようです**。

There is not much of a possibility that my team will fail.
私のチームが失敗する**可能性はほとんどありません**。

It is very improbable that our company will cancel this development project.
弊社がこの開発プロジェクトを中止することは、**可能性としてあり得ないでしょう**。

同意する表現① | 賛成する

単純な「同意します」「賛成です」という言い方に加え、「考えは理解できます」のような含みを持たせた表現や、「まったく賛成です」という強い賛成の表現がある。

EXAMPLE

As I understand that you yourself are in the position to work against that deadline, I think that we are in agreement on the main points of how many days we are allowed to spend to fix this bug.

貴社もその期日に間に合わなければならない立場にあるということは理解できますので、このバグを何日で修正しなければならないかについて、我々は大筋で合意していると思います。

VARIATIONS

I agree one hundred percent on Manager Keita Yasuda's suggestion to let programmers take a 10 minute break every 2 hours.
プログラマーに2時間ごとに10分の休憩を取らせるという安田敬太課長の提案に、**私は100％賛成です**。

I can understand your thoughts on the issue of our staff's working overtime every night.
スタッフが毎晩残業して働いている件についての、**あなたの考えは理解できます**。

I agree with your opinion that the bug report should include the description of the phenomenon when the problem occurs.
バグレポートには、その問題が発生した時の現象の記述を含めるべきだ、**というあなたの意見に同意します**。

This development team **is of the same opinion as** Manager Hideki Harada.
当開発チームは、原田英樹課長**と同意見です**。

About continuing this development, I think that **we are of one mind.**
この開発の続行に関して、**我々の考えは同じだ**と私は思います。

We are in total accord on the goals of this development project team.
この開発プロジェクトチームの目標に関して、**我々は完全に一致しています**。

I am in total agreement with your decision to remove Kent Morris from the development team.
ケント・モリスを開発チームから外すというあなたの決定に、**私はまったく賛成です**。

同意する表現② | 部分的に合意する

相手の考えに完全に反対ではないが、さりとて全面的に同意しているわけでもないという微妙な立場のときに、こうした表現が使える。

EXAMPLE

In principle I agree with the chief engineer's idea about how to set up a P2P server, but I wonder if it will work as he explained at the meeting last night.

P2Pサーバーをどのようにセットアップするかについては、技術主任の考えに同意しますが、彼が昨晩の会議で説明した通りに実際にうまく動作するかは疑問だと思います。

VARIATIONS

Although **I agree with most of** what you've described in your email of July 15 about how to market our email server software in Taiwan, **I find it difficult to agree with you on** the issue of customizing the software by ourselves.
弊社のメールサーバーソフトを台湾向けにどのように販売するかについて、あなたが7月15日付けのメールで示した内容の**大部分に私は賛成します**が、このソフトウェアを自分たちでカスタマイズするという件**については賛成しかねます**。

We are in agreement on the methodology that we should adopt, but **I can't agree with** your implementation plan.
採用すべき方法論では**あなたと意見が一致しています**が、あなたの実装計画には**同意しかねます**。

Concerning continuing this development project, **I would tend to agree with your opinion**, but **there are certain points where I have my doubts**.
この開発プロジェクトの継続に関して、**あなたの意見に賛成したいのですが**、**いくつか疑問点があります**。

About bringing more programmers into this project, **I am inclined to agree with you** although **we may differ on a couple of points.**
このプロジェクトにプログラマーをもっと追加する件に関して、**あなたに賛成したいところ**ですが、**2、3考えが違うところがあるようです**。

Regarding this development plan, I think **we agree for the most part**, but the following 3 points **should be discussed further.**
この開発計画に関して、**大筋で我々は合意している**と思いますが、次の3点は**もっと話し合うべきでしょう**。

同意する表現③ ▍ 提案を全面的に支持する

相手の考えに賛成するという自分の立場を明確にし、その上で相手の考えを強く支持するときに使う表現。

EXAMPLE

Regarding how to change the basic development plan, I am fully in favor of asking the chief engineer to help us.

基本開発計画をどのように変更するかについてですが、技術主任の助けを借りることに私はまったく賛成です。

VARIATIONS

Because we **will support** the development division **all the way** on this project, you can count on us.
このプロジェクトに関しては、我々は開発部門を**最後まで支持します**ので、ご安心ください。

I am behind Lester Grant's proposal **100%.**
レスター・グラントの提案を**100％私は支持します**。

We **firmly support** your team's position, too.
我々も、あなたのチームの立場を**固く支持します**。

I give my total support to the idea of changing the basic specifications.
基本仕様を変更する考えに、**私は全面的に賛成です**。

I would like to **express my total support** for the chief engineer's action.
私は技術主任の行動を**全面的に支持することを表明**したいと思います。

The Santa Clara office's proposal **has my full support.**
私はサンタクララ・オフィスの提案に**大賛成**です。

The project group has our **total and unconditional support.**
我々はプロジェクトグループを**全面的かつ無条件で支持します**。

同意する表現④ 提案を基本的には支持する

相手が出してきた提案や考え方を基本的に、あるいは若干の条件付きで支持することを伝えるときの表現。

EXAMPLE

With certain conditions, we would support the Cupertino office's proposal that we will use more than five programmers.

条件付きながら、我々は、5人以上のプログラマーを使うというクパチーノ・オフィスの提案を支持します。

VARIATIONS

I like the basic idea behind Mr. Clark Stillman's instruction, but I can't help wondering about some of the particulars.
クラーク・スティルマンさんの指示の**基本的な考えは気に入っています**が、個別的には疑問に思う点がいくつかあります。

I am **basically in favor of** the San Mateo office's proposal.
サンマテオ・オフィスの提案に**基本的には賛成**です。

Basically I support the idea of letting contracted programmers work overtime.
契約プログラマーに残業させる**という考えを、私は基本的に支持します**。

I would not oppose the idea of leaving tomorrow instead of the day after tomorrow.
明後日ではなく、明日出発する**という考えに私は反対しません**。

Basically, we support the product group's proposal.
基本的には、プロダクトグループの提案を**我々は支持します**。

With a few changes, we would support your development plan.
いくつかの変更をするのであれば、我々はあなたの開発計画を**支持します**。

Our overall reaction to LuxTech's proposal **is favorable**, but we need to talk about a couple of points.
我々はLuxTech社の提案に対して**全体的には賛成ですが**、2、3の点については話し合う必要があります。

反対する表現① | **意見の不一致を表明する**

相手の考えに対して「私は考えが違う」「見方が違う」と言いたいときの表現の仕方。

EXAMPLE

Mr. Silversteen, thank you for drawing my attention to the bug and I am sorry to hear that our system does not function properly because of it. But I don't agree with your assertion at all that I should fix the bug because it is located in a module which I have nothing to do with.

シルバースティーン様、バグの存在を知らせていただきありがとうございます。また、そのバグのせいでシステムが正しく動作しないことは残念ですが、それを修正するのは私だ、というあなたの指摘にはまったく同意できません。そのバグは、私がまったく関知しないモジュール内にあるからです。

VARIATIONS

I can't say that I share your idea on how to implement this function.
この機能をどのように実装するかについての**あなたの意見には、賛成だとは言えません**。

I really can't agree with you that this month is the best timing to halt the development plan.
今月が開発計画を中止する一番いいタイミングだという**あなたの意見に、私は賛成できません**。

Regarding how to proceed with the development plan from now on, **I am afraid we don't see things the same way.**
開発計画を今後どのように推進するかについては、**残念ながら我々は見解が違います**。

I can't help feeling that you are not quite right about how to fix this bug.
このバグをどのように修正するかについて、**あなたは間違っていると思わざるを得ません**。

I do not share your view on the best method that we should adopt for this project.
このプロジェクトで採用すべき最善の方法についての**あなたの考えには同意しかねます**。

I feel that I really must disagree with Matthew Hawkins' opinion.
マシュー・ホーキンスの意見には、**反対しなくてはならない、と思います**。

I don't completely agree with Mr. Taguchi's view that this is the best time to get into the Vietnam market.
現在がベトナム市場に参入する一番いい時期だという、田口氏の意見に**全面的に賛成するわけではありません**。

反対する表現② 意見の不一致を強調する

意見の不一致を、前項よりもさらに強調して伝えるときの表現である。

EXAMPLE

Mr. Oscar Feldman, thank you for your email dated July 20, in which you proposed to change the basic design of this project completely. Unfortunately, my development group and I are **in total disagreement** with you because it does not seem practical to start doing it at this stage of the development process.

オスカー・フェルドマン様、このプロジェクトの基本設計を徹底的に変更してはどうかという 7 月 20 日付けのメールを拝見いたしました。残念ながら、弊社の開発グループも私も、あなたの意見に**まったく反対**です。開発作業のこの段階になっての基本設計の変更は実際的でない、と思えるからです

VARIATIONS

I am **in total disagreement** with your programming approach.
あなたのプログラミング手法に、私は**まったく反対**です。

I totally disagree with his opinion on this solution.
このソリューションに関して、私は彼の意見に**まったく反対**です。

Mr. Paul Jenkins, I hate to disagree with you, but **I don't think that** Mr. Taguchi **understands our perspective at all.**
ポール・ジェンキンス様、あなたの意見に反対したくはないのですが、私は田口氏が**我々の見識をわずかなりとも理解しているとは思いません**。

I think that it's a bad idea to accept EdgePeople's excuse for this delay.
この遅れについての EdgePeople 社の弁解を受け入れるのは、**まずい考えだと思います**。

What you are proposing **just isn't feasible** to implement at all.
あなたの提案を実装するのは**まったく無理**です。

With all due respect to the chief engineer's suggestion, **I just don't think it would work.**
技術主任のご意見は誠にごもっともですが、私は**それがうまくいくとは思いません**。

I respect the Santa Cruz office's opinion, however, **I can't agree with the idea that** we should continue our contract with SilcotSoft Co.
サンタクルーズ・オフィスの意見はもっともですが、(株) SilcotSoft 社との契約を継続すべきだ**という考えに私は同意できません**。

反対する表現③ ｜ 反対意見を巧みに表現する

まず相手の立場を認めてから、自分の考えが相手と違うことを示す。

EXAMPLE

Mr. Neal Ferguson, thank you for sharing your idea about how to implement changes into this project, and I want you to know that I agree with your idea up to a certain extent. However, it seems that we need to deal with a couple of issues before we finalize our plan.

ニール・ファーガソン様、このプロジェクトをどのように変更するかについて、あなたのご意見をお知らせくださり、ありがとうございました。あなたのご意見には、私もあるところまで賛成であることをご承知ください。しかし、我々の計画を最終決定する前に、まだ2、3の問題を片付ける必要があるかと思います。

VARIATIONS

We think that the chief engineer **has a point, but** this group doesn't think that we need to worry about how it will be implemented.
技術主任の**意見はごもっとも**だと思いますが、実装方法を心配する必要はない、と当グループは思います。

I understand your point, Mr. Fitz Manchester, **but** have you considered the time for carrying out what you have proposed?
フィッツ・マンチェスターさん、**あなたのご指摘はもっとも**ですが、あなたの提案を実行するのに要する時間を考えたことはありますか。

I don't mean to disagree with you, Project Manager, but it seems to me that there are certain things that you have completely forgotten.
プロジェクトマネジャー、**あなたに反対するつもりはありません**が、あなたが完全に忘れてしまっていることがあるように思えます。

I can see your point of view, Chief Engineer, **but** I think you ought to consider my team's position.
技術主任、**あなたの立場はわかります**が、私のチームの立場も考慮していただきたい、と思います。

I see your point, but I don't think that we should cancel this development project immediately.
あなたの仰りたいことは理解できますが、この開発プロジェクトを直ちにキャンセルすべきではない、と私は考えます。

反対する表現④ 提案／対案を出す

やみくもに反対するのではなく、こちらから提案や対案を提示して、相手の理解を求めるという戦略もある。

EXAMPLE

Now that I have pointed out the problems of Mike Washington's original proposal about how to implement this function, I would like to present the counterproposal of our team.

この機能をどのように実装するかについてのマイク・ワシントンの提案の問題点を指摘しましたので、今度は我がチームの対案を提示したいと思います。

VARIATIONS

I feel it would be better to add more programmers to the project rather than to hire a system consultant.
システムコンサルタントを1人雇うより、プログラマーをプロジェクトに複数追加する方がいい、**と私は思います**。

Regarding this problem, **allow us to suggest a new approach** which is different from that of Mr. Taka Miyoshi's team.
この問題については、三好高さんのチームとは**異なるアプローチを提案させてください**。

I would like to propose that we hold a meeting every Tuesday and discuss this development project.
毎週火曜日に会議を開催して、この開発プロジェクトについて話し合う**ことを提案します**。

Why don't we all get together and talk about this specification next week when I will be visiting the Fremont office**?**
来週、私がフレモント・オフィスを訪問するので、その時、全員で集まって、この仕様について話し合うの**はいかがでしょう**。

My proposal is that we promote Kent Morris to the project manager of this development plan.
私の提案は、ケント・モリスをこの開発計画のプロジェクトマネジャーに昇進させる**ことです**。

I would like to put forward a proposal that we add more servers.
サーバーをもっと追加すること**を、私は提案したいと思います**。

反対する表現⑤ ｜ 提案に対する不支持の表明

議案などに対して疑問を呈し、支持できないことを述べるのに使う。

EXAMPLE

With respect to the plan that CoolClick Co. made, I think it needs major revisions. Without substantial changes, I cannot support their plan. Therefore, as it stands, I would not be able to give my backing to it.

（株）CoolClick 社が作成した計画についてですが、大幅な修正が必要だと思います。大幅な変更なしに支持することはできません。従って、現状では、（株）CoolClick の開発チームが提案した計画を私は支持できません。

VARIATIONS

I am afraid **I cannot support** Paul Jenkins**'s proposal**.
残念ながら、**私はポール・ジェンキンスの提案を支持できません**。

There seem to be a couple of problems with the development schedule.
その開発スケジュールに関しては、**問題が2、3あるように思います**。

I can see some problems in adopting this design.
この設計の採用には、**いくつかの問題が予測されます**。

I am not sure if Arnold Holgate's plan is feasible.
アーノルド・ホルゲートの計画が実行可能**かどうか、私にはわかりません**。

I am not convinced that acting on this plan is in the best interest of my team.
この計画が現時点で私のチームのためになる**との確信が私にはありません**。

It seems to me that Fred Murphy's approach to this problem **doesn't take into account certain important factors.**
フレッド・マーフィーのこの問題に対するアプローチですが、**重要な要素を考慮に入れていないように思えます**。

反対する表現⑥ 全面的な不支持の表明

相手の計画や提案に強く反対し、支持できないことを伝える表現である。

EXAMPLE

I think implementing it as Koga suggested would be totally counterproductive. I am totally against his suggestions.

古賀の提案通りに実装するのは、まったく非生産的だと私は思います。私は彼の提案に全面的に反対です。

VARIATIONS

I am **absolutely opposed** to Kiyota's idea of letting Adam Larsen go.
アダム・ラーセンを解雇するという清田の考えに、私は**絶対に反対**です。

I don't agree at all with your suggestion, Mr. Simon Cooper.
サイモン・クーパーさん、**私は**あなたの提案に**まったく賛成できません**。

I see no reason for you supporting Nagasawa's plan whatsoever.
私には、長沢の計画を**あなたが支持する理由がまったくわかりません**。

I am firmly convinced that we must reject SmartPro Co.'s proposal for the benefit of our company.
(株)SmartPro社の申し出は、弊社の利益のために**却下すべきだと、私は確信します**。

To pick the plan that BestSonic Co. suggested **would be the worst option** that we could take for this company at this time.
(株)BestSonic社が提案した計画を選択することは、現時点では弊社にとって**最悪のオプション**です。

It is my opinion that Kiyota **is precisely the kind of** person **we need to avoid** in organizing a design team for large scale systems.
大規模システムの設計チームの編成に当たって、清田**こそ我々が避けるべき人間である**、というのが私の意見です。

I feel very strongly that we should not promote Tabata to the chief engineer at the collaboration system unit.
田畑をコラボレーションシステムユニットの技術主任に昇進させるべきではない、と私は強く思っています。

反対する表現⑦ 再考を求める

決定が下された後で、もう一度考え直してほしいと頼むときの表現。

EXAMPLE

Since we are hoping that JugglerNet Co. might reconsider their decision, would you please reconsider your decision not to award the contract to them?

我々は（株）JugglerNet社が彼らの決定を考え直してくれることを望んでいますので、彼らとは契約を結ばないというあなたの決定を再考していただけないでしょうか。

VARIATIONS

I would like to sincerely urge you to reconsider your decision to remove me from the Web service development project team.
私をWebサービス開発プロジェクトチームから外す、**という決定を考え直してくださることを心からお願いします。**

Can you reconsider your decision to put the development project on a temporary freeze**?**
開発プロジェクトを一時停止するという、**あなたの決定を考え直していただけませんか。**

Director Alex Bertland, **I would appreciate it very much if you would reconsider your decision** to cut our budget.
アレックス・バートランド部長、我々の予算を削減するという、**あなたの決定を考え直していただければ、とてもありがたいです。**

We were very disappointed to receive the email from your company on August 10, and **we are hoping that you might reconsider** your decision concerning the contract with us.
8月10日に貴社からメールを受け取って非常に落胆しました。我々との契約に関するあなたの決定を**考え直してくださるようにお願いいたします。**

Mr. Yamada, **wouldn't you reconsider** your refusal to work at the Silicon Vally office starting next month**?**
山田さん、来月からのシリコンバレー・オフィス勤務、**もう一度考え直してくれませんか。**

If we were to give you a raise, **might you reconsider your decision?**
昇級させれば、**決定を考え直しますか。**

妥協の表現① │ 妥協案の提示／受け入れ

相手との交渉において妥協案を提示する、あるいは妥協案を受け入れるときに使う表現。

EXAMPLE

Director Bill Trump, I think that our company could add more programmers, provided that your company would pay for the extra expenses to hire them.

ビル・トランプ部長、御社が彼らを雇うのにかかる費用をもってくれるのであれば、弊社はもっとプログラマーを追加できる、と思います。

VARIATIONS

I think that **the alternative solution we suggested** in our email of September 15 **is very reasonable.**
9月15日付で**提案した代替案は非常に妥当**だと私は思います。

As for this matter, **let us agree** to Lauri Pinker's conditions **to meet you halfway**.
この件について、ローリー・ピンカーの条件**に同意して、貴社と妥協させてください**。

My group **will try our best provided that** you will support our company financially.
金銭の面で弊社をサポートしていただけるなら、私のグループは**御社のために全力を尽くします**。

We think that **the compromise solution** sent from the development division **would be perfectly acceptable.**
開発部門が送って来た**妥協案で結構**だと我々は思います。

The Steven Creek office's **proposal seems to me to be reasonable.**
スティーブンクリーク・オフィスの**提案は妥当のように私には思えます**。

The chief engineer's **plan is acceptable** to my project group.
技術主任の**案**で私のプロジェクトグループは**結構です**。

Our company **is prepared to** continue this project **on the condition that** your company would add three more programmers.
御社がプログラマー3人を追加する**ということを条件に**、当社はこのプロジェクトを継続す**ることにします**。

妥協の表現② | 妥協案を受け入れられないとき

妥協案を提示されたが、それでも受け入れられないときは、相手の立場を一応考慮したうえで提案を断る。

EXAMPLE

Regarding solutions for this bug, this project team is not satisfied with the original proposal that the Newark office submitted. We are not entirely convinced that Mr. Yamada's team's counterproposal is a viable solution either.

このバグの解決策ですが、当プロジェクトチームはニューアーク・オフィスが提案した原案に満足していません。山田さんチームの対案も有効なソリューションだとの確信が持てません。

VARIATIONS

Although the development division of our company wants to avoid a deadlock as much as your company does, **we found** Barry Porter's counterproposal **totally unsatisfactory**.
御社と同様、弊社の開発部門も行き詰まりを避けたいのですが、バリー・ポーターの対案は**我々にとってまったく満足のいくものではありません**。

I have some doubts as to **whether** the product division's **compromise is a viable solution.**
プロダクト部門の**妥協案が有効な解決策かどうか**、私には疑問です。

I feel that the change the network management division suggested yesterday **is somewhat unfair.**
ネットワーク管理部門が昨日提案した変更は、**いくぶん不公平だと私は思います**。

If the solution your company emailed us this morning **is your final offer,** very reluctantly, our company has to cancel this project.
今朝、御社からメールされてきたソリューションが、**そちらの最終的な申し出であるなら**、非常に残念ながら、弊社はこのプロジェクトをキャンセルせざるを得ません。

We are afraid that **we won't be able to accept the compromise** that SuperLinkPro Co. suggested.
我々としては、SuperLinkPro社ご**提案の妥協案は受諾しかねます**。

妥協の表現③ ｜ 要求を条件付きで受け入れる

「～なら、～します」と、こちらの条件が満足されれば相手の要求を受け入れる、と伝えるときの表現。

EXAMPLE

Mr. Douglas Foothill, our participation to this project would be conditional on whether or not your company will cover the cost. We are willing to send several programmers immediately if you would agree to pay for the expense.

ダグラス・フットヒル様、弊社が本プロジェクトに参加するかどうかは、御社に費用を負担していただけるかどうかによります。費用をお支払いいただけることに合意していただければすぐに、プログラマーを数人派遣いたします。

VARIATIONS

We will be willing to show you any technical document **as long as** your company sends us your NDA first.
弊社といたしましては、御社が最初に秘密保持誓約を送って**くだされば**、技術文書を**喜んでお見せします**。

We see no objection whatsoever to fix the bug, **provided that** you will pay us first.
最初にお支払いいただける**のであれば**、そのバグを修正することについて、**我々は何の異存もありません**。

Manager James Brown, I understand that you want me to attend the meeting next month. **The only way I could do it would be to** go to the San Jose office this week.
ジェームズ・ブラウン課長、来月の会議に出席するようにとのお話ですが、**私が出席できる唯一の方法は**、今週中にサンノゼ・オフィスに行く**ことです**。

If your company **would be prepared to** pay a 10 % deposit, **we could** send 3 programmers right away.
もし御社に10％の手付金を支払う**用意があるのであれば**、3人のプログラマーをすぐに派遣できます。

Unfortunately, **there is no way we can** continue this development plan unless your company will pay one million dollars in advance.
残念ながら、御社に100万ドル前払いしていただけないと、本開発計画は継続**できません**。

問題が生じたとき① ┃ 警告を発する

「こちらの指摘を無視すると大変なことになりますよ」という意図を込めて警告するときに使う表現。用件の性格上、やや高圧的な文面になる。

EXAMPLE

I want to give you a word of caution about how to configure your in-house network. If you don't set up your firewall properly, you may be visited by unauthorized persons looking for proprietary information on the server.

社内ネットワークの設定に関して、ひと言ご注意いたします。ファイアウォールを正しく設定しないと、部外者がサーバー上の機密情報を求めて侵入してくるかもしれません。

VARIATIONS

Let this serve as fair warning --- if you continue to bad mouth co-programmers, you will be asked to leave this company.

あらかじめ警告しておきます。同僚プログラマーの悪口をこれからも継続した場合、弊社を辞めていただきます。

If you damage our workstation, your company **will be asked to** reimburse us for the total cost of repair.

あなたが弊社のワークステーションを破損した場合には、修理費用全額をあなたの会社に**負担していただきます**。

This is to inform you that you are using our Web content without our permission, and if this situation is not corrected, we **will be forced to take legal action**.

お知らせいたします。あなたは、弊社のWebコンテンツを、弊社の承諾なく使用しております。この状況が改善されなければ、弊社は**法的手段をとらざるを得ません**。

Regarding this Web service development contract, this will be your last chance to pay your account before we **will be forced to take the matter to the court**.

本Webサービスシステムの開発契約に関して、今回、弊社への未払金をお支払いいただかなければ、**訴訟に訴えざるを得ません**。

問題が生じたとき② | 落胆の意を表明する

期待が裏切られたとき、「不本意だ」という自分の気持ちを伝える表現。

EXAMPLE

Since we trusted that you would make every effort to clear up this matter, we are very disappointed to learn that PeerOneCOM Co. canceled the Web service development contract with us so suddenly.

弊社といたしましては、御社があらゆる努力を講じてこの事態を是正してくださると信頼していましただけに、(株) PeerOneCOM社が弊社とのWebサービス開発契約を突然解消いたしましたので、非常に落胆しております。

VARIATIONS

Mr. Chris Trent, **I can't tell you how disappointed I am** to hear that you will not be able to make it to the project meeting tomorrow.

クリス・トレントさん、君が明日のプロジェクト会議に出席できないと聞いて、**心底がっかりしている**。

Vice President Troy Harrison **is really disappointed** to find out how InfoBank4U Co. treated some of our programmers.

弊社の一部のプログラマーに対する(株)InfoBank4U社の対応の仕方を知って、トロイ・ハリソン副社長は**非常にがっかりしています**。

I am **not satisfied** with the decision to promote Mr. Taguchi to a project manager ahead of Mr. Arnold Rankine.

アーノルド・ランキン氏よりも先に田口氏をプロジェクトマネジャーに昇進させるとの決定に、私は**不満があります**。

Regarding the system that your Web service project team developed, **I must say that** the overall performance of it greatly **disappointed me.**

御社のWebサービスプロジェクトチームが開発したシステムですが、その全体的な性能には**落胆した、と私は言わざるを得ません**。

We **are very disappointed** not to receive any information from your company concerning your programmer training.

御社のプログラマー研修に関して、何の情報も御社から得られなかったので、**がっかりしています**。

問題が生じたとき③ | 驚きを伝える

予想外の出来事に出会ったときの気持ちを述べるときの表現の例である。

EXAMPLE

We can't tell you how surprised we were to learn that your company is closing your Dallas branch. May we direct your attention to the fact that your Dallas office still has an unpaid balance for the previous services with us.

御社がダラス支社を閉鎖すると知って、非常に驚きました。ダラス支社は弊社のサービスに対するお支払いに未払いがございますので、ご案内申し上げます。

VARIATIONS

I was very surprised by your suggestion that we discontinue this Web service development project.
このWebサービス開発プロジェクトを中止するとのあなたの提案には、**大変びっくりしました**。

I have been caught off guard by the San Jose office's decision that they will be awarding this development contract to OrbisExpress Co.
この開発契約を（株）OrbisExpressと結ぶというサンノゼ・オフィスの決定は、**寝耳に水でした**。

I am really surprised by the news that Bill Sandberg has quit AntiCloseTech Co. and is about to start his own software house.
ビル・サンドバーグが（株）AntiCloseTech社を辞めて自分でソフトハウスを始めるところだ、**という知らせにはとても驚いています**。

I was speechless to hear the news that Mr. Taguchi, collaboration analyst, had been fired.
コラボレーションアナリストの田口さんが解雇されたと聞いて、**言葉もありませんでした**。

I can't believe that they have promoted David Skyport to chief engineer.
デビッド・スカイポートを技術主任に昇進させた**なんて信じられません**。

I am surprised to hear that Santa Cruz Operations (SCO) is suing IBM for more than $1 billion.
Santa Cruz Operations社（SCO）がIBM社に対して10億ドル超の訴訟を起こしている、**と聞いて大変驚きました**。

問題が生じたとき④ 苦情を述べる

苦情を述べる場合でも、ビジネス上の関係に配慮し、あまりに感情的な物言いは避けるようにしたい。

EXAMPLE

Dear SouthenNet2Go Co.,

We are very disappointed with the performance of your programmers. Consequently, we are requesting a total refund of the payment we made.

(株) SouthenNet2Go殿、

貴社のプログラマーがまったく役立たずだったことに驚かされました。つきましては、全額払い戻してくださるようお願いいたします。

VARIATIONS

I am sending this email to complain that it has been 8 months now since your programmers started working, and they still haven't completed the project.
御社のプログラマーはすでに8カ月も作業を行っているのに、まだ本プロジェクトを完了していないので、**苦情を申し上げたく、このメールを差し上げています**。

I am writing this email to complain to you that the engineers who work at your user support center are not only rude but also unhelpful.
御社のユーザーサポート窓口で働く技術者は、対応が失礼なだけでなく、役立たずでもある**ことを指摘したく、この苦情メールを書いています**。

I regret to say that I was a little disappointed with your performance while you were on this development project.
残念ですが、この開発プロジェクトでのあなたの仕事ぶりには、**少しがっかりしています**。

It is with reluctance that I am sending this email to inform you that we are very disappointed with the service that your engineers provided to us.
残念ですが、御社の技術者のサービスに不満を感じていると、**このメールで申し上げなければなりません**。

Regarding the quality of this open source UML design tool, **I am afraid that it was far below our expectations.**
このオープンソースのUML設計ツールの品質ですが、**我々の期待を大きく下回っています**。

問題が生じたとき⑤ ■ 陳謝する

自分の怠慢、過失、不注意で、相手に迷惑や損害を与えてしまい、それを謝るときの表現。

EXAMPLE

Please accept our apologies for not being able to send our engineers to the Palo Alto office sooner. It was due to our mistake in arranging their plane tickets. We are sorry that you were inconvenienced.

私どもの技術者をパロアルト・オフィスにもっと早く派遣できなかったことをお詫びいたします。原因は航空券手配の手違いによるものでした。ご不便をおかけし、お詫び申し上げます。

VARIATIONS

We are sorry about the delay in completing this Web system **and sincerely hope that** it did not cause serious business inconvenience.

本Webシステムの完成が遅れたことを**お詫び申し上げますとともに**、ビジネス上、多大なご迷惑をおかけしなかった**ことを心から願っております**。

Everybody, a server malfunction was responsible for the slow traffic you experienced yesterday, and we regret **any inconvenience it may have caused you.**

皆さん、昨日のスロートラフィックは、サーバーの誤作動によるものでした。**ご迷惑をおかけして**申し訳ございませんでした。

I apologize for the delay in implementing this function.

この関数の実装が遅れたことを**お詫びいたします**。

We would like to apologize for the delay in taking care of this bug.

このバグへの対応が遅れたこと**をお詫び申し上げます**。

Please forgive me for not emailing you my progress report sooner.

私の進捗報告書をもっと早くメールしなかった**ことをお許しください**。

We are very sorry for the inconvenience this bug has caused you.

このバグによりご迷惑をおかけしました**ことをお詫びいたします**。

We are very sorry to learn from your email that the server system we implemented does not function properly.

私どもが実装したサーバーシステムが正常に動作しないとの**ご連絡をメールでいただき、大変申し訳なく思っております**。

問題が生じたとき⑥ 間違いを通知する

自分以外、特に相手の間違いを指摘するのには神経を使う。あまりストレートな言い方は避け、「～ようです」「～によれば」のような間接的な表現を使うのも1つの手である。

EXAMPLE

Mr. Dennis Homestead, my apologies. It appears that Phil Green has overlooked a few critical routines in the CompositeState.java program that he created. I am sorry for the inconvenience caused.

デニス・ホームステッドさん、申し訳ありません。フィル・グリーンの作成したCompositeState.javaプログラムに致命的な見落としがいくつかあったようです。ご迷惑をおかけしたことをお詫び申し上げます。

VARIATIONS

According to what Dexter Harris, the chief engineer, is saying, **there appears to be an error** in the program you emailed to him last Tuesday. You owe him some apologies.

技術主任デクスター・ハリスの説明**によれば**、君が先週の火曜日にメールしたプログラムに**エラーがあるようだ**。彼に謝った方がいい。

It appears that **by some oversight,** John **didn't** code a few important functions.

うっかりして、ジョンが重要ないくつかの関数のコーディング**をしませんでした**。

Based on the investigation done by Mr. Hideki Matsumoto of the development division, **a serious error has been made** in designing the system.

開発グループの松本秀樹さんの調査**によれば**、システムの設計に**重大な間違いがありました**。

Please excuse me, but there has been a semantic **error** in the design of the client system.

申し訳ありません。クライアントシステムの設計にセマンティックな**間違いがありました**。

I believe there are 3 errors in the Web service system program.

Webサービスシステムのプログラムには、**間違いが3つある、と思います**。

It is a mistake to think that we need to add programmers.

プログラマーの補充が必要だ、**と考えるのは間違っています**。

It has come to our attention that several programmers of this project are totally confused.

このプロジェクトの何人かのプログラマーが完全に混乱している**ことが判明しました**。

問題が生じたとき⑦ | 問題点を指摘する

何が問題になっているかは、明確に示す必要がある。問題解決の出発点として重要な情報なのだから、曖昧な言い方はせず、簡潔に言い切ってかまわない。

EXAMPLE

Although NetSolutions4U is wondering how long it will take to develop the Web service system program, what I am concerned with most is whether or not the development can be completed on time.

NetSolutions4U 社の質問は、その Web サービスシステムのプログラムを開発するのにどれだけ時間がかかるかということですが、私が最も心配しているのは開発が期日通りに完了するかという点です。

VARIATIONS

The only problem is that the server development group has already sealed the contract with Mr. Hiroyuki Nishikino.
唯一の問題は、サーバー開発グループが錦野博之さんとその契約を取り交わしてしまった、ということです。

The difficulty lies in finding a programmer who has skills to debug the Web server system.
難しいのは、その Web サーバーシステムをデバッグできるスキルを持ったプログラマーを見つけることです。

There seems to be a problem with the design of the Web server system.
その Web サーバーシステムの設計に**問題があるようだ**。

There is only one problem with the Web server project group's plan. The cost would surely exceed our budget.
Web サーバープロジェクトグループの計画には**1つだけ問題がある**。それはコストが我々の予算を上回る、ということだ。

問題が生じたとき⑧ ┃ 誤解を解消する

トラブルがお互いの誤解に起因するとき、どこが誤解されているかを相手に伝えて、その解消を図る。

EXAMPLE

Director Fred Bascom, I would like to report Edwin Fisher's misunderstanding about me. I think that his misunderstanding occurred when I said "there are some bugs in the program that OrchidSoft developed." I am afraid that I failed to make myself clear to him.

フレッド・バスコム部長、エドウィン・フィッシャーの私に対する誤解についてご報告いたします。私が「OrchidSoft社の開発したプログラムにはバグがある」と言ったとき、彼は私を誤解したと思います。私の言いたかったことが正確に伝わらなかった可能性があります。

VARIATIONS

I am afraid that there seems to have been a slight misunderstanding about what I pointed out about the design of the Web server system. Could you please read my email of February 16 one more time?

私がそのWebサーバーシステムの設計について指摘したこと**について、多少の誤解があったのではないかと思います**。2月16日付けのメールをもう一度読み直していただけませんか。

There seems to be some misunderstanding about the fact that the server development group has already sealed the contract with Mr. Masaaki Ishida.

サーバー開発グループが石田正明さんとその契約を取り交わしてしまったこと**について誤解があるようです**。

We seem to be **not communicating with each other accurately.**
正確にコミュニケーションしていないようです。

What I wanted to tell you in the development meeting **is not that** we should cancel this project.
私が開発会議で**言いたかったのは**、このプロジェクトを中止せよ、**ということではありません**。

I never intended to say that the quality of the program that Mr. Fredrik Copeland developed is bad.
フレデリック・コープランドの開発したプログラムの品質が悪い、**などと私は決して言うつもりはありませんでした**。

8

第 8 章
エンジニアが よく使う表現

概要を打ち合わせる 》P.206 - P.209

問題解決策を探る 》P.210 - P.213

環境や条件 》P.214 - P.216

ユーザーサポート 》P.217 - P.218

個別技術で使う表現 》P.219 - P.221

概要を打ち合わせる① | **セールスポイントを強調する**

システムの概要について打ち合わせる際、受注側と発注側で、互いの意向を確認するため、覚えておくと役立つ表現がいろいろある。この項は受注側の売り込みの際の表現である。

EXAMPLE

Dear Mr. Linden McCullough,

In our efforts to help customers automate their corporate transactions, it is important to provide a high-speed Web service function. We are a hightech company specializing in that field.

リンデン・マカロフ様、

お客さまの企業決済の自動化のお手伝いをするに当たって、高速Webサービス機能の提供は重要です。弊社はその分野を得意とするハイテク企業です。

VARIATIONS

We are contacting you to inquire whether you would be interested in our new product that **can greatly benefit your company** by **automating the business processes**.
ビジネスプロセスを自動化することで、**貴社にかなりの恩恵を与えることができる**弊社の新製品をご検討していただきたく、ご連絡申し上げる次第です。

From the perspective of intranet users in our company, **this new function is quite effective.**
弊社のイントラネットユーザーの観点から見ると、**この新しい機能は非常に有効**です。

This is **one of the merits for your company to use** IPv6. As we are a high-tech company specializing in Internet technologies, we are very familiar with IPv6, too.
これは御社がIPv6を**利用するメリットの1つ**です。弊社はインターネット技術を専門とするハイテク企業ですので、IPv6についても熟知しております。

Because it is always our pleasure doing business with you, **we are willing to grant you a reduction.**
貴社とお取り引きするのは私どもの喜びとするところですので、**値引きのご用意がございます**。

If it is impossible for you to finalize the agreement, **we are prepared to offer you another** 5% **reduction.**
先日の値引き率で契約をお願いするのが難しいということであれば、**さらに5%値引き**させていただくつもりです。

概要を打ち合わせる② | 具体的効用を訴える

EXAMPLE

This Web service can provide an efficient and cost-effective model for accomplishing various tasks for your company.

このWebサービスは、御社のさまざまなタスクをこなすうえで、効果的かつコスト効率の高いビジネスモデルを提供できます。

VARIATIONS

With the addition of this new feature, any user can install an application on a server machine very easily.
この新機能の追加によって、どのユーザーもアプリケーションをサーバーマシンに簡単にインストールできます。

The system that our company designed **provides functions in modules.**
弊社の設計したシステムは、**モジュール形式で機能が分割されて**います。

The email system that our company developed **is very stable.**
弊社が開発したメールシステムは**非常に安定性があります。**

The main scope of this program **is to integrate** the existing legacy system with a new database system.
レガシーシステムと新規データベース**を統合させるのが、**このプログラムの**主目的です。**

With our application **you can plug-in** a function that you want.
弊社のアプリケーションには、**プラグイン形式で**ほしい機能を**追加することができます。**

No particular performance problem has been noted about this server software even at sites whose daily accesses can exceed 500,000.
このサーバーソフトウェアは、1日に50万以上のアクセスがあるサイトにおいても、**パフォーマンスの問題は特に報告されていません。**

概要を打ち合わせる③ ┃ 何が効用かを尋ねる

VARIATIONS

Does this solution provide any **technical advantages** over other methods?
この解決策は、他の方法に比べて、**技術面で優れて**いますか。

What kind of special features does this new product have?
この新製品には、**どんな特殊機能**があるのですか。

Can this system provide effective Web services to our company?
このシステムは弊社に対して効率的な Web サービスを**提供できますか**。

Can this system **change the way we do business** in our company?
このシステムは、**弊社のビジネス手法を変えさせる**ことができますか。

What kind of a business model can this Web service **provide?**
この Web サービスは**どんなビジネスモデルを提供**できますか。

What kind of problems can IPv6 **solve?**
IPv6 は、**どんな問題を解決**できますか。

How much data can this program **process** per hour?
このプログラムは、1時間当たり、**どれくらいのデータを処理**できますか。

What kind of information can I find by using the Web service of your company?
御社の Web サービスを使った場合、**どんな情報が検索**できますか。

What kind of information can I entrust to this Web service?
この Web サービスに対して、**どんな情報を託す**ことができますか。

概要を打ち合わせる④ ｜ 技術的詳細を確認する

EXAMPLE

Regarding the system that you developed for us, where is the bottleneck as far as its performance is concerned?

御社が当社のために開発したシステムですが、パフォーマンスに関してネックになっている部分はどこですか。

VARIATIONS

Can the new system **read the data** that was made by the previous version?
新しいシステムは、前バージョンで作成した**データを読み込む**ことはできますか。

Can this problem **be fixed in** the next version?
この不具合は次期バージョン**では解決されます**か。

Please tell me whether this program calculates the product discount rate every time when a customer purchases something.
このプログラムは、お客さまが何かを買うたびに商品の割引率を計算する**か教えてください**。

What is this use case diagram **supposed to describe?**
このユースケース図は**何について記述した**ものですか。

About this use case diagram, is it **supposed to show the system requirements of** BayTech's automatic transaction system?
このユースケース図ですが、それはBayTech社の自動決済**システムの要件についてまとめた**ものですか。

What kind of an OS should we install on our workstation **to try to see what** this program **can do**?
このプログラム**で何ができるか試してみる**には、我々のワークステーションにどのOSをインストールすればよいですか。

What is the **main scope** of this program?
このプログラムの**主な目的**は何ですか。

What is this function **supposed to support** in the existing program**?**
この機能は、従来のプログラムの**何をサポートする**ためのものですか。

What can the specifications of your company **support?**
御社の仕様は、**何をサポート**できますか。

問題解決策を探る① 状況を知る

システム開発上の問題が起きたときは、状況を明確にして解決策を探り、何らかの手を打つ必要がある。

EXAMPLE

Mr. Henry Miller, we are experiencing network trouble. What should we do first to solve this problem?

ヘンリー・ミラーさん、ネットワーク障害が発生しています。この問題を解決するには最初に何をすべきですか。

VARIATIONS

Please inform us **what must clearly be done** to complete this system.

このシステムを完成させるために、**明らかに実行されなければならないこと**を知らせてください。

What kind of **an approach is needed to solve this problem**?
この問題を解決するのに必要とされるアプローチは何ですか。

Regarding the need to change the basic design that AnnexInfo Co. has pointed out, **how many technical solutions** can you think of to take care of this problem?
AnnexInfo社が指摘した基本設計変更の必要性についてですが、この問題に関しては**いくつの技術的解決策**が考えられますか。

The Web service development project that LexusWebCom has been working on for us is getting behind schedule. If we ask your company to alter its design, **how much do you charge for it?**
LexusWebCom社が弊社向けに行っているWebサービス開発プロジェクトが予定より遅れています。御社にお願いして、設計を変更してもらう場合、**費用はどのくらいかかりますか。**

問題解決策を探る② ▍要望や回答を述べる

EXAMPLE

Mr. Joe Weisenberger, I am writing this email in the hope that we could have the benefit of your suggestions. Would you be so kind as to propose a solution that we can use to automate the database system of our company?

ジョー・ワイゼンバーガー様、あなたのお知恵を拝借できればと思い、このメールを書いています。弊社のデータベースシステムを自動化するために使用できる解決策を提案していただけないでしょうか。

VARIATIONS

Mr. James Brown, in order to carry out the change we **need to take the system down** for about (at least) 2 hours.
ジェームズ・ブラウン様、その変更を行うためには、2時間ほど(最低2時間)**システムを停止させる必要があります**。

Why don't we start with 10 elements and 1000 daily accesses**?**
取り敢えず、10個の要素、1日のアクセス数1000件で**始めてみませんか**。

This problem can be solved either by using an open source program or by developing a utility tool internally.
この問題は、オープンソースのプログラムを使用するか、自前でツールを開発するか**すれば解決できます**。

Our answer to your inquiry is that **we would like to take care of this problem by** entering all the user information manually.
ユーザー情報を手作業で入力**することでこの問題に対処したい**、というのがあなたの問い合わせに対する我々の回答です。

Please give us a couple of days as we will **consider these two options** before we decide which option we will choose.
これらの2つのオプションの両方を検討してから、どちらにするかを決定しますので、2、3日お待ちを。

問題解決策を探る③ ｜ 機能の追加や変更

EXAMPLE

Mr. John Newhall, in order to implement the function that you want, we must add 3 new programs in two months.

ジョン・ニューホール様、あなたのご希望の機能を実装するためには、新しいプログラムを2カ月で3本追加しなければなりません。

VARIATIONS

About changing the specifications, we are currently considering several options.
仕様変更については、現在、いくつかの案を検討中です。

What kind of a function is needed **in order to greatly enhance the usability** of this system?
このシステムの**使い勝手を大きく高めるために**必要な機能は何ですか。

In order to greatly enhance the performance of the system, we need **to customize** the data transfer part **and speed it up.**
このシステムの性能を高めるためには、データ転送部分を**カスタマイズして高速化する**必要があります。

What can we do **with the addition of this new feature**?
この新機能の追加によって、我々は何ができますか。

Please add and provide, at least, the message sorting function.
少なくとも、メッセージの並び換え機能は**付け加えて提供してください**。

In order to fix this bug, **we must make** three **changes** to the source.
このバグを修正するためには、ソースを3カ所**変更しなければなりません**。

In our company, we **have added attributes** to each of those 10 elements to differentiate whether they are for domestic or overseas uses.
弊社は、「国内用」と「国外用」を区別するために、その10個の要素に**属性を追加しました**。

問題解決策を探る④ 期限の延長を求める

EXAMPLE

Mr. John Smith, if it is possible, we are hoping that you will allow us 10 more days because this project is so close to completion. Thank you in advance for your understanding and cooperation.

ジョン・スミス様、この開発プロジェクトは完成間近ですので、もし可能であれば、あと10日間、時間をいただければと思います。ご理解、ご協力いただけるものと前もってお礼申し上げます。

VARIATIONS

Because we are getting 3 more new programmers today, we would be most grateful if you would grant us a **one-month extension of the original deadline.**
本日から3人プログラマーが新たに加わりますので、**最初の締め切り期限をあと1カ月延長**していただければうれしいです。

Regarding the Web server development, I believe that **it is going to take a little longer** to draw up a plan **than I estimated.**
Webサービスの開発ですが、計画立案には、**私の予測より多少時間がかかると思います**。

I am afraid that the project team **is going to ask for 10 more days** to complete the Web service system.
あと10日いただかないと、プロジェクトチームはWebサービスシステムを仕上げられそうにありません。

Mr. Kent Morris, **would you grant us** a two-week **extension** on the March 10 deadline**?**
ケント・モリス様、3月10日の納入期限を、2週間**延長していただけませんでしょうか**。

About fixing this bug, we would appreciate it very much **if you could extend the deadline for 5 more days.**
このバグを修正する件ですが、**締め切り期限をあと5日間、延ばしていただけるならば**、弊社としてはありがたいです。

Could we have one more month as my team is going to study the bug report carefully**?**
私のチームがバグレポートを慎重に検討いたしますので、**あと1カ月いただけますか**。

環境や条件① | 動作環境について

EXAMPLE

Is your company's program **environment-neutral or not**? Is a PC with a Core 2 2 GHz pocessor or above and 2 GB or more in RAM recommended?

御社のプログラムは、**特定の環境にこだわりませんか、こだわりますか？** 推奨するマシンは、Core 2（2 GHz）以上のCPU、2 GB以上のメモリを搭載したPCですか。

VARIATIONS

On what OS does this program **run most stable**?
このプログラムはどのOS上で**一番安定して動作します**か。

Does your company's program **require any specific environment to run**?
御社のプログラムは、**特定の動作環境を要求します**か。

Regarding the applet that your company developed, can it **run under** 32 MB?
御社の開発したアプレットですが、32 MB以下で**稼動します**か。

Do I have to use an ssh **to connect to** a server outside of the in-house LAN?
会社のLANから外部のサーバーに**接続する場合は**、sshを利用しなければなりませんか。

How much memory is needed to run this program**?**
このプログラムを動作させるには、**メモリはどれだけ必要でしょう**か。

This program uses **memories only as much as needed.**
このプログラムは、**必要なだけしかメモリを使いません。**

To what kind of devices can this Web service deliver content?
このWebサービスは、**どんなデバイスに対して**、コンテンツを提供できますか。

You can **use a variety of devices** to connect to the Web.
さまざまな機器を使ってWeb接続できます。

環境や条件② | 開発環境について

EXAMPLE

Can we create an application without regard to specific runtime constraints if we use your company's component software tool? And, how much improvement in the system development productivity will there be if we introduce it?

御社のコンポーネントソフトウェアツールを使えば、実行時の制約を気にせずにアプリケーションを作成ができますか。そして、これを導入することで、開発作業の効率がどれくらい上がりますか。

VARIATIONS

Can this program communicate with a server **located outside** the firewall?
このプログラムはファイアウォール**の外側にある**サーバーと通信することができますか。

Is this a **mature** application on Linux?
これは、Linux上で**十分枯れている**(十分実績のある)アプリケーションですか。

On that workstation, please install Linux, **which you can use for free**.
そのワークステーションには、**無料で自由に使える**Linuxをインストールしてください。

Please install Linux on the PC on the rack **and run** this program on it.
ラックにあるPCにはLinuxを**インストールして、**このプログラムを**動作させてください**。

Please let us know whether the program **is written in** Java.
そのプログラムがJavaで**書かれているか**教えてください。

Can this graphics application **show** our experimental model **in three dimensions**?
このグラフィックアプリケーションは、我々の実験モデルを**3Dで表示**できますか。

環境や条件③ | 開発者のスキルや資格

EXAMPLE

Dear Mr. Lester Grant,

We appreciate you emailing us your resume. Incidentally, have you ever developed a Linux application?

レスター・グラント様、

このたびは履歴書をメールしていただきありがとうございました。ところで、あなたはLinux用アプリケーションを開発したことがございますか。

VARIATIONS

If I want to take part in your company's system development plan, **would it be enough if I can write** C language programs**?**
もし私が御社のシステム開発計画に参加する場合、C言語のプログラム**を書けるだけで十分ですか**。

What kind of knowledge and skills do I need to have if I want to learn about your company's system**?**
御社のシステムについて学ぶ場合、**どんな知識と**スキル**が必要ですか**。

Our company **requires** all the engineers **to learn** Java programming.
弊社では、全エンジニアに対してJavaプログラミング**の履修を科しています**。

Can a UML certification be **a big advantage for a person who wants to find a job in** the US?
UML認定資格は、米国で**就職活動するのに有利**ですか。

What kind of IT certification **will look good on my resume**?
どんなIT認定資格を持っていると、**自分の経歴書に箔が付きますか**。

ユーザーサポート① ｜ 一般消費者からの問い合わせ

EXAMPLE

Thank you for your email of inquiry dated December 14 in which you expressed your interest in our encryption software. Attached is our brief pamphlet. For details, please download its manual to your PC and read it.

この度は、12月14日付けで、弊社暗号化ソフトウェアについてのお問い合わせいただき、ありがとうございました。このメールに簡単なパンフレットを添付いたしました。詳しくは、ソフトウェアのマニュアルをご自分のPCにダウンロードしてお読みください。

VARIATIONS

Before I try to answer your question, **please let me know what kind of a computer** you have on your office desk.

ご質問にお答えする前に、お客さまのお手元にあるマシンは**どんなコンピューターか教えてください**。

CondorVersa's library **is now used at** 30 Web sites.

CondorVersa社のライブラリは、現在30のWebサイト**にて利用されています**。

No, **we don't guarantee** our application **to work properly on** Windows 7.

はい、弊社のアプリケーションはWindows 7**上での動作は保証していません**。

Mr. John Bishop, **our answer is** that MadrasNavi's application can let you use streaming audio and video over an Internet connection. **If you want to have further details,** please do not hesitate to contact us by email.

ジョン・ビショップ様、**お答えします**。MadrasNavi社のアプリケーションでは、インターネットに接続してストリーミング音声とビデオを使うことができます。**より詳しい情報をご希望の場合は、**メールにてご遠慮なくお尋ねください。

In answering your question of what you need to enjoy our game, I would say you need a PC with a Core 2 2 GHz processor or above and RAM 2 GB or above.

弊社のゲームを楽しむには何が必要か**とのご質問ですが、**Core 2（2 GHz）以上のCPU、2 GB以上のメモリを搭載したPCが必要です。

You only need a sound card and a Direct 3D compliant video card **to enjoy** this game.

このオンラインゲームは、サウンドカードとDirect 3D互換ビデオカード**さえあれば楽しめます**。

ユーザーサポート② ▎技術的な対応

EXAMPLE

Mr. Haward Campbell, please let me know the specs of the PC you are using. If you know the model number/name, please let me know it, too.

ハワード・キャンベル様、お使いのPCのスペックを教えてください。機種番号や機種名がおわかりでしたら、それも教えてください。

VARIATIONS

In order to upgrade this system to the latest version, **you need the resources described in** the attached file.

このシステムを最新バージョンにアップグレードするには、添付ファイル**に記述されているリソースが必要**です。

To answer your question of **how our company plans to distribute data,** we intend to do it online.

データをどうやって配布する計画かとのご質問ですが、弊社はデータをオンラインで配付します。

We intend to release products that comply with the latest version this fall.

弊社は、最新バージョン対応製品をこの秋に**リリースするつもり**です。

You can use the Web service that our company is supporting **when your network security is secured.**

弊社がサポートしているWebサービスは、**御社のネットワークセキュリティが確保できた**ら利用できます。

Please refrain from using this function because **it may affect network performance greatly.**

ネットワークパフォーマンスに大きな影響を及ぼす可能性がありますので、この機能は使わないでください。

Please **use the XML format when you describe** the system configuration file.

そのシステムの設定ファイルは**XML形式で記述して**ください。

It does not seem to take much time **to network deliver** this data because it is very small.

このデータは小さく、**ネットワーク配信する**のにさほど時間がかかるとは思えません。

個別技術で使う表現① | Webアプリケーション関係

EXAMPLE

I understand that your program guarantees smooth interactivity with Web applications. How many illegal attacks can its authentication method withstand?

御社のプログラムはWebアプリケーションとの双方向性を保証しているそうですが、その認証方式はどれくらい不法な攻撃に耐えられますか。

VARIATIONS

Nobody can construct a Web system without **assuring its network security**.

Webシステムを構築する上で、**ネットワークセキュリティの確保**は避けては通れない問題です。

By using this clustering software, can you use the in-house intranet system **as if it were one big computer system**?

このクラスタリングソフトウェアを使うと、社内イントラネットを**1つのコンピュータのよ うに**使うことができますか。

This program can **provide services to a variety of Web-enabled devices**.

このプログラムは、**Webを使用する各種のデバイスに対して、サービスを提供**できます。

Although this system cannot let you **browse the Web with your smartphone** right now, you will be able to do so when the next version is released.

現在のところ、このシステムは**スマートフォンでWeb検索**ができませんが、次期バージョンではできるようになります。

What kind of mobile devices should users of your application use **to connect to the Web**?

御社のアプリケーションを使用しているユーザーが**Web接続する場合**、どんなモバイル機器を使用すべきですか。

個別技術で使う表現② ｜ データベース関係

EXAMPLE

This application requires access to a large-scale database system. The database service of our company is available whenever you connect to the Internet. Please do use it.

このアプリケーションは大規模データベースシステムへのアクセスが必要です。弊社のデータベースサービスはインターネット接続すればいつでも利用できます。ぜひ、ご利用ください。

VARIATIONS

Mr. M. Hawkins, **what kind of a data format do you want to use to describe** customer information?
M・ホーキンス様、顧客情報は**どんなデータフォーマットで記述**したいのですか。

We at this section are using an application that **saves our customer data in the XML format**.
当部署では、**XML形式で顧客データを保存する**アプリケーションを使っています。

How many elements should we use for this customer database?
この顧客データベースでは、**要素をいくつ使うべき**ですか。

Regarding the algorithm that is used in your application, can it **find a matching pattern** out of a huge database **very fast**?
御社のアプリケーションが使用しているアルゴリズムですが、膨大なデータベースの中から**同じパターンを素早く見つける**ことができますか。

Manager Alan Simmons, I have a question. In which database should we enter **the results of the data mining**?
アラン・シモンズ課長、質問があります。**データマイニングの結果**はどのデータベースに入力すべきでしょうか。

This program can **pull the right records out of** our customer database.
このプログラムは、**正しいレコードを**当社の顧客データベース**から抽出**できます。

Please implement this database system **by utilizing** your existing program(s).
このデータベースシステムは、御社の既存の（複数の）プログラム**を利用して実装してください**。

個別技術で使う表現③ ｜ ネットワーク関係

VARIATIONS

Everybody, we need to **shut down the in-house network system** for maintenance today from 9:00 a.m. to 9:00 p.m.
皆さん、本日は保守作業のため、午前9時から午後9時まで、**社内ネットワークを停止する**必要があります。

Mr. Paul Jenkins, if you want to find out something **about the RSA public-key cryptosystem**, you can obtain detailed information from the sites below.
ポール・ジェンキンスさん、**RSA公開鍵暗号方式**に関連した情報をご希望でしたら、以下のサイトから詳しい情報を入手できます。

Mr. Mark Austin, the anomaly you are experiencing is one of the phenomena that occur **when more than one operation is performed on the network concurrently**.
マーク・オースティン様、現在そちらで発生している不具合は、**ある特定の操作がネットワーク上で同時に行われると**発生する現象の1つです。

The security function that ClusterShell Co. developed **does not encrypt the message it sends**. Therefore, it does not seem as secure as they advertise.
ClusterShell社の開発したセキュリティ機能は**通信を暗号化していません**。同社が宣伝するほど安全ではないと思います。

Russell, please send your summary of **what caused the network trouble** that we experienced last night.
ラッセル、昨晩発生した**ネットワークトラブルの原因**についてまとめて、報告してください。

Mr. Jonathan Perlman, the specification you were talking about can **assign IPv6 IP-addresses**. However, please use existing IPv4 addresses because they are compatible with IPv6.
ジョナサン・パールマン様、お尋ねの仕様は**IPv6のIPアドレスを割り当てる**ことができます。しかし、既存のIPv4アドレスはIPv6と互換なので、IPv4アドレスを使ってください。

How will this security function **affect network performance**?
このセキュリティ機能は、**ネットワークパフォーマンス**にどの程度**影響を及ぼし**ますか。

Can this program **access objects** thought the Internet?
このプログラムは、インターネット経由で**オブジェクトへのアクセス**ができますか。

Concerning the software that your company is selling, can it solve **the problems of transmission priority**?
御社の販売しているソフトウェアは、**転送優先度の問題**を解決できますか。

This function is supposed to **support data transfer** in the existing program.
この機能は、従来のプログラムの**データ転送をサポートする**ためのものです。

用例索引

あ

アイデア

何かいいアイデアを提案していただければ … 156
if you could suggest some idea(s)

〜ことは良いアイデアです …………………… 176
it is a good idea for you to ...

あいにく

あいにく ……………………………………… 31
we are sorry

会う

最後にお会いしたのは ……………………… 28
since I saw you last

お会いすることは可能 ……………………… 102
possible for me to see

お会いして、話し合うことは
可能でしょうか …………………………… 102
set up an appointment with you and discuss ...

喜んでお会いいたします …………………… 106
I will be happy to meet with

また別の機会にお会いできればと思います … 106
I hope that I can see you some other time

お会いする場所 ……………………………… 107
the place where you want to meet

お会いする場所 ……………………………… 107
where we will be meeting

お会いできなくなりました ………………… 111
I won't be able to keep our appointment

直接お会いして、話し合いたい …………… 171
would like to meet you and talk

空き

空いています ………………………………… 106
I will be free

〜なら空いています ………………………… 108
I have an opening on ...

どの時間帯も空いています ………………… 108
will be free anytime

空いていますか ……………………………… 108
Are you free ... ?

空いています ………………………………… 108
I will be available

空いています ………………………………… 108
I will be free

〜は空いていますか ………………………… 116
Do you have ... available?

定員に空き …………………………………… 117
accepting applicants

圧縮

圧縮してメールします ……………………… 43
going to compress ... and email it to you

宛て

あなた宛てと思われます …………………… 44
It seems that it was intended for you

後

後で送ることができます …………………… 67
we can send you at a later time

アドバイス

貴重なアドバイスをいただき ……………… 24
gave me important pieces of advice

アドバイスをいただきたいです …………… 156
would like to ask your advice

〜というのが私のアドバイスです ………… 157
my advice would be to ...

〜のアドバイスを受け入れて ……………… 159
take the advice of ...

アプローチ

異なるアプローチを提案させてください … 89
allow us to suggest a new approach

この問題を解決するのに必要とされる
アプローチ ………………………………… 210
an approach to solve this problem

[余って]
もし〜が余っていて、使わせていただける
ようでしたら ……………………………… 89
if you have an extra ... that you can let us use

[誤り]
誤った情報を送ってしまい ……………… 36
that I sent you the wrong information

[洗い出す]
洗い出してみて ……………………………… 114
try to identify

[ありがたい]
〜していただけるとありがたいのですが … 154
I would be grateful if ...

[案]
何かいい案がありましたら ………………… 156
if you have any advice or suggestions

[安心]
〜ので、ご安心ください……………………… 166
please rest assured that ...

[安定]
非常に安定性があります……………………… 207
is very stable

一番安定して動作 ……………………………… 214
run most stable

[案内]
ご案内までに ……………………………… 65
for your guidance

い

[言う]
言いたかったのは〜ということでは
ありません ……………………………… 203
what I wanted to tell you is not that ...

〜などと私は決して言うつもりは
ありませんでした ……………………… 203
I never intended to say that ...

[いかが]
〜してみたらいかがでしょうか …………… 157
I advise you to ...

いかがでしょうか …………………………… 170
please let me know what you think

[意見]
意見を交換する ……………………………… 104
to exchange our opinions

〜の意見を取り入れて ……………………… 159
by following the suggestions from ...

素晴らしい意見を出してくれました ……… 159
has made an excellent point

あなたの意見を伺いたいと思います ……… 170
would like to hear your opinion

〜の意見を聞きたい ………………………… 170
I am interested in hearing ...'s view.

あなたの意見をぜひとも知りたい ………… 170
need to have your opinion

私の意見としては …………………………… 171
from my point of view

というのが〜の意見です …………………… 171
it is the opinion of ...

特に意見はありません ……………………… 173
I don't have an opinion

意見を述べる前にもっと考えたい ………… 173
would like to think more about it before
giving an opinion

[遺失物]
遺失物室で保管されています ……………… 90
It is being kept at the lost/found

[忙しい]
いま忙しい …………………………………… 58
I am occupied right now

[異存]
もしご異存がなければ ……………………… 153
if it is all right with you

〜であれば何の異存もありません ………… 195
see no objection whatsoever provided that ...

[いただく]
〜していただくことにしました …………… 126
I have decided to ask ...

223

皆さん方のうちのどなたかが
〜していただけませんか ……………………… 154
Would one of you be so kind as to ... ?

〜していただけませんか ……………………… 154
would you ...

〜していただけますでしょうか …………… 154
Would you please ... ?

〜していただきます ……………………………… 196
will be asked to ...

あと1カ月いただけますか ……………………… 213
Could we have one more month?

[一番]
一番いいのは〜ことです …………………… 157
the best thing for you to do is to ...

〜が一番いいと思います ……………………… 160
I like ... the best

[いつ]
いつがよろしいですか ………………………… 106
When do you prefer?

[一致]
我々は完全に一致しています ……………… 182
we are in total accord

〜ではあなたと意見が一致しています …… 183
we are in agreement on

[以内]
3日以内にお知らせください ………………… 132
please let us know your solution within three days

[祈る]
〜ことを祈っています ………………………… 131
I hope and pray that ...

〜ようお祈りしております …………………… 145
I am praying that ...

[依頼]
ご依頼のありました〜です …………………… 42
here is ... you requested

ご依頼にお応えする …………………………… 124
comply with your request

[インタビュー]
〜というテーマでインタビューさせて
いただければ ……………………………………… 104
have an interview with you on the subject of ...

う

[伺う]
〜から伺いました ……………………………… 99
I learned from ...

それについては〜から伺いました ………… 99
I heard about it from ...

御社に伺います ………………………………… 105
will visit your company

御社に伺います ………………………………… 107
coming to your place

〜について、あなたの意見を伺いたい …… 170
would be interested to find out your opinion about ...

[請け負う]
〜ことを請け合います ………………………… 166
let me assure you that ...

[受付]
〜と約束があると、受付で仰って ………… 109
tell the receptionist that you have an appointment with ...

受付を受け持つ ………………………………… 121
take care of the reception

[受け取る]
受け取り次第 …………………………………… 22
as soon as we receive

メールを受け取りましたので ………………… 66
now that I received your email

〜からのメールを受け取りましたので、
お知らせいたします …………………………… 66
I want to inform you that I have received an email from ...

〜との確認メールを受け取りました ……… 66
I received an email which confirms that

[受ける]
喜んでお受けする ……………………………… 124
happy to accept

疑う
～に疑いの余地はありません ……………… 172
there is no doubt that ...

うっかり
うっかりして ……………………………… 201
by some oversight

うまく
それがうまくいくとは思いません ………… 187
just don't think it would work

うれしい
～だとうれしいのですが …………………… 30
we will be glad if ...

～とお聞きし、うれしく思います ………… 30
we are pleased to learn that ...

～ことを大変喜んでおります ……………… 30
we are very pleased that ...

大変うれしく思いました …………………… 30
we had the great pleasure

え

影響
ネットワークパフォーマンスに大きな影響
を及ぼす可能性があります………………… 218
it may affect network performance greatly

ネットワークパフォーマンスに影響を
及ぼす ………………………………………… 221
affect network performance

延期
延期されました ……………………………… 81
has now been postponed

延長
延長していただけませんでしょうか ……… 213
would you grant us extension

遠慮
どうぞご遠慮なく、
いつでもお電話ください…………………… 34
please do not hesitate to call us any time

～までメールにて、ご遠慮なく
ご連絡ください ……………………………… 34
please do not hesitate to contact us by email

ご遠慮なくご連絡ください………………… 40
please do not hesitate to contact us

ご遠慮なくメールをください ……………… 40
please feel free to email me

ご遠慮なくメールを送ってください ……… 40
please do not hesitate to send us an email

お

お祝い
お祝いを述べさせてください……………… 150
allow me to congratulate you

お祝いを述べさせてください……………… 150
let me congratulate you

応募
奮って応募してください…………………… 91
we are encouraging ... to submit

奮ってご応募ください……………………… 92
are encouraged to apply

大筋
大筋で我々は合意している ……………… 183
we agree for the most part

お返し
お返しができれば …………………………… 148
look forward to repaying

お悔やみ
謹んでお悔やみ申し上げます…………… 144
want to express our heartfelt sympathy

謹んでお悔やみ申し上げます…………… 144
would like to express our condolences

お悔やみ申し上げます …………………… 144
we would like to extend our deepest sympathy

送る
送っていただき、ありがとうございます … 24
thank you for sending

お送りいたします …………………………… 42
I am pleased to send you

3回に分けて送る …………………………… 43
segment it into 3 files and send them as 3 separate mails

225

もう一度送ってくださいませんか ………… 44
can you send it again

メールでお送りいたします……………… 62
I am pleased to send you by email

メールでお送りいたします……………… 62
we are pleased to email you

〜を下記アドレスまで送っていただけますか … 64
will you please send ... to the following address

当部署まで送ってください ……………… 64
please send to this office

私までお送りください……………………… 64
need to send to me

追って送ります ……………………………… 67
will follow

来週、送ることができます ………………… 67
I can send next week

[遅れ]
予定より若干遅れ気味………………… 114
going a little behind schedule

[お越し]
弊社にお越しくださされば大変助かります … 103
it would help me a lot if you could come to our place

弊社にお越しください ……………… 103
please come to our office

こちらにお越しいただく ……………… 107
for you to come to our place

こちらにお越しいただければ…………… 107
if you could come to our place

〜に直接お越しください……………… 109
please come directly to ...

[教える]
ご存じでしたら教えていただれば
ありがたいです ……………………… 88
I would very much appreciate any information you could send me

教えていただけますか ………………… 97
Can you let me know?

あなたのことは〜から教えていただき
ました ……………………………… 99
I got your name from ...

あなたのメールアドレスは〜から
教えていただきました……………… 99
I got ... from ...

教えていただければ ………………… 104
hear your view on ...

〜は誰か、教えていただけるでしょうか … 165
Could you tell me who is ... ?

どんなコンピュータか教えてください …… 217
please let me know what kind of a computer

[お知らせ]
このメールは、〜をお知らせするための
ものです ……………………………… 29
this email is to inform you that ...

お知らせできることをうれしく思います … 30
I have the pleasure of informing you

お知らせでき、うれしく思います ………… 30
we are happy to inform you

お知らせいたします ………………… 32
I would like to report

お知らせいたします ………………… 32
this message is to let you know

[お世話]
いろいろとお世話になりました ………… 136
thank you for everything you have done for me

本当にお世話になり、
ありがとうございました ……………… 138
thank you very much for all your help

[おそらく]
おそらく〜でしょう ………………… 180
it is very likely that ...

[落ち着く]
落ち着き先が決まりましたら…………… 136
once I am settled

[おつき合い]
おつき合いさせていただいていた ………… 144
I had the privilege of knowing him

[お手数]
お手数ですが ………………………… 152
I hate to put you to the trouble of ... but

[驚く]

〜と聞き、お気の毒に思っています ……… 145
I am sorry to hear the news of ...

〜という知らせにはとても驚いています … 198
I am really surprised by the news that ...

〜と聞いて大変驚きました …………………… 198
I am surprised to hear ...

[お願い]

お願いしたく、連絡を差し上げています … 32
we are writing to request

[お見舞い]

私の様子を案じてお見舞いに来る ………… 146
to see how I was doing at the hospital

[おめでとう]

おめでとう、と〜にお伝えください ……… 39
please convey our congratulations to

おめでとうございます …………………………… 150
I want to congratulate you

[お目にかかる]

〜でお目にかかりましょう …………………… 107
why don't we meet at ...

喜んでお目にかかりたい ………………………… 124
be delighted to meet you

[思う]

〜と思ってよろしいでしょうか …………… 129
Am I correct in assuming that ...

〜したいと思っています……………………… 131
I hope to ...

〜と私は思います ……………………………… 172
it seems to me that ...

〜べきではない、と私は強く思っています … 191
I feel very strongly that we should not ...

[折り返し]

メールで直ちに折り返しご連絡ください … 33
please let us know by return email right away

大至急、折り返しメールで返事をください … 33
you need to reply by return email ASAP

折り返しご連絡ください……………………… 132
please let us know by return mail

[お礼]

お礼の印として ……………………………………… 91
as a token of our appreciation

[お詫び]

お詫びし、ご報告いたします ……………… 31
we are very sorry to inform you

〜をお詫びいたします………………………… 36
we would like to apologize for ...

〜をお詫びいたします………………………… 200
we are very sorry for

[終わる]

〜が終わったら ………………………………… 22
when you are done with ...

[恩義]

何かアドバイスをいただけたら、
恩義に感じます ………………………………… 156
would be greatly indebted to you if I could get any advice

[恩恵]

貴社にかなりの恩恵を与えることが
できる ……………………………………………… 206
can greatly benefit your company

か

[解決]

どんな問題を解決できますか ……………… 208
What kind of problems can ... solve?

いくつの技術的解決策………………………… 210
how many technical solutions

この問題は〜すれば解決できます ………… 211
this problem can be solved either by ...

[開催]

〜を開催いたしますので、
あなたもご参加ください……………………… 78
you are invited to attend ... which is going to be held

[会社案内]

新しい会社案内ができました ……………… 92
corporate brochure is now ready for distribution

227

[解釈]
〜と理解しました ……………………… 127
it is my understanding that ...

[開設]
〜に開設されました ……………………… 72
I am pleased to inform you that ... has been opened in ...

[解凍]
解凍できません ……………………… 43
cannot expand

〜で解凍できるはずです ……………… 43
should be able to open it with ...

解凍できない場合は〜を使ってみてください… 43
if you cannot open it, please try it with ...

[開発]
開発元はどこでしょうか ……………… 117
who is the developer

[回復]
素早い復旧を願っております ………… 145
want to wish you a speedy recovery

[書く]
〜で書かれている ………………………… 215
is written in ...

[確実]
確実に終了します ……………………… 166
we will be done for sure

〜のは確実だと私は思います ………… 172
I am absolutely certain that ...

〜ことは確実だ、と私は思います ……… 179
I have every confidence that ...

〜ことは確実だ ……………………… 179
It is beyond question that ...

〜のは確実だ ………………………… 179
we have every reason to believe that ...

ほぼ確実だろう、と私は思います ……… 180
I am almost positive

[確信]
〜だと確信しています ………………… 158
I am convinced that ...

〜との確信が私にはありません ………… 190
I am not convinced that ...

[確認]
確認したいのですが ……………………… 127
I just want to make sure

〜ことをご確認ください ……………… 128
please be reminded that ...

確認のお知らせです …………………… 128
this is just a reminder

確認させていただきますと、〜ということですね ……………………… 129
I would like to make sure, if I may ... Won't we?

[確保]
ネットワークセキュリティが確保できたら … 218
when your network security is secured

ネットワークセキュリティの確保 ………… 219
assuring its network security

[がっかり]
残念ですが〜には、少しがっかりしています ……………………… 199
I regret to say that I was a little disappointed with ...

心底がっかりしている ………………… 197
I can't tell you how disappointed I am

非常にがっかりしています …………… 197
is really disappointed

[画期的]
画期的な〜を開発しました …………… 161
have developed an innovative ...

[活動]
以下の活動を展開します ……………… 91
carry out the following activities

[活躍]
どうぞお元気にご活躍ください ………… 38
I wish you the best of luck with everything

[稼動]
〜以下で稼動 …………………………… 214
run under ...

228

[必ず]
必ず〜するように ……………………… 169
just make sure to ...

[可能]
それは可能でしょうか ………………… 160
would it be possible

[可能性]
可能性が大いにあります ……………… 180
it could very well be that

可能性が高い …………………………… 180
there is a good chance

可能性は十分にある …………………… 180
there is every possibility

可能性は少ない ………………………… 181
it is very unlikely

可能性は少ない ………………………… 181
it is not likely

〜できる可能性はほとんどありません …… 181
the chances of ... are extremely remote

可能性はほとんどありません ………… 181
there is not much of a possibility

可能性としてあり得ないでしょう ……… 181
it is very improbable

[考え]
どうお考えか、お聞きしたいと思います … 104
I would like to hear how you view ...

私の考えでは〜だと思います ………… 158
in my view ...

〜の考えでは …………………………… 158
in the view of ...

私としては〜という考えです ………… 171
as far as I am concerned ...

私の考えでは …………………………… 171
in my opinion

考えがまとまって ……………………… 173
to consider it to form an opinion

〜と考えていいでしょう ……………… 180
we can be fairly certain that ...

我々の考えは同じ ……………………… 182
we are of one mind

2、3考えが違うところがあるようです …… 183
we may differ on a couple of points

[考え直す]
決定を考え直してくださることを
お願いします …………………………… 192
would like to sincerely urge you to reconsider your decision

あなたの決定を考え直して
いただけませんか ……………………… 192
Can you reconsider your decision?

あなたの決定を考え直していただければ、
とてもありがたい ……………………… 192
I would appreciate it very much if you would reconsider your decision

〜を考え直してくださるように
お願いいたします ……………………… 192
we are hoping that you might reconsider ...

もう一度考え直してくれないか ……… 192
wouldn't you reconsider

決定を考え直しますか ………………… 192
Might you reconsider your decision?

[環境]
特定の動作環境を要求 ………………… 214
require any specific environment to run

[関係]
私は関係していません ………………… 44
I am not involved

[歓迎会]
略式歓迎会が開催されます …………… 85
an informal luncheon will be held

[観察]
私が観察できる限りでは ……………… 172
as far as I am able to observe

[感謝]
ご助言およびご協力に深く感謝して
おります ………………………………… 37
I really appreciate all the advice and cooperation you gave me

あなたには心より感謝しております …… 148
I am greatly indebted to you

〜していただければ感謝いたします ……… 152
I would be most grateful if ...

〜には本当に感謝しています ……………… 159
I really appreciate ...

〜のアドバイスには感謝しています ……… 159
I appreciate ... 's advice

感心
〜に非常に感心していました ……………… 149
were very impressed with ...

〜なので感心しました …………………… 149
we have been impressed by ...

関心
私の関心は〜にあります …………………… 162
I am concerned with ...

関する
〜に関してこのメールを書いています …… 29
I am writing this email about ...

このメールは、〜に関するものです ……… 29
this email is in reference to ...

〜に関して、何か私にできることがあれば … 163
if there is anything I can do for ...

間髪
間髪を入れず ……………………………… 155
waste no time

頑張る
スタッフ一同頑張りたい…………………… 147
all of us here will try our best

き

記憶
〜ことはご記憶でしょうか ……………… 128
Can you recall that ...

聞かせる
あなたのご意見を聞かせてください ……… 170
I am curious to hear your opinion

機器
さまざまな機器を使って…………………… 214
use a variety of devices

期限
締め切り期限をあと５日間、延ばして
いただけるならば ………………………… 213
if you could extend the deadline for 5 more days

寄稿
簡単な解説記事をご寄稿 ………………… 120
provide a short explanatory article

記述
〜は何について記述したものか ………… 209
what is ... supposed to describe

XML形式で記述 ………………………… 218
use the XML format when you describe

どんなデータフォーマットで記述したいの
ですか ……………………………………… 220
what kind of a data format do you want to use to describe

議事録
議事録の作成には、予定より少し時間が
かかりそうです …………………………… 84
completing the minutes will take a little longer than I thought

議事録が完成し、本メールに添付
されている ………………………………… 84
the minutes are now completed and attached to this email

正しく直した議事録を添付いたします …… 84
the correctly worded minutes are now attached

その日のうちに議事録を私にメール
してください ……………………………… 84
please email me the minutes within the day

期待
〜を期待して、このメールを書いています … 32
we are writing with the hope ...

議題
主たる議題は ……………………………… 82
this is to announce that the main agenda is ...

議題原案を添付いたします ……………… 82
I am attaching the draft agenda

取り上げる議題は次の通りです ………… 82
we will discuss the following subjects

議題は〜です ……………………………… 82
the agenda is ...

[気づく]
たぶんお気づきでしょうが……………… 32
as you are probably aware

[きっと]
きっと〜でしょう ………………………… 180
it is quite likely that ...

[気に入る]
〜を気に入ってくれるといいのですが …… 131
I hope you like ...

[機能]
この新機能の追加によって ………………… 207
with the addition of this new feature

モジュール形式で機能が分割されて ……… 207
provides functions in modules

どんな特殊機能 ……………………………… 208
what kind of special features

[寄付]
寄付は〜に送ることができる ……………… 143
donations can be sent to ...

[希望]
希望はある、と思います…………………… 131
I think that there is some hope

〜ことが我々の希望です…………………… 131
it is our hope that ...

[基本的]
〜の基本的な考えは気に入っています …… 185
like the basic idea behind ...

〜に基本的には賛成 ……………………… 185
basically in favor of ...

〜という考えを私は基本的に支持します … 185
basically I support the idea of ...

基本的には〜を我々は支持します ………… 185
basically, we support ...

[義務]
〜するのはあなたの大切な義務です ……… 176
it is your important duty to ...

[決める]
〜ことに決めました ……………………… 126
it is my decision ...

[疑問]
少々疑問です ……………………………… 165
there is some question as to ...

いくつか疑問点があります…………………… 183
there are certain points where I have my doubts

[却下]
却下すべきだと、私は確信します ………… 191
I am firmly convinced that we must reject

[キャンセル]
キャンセルしたいと思います……………… 119
would like to cancel

キャンセルして、確認の連絡を
してください ……………………………… 119
please cancel it and confirm this

[キャンペーン]
本キャンペーンの募集締め切り ………… 91
the deadline date for this campaign

[急]
急務を要します …………………………… 155
it is urgent

〜にとってこれは急を要します …………… 155
this is urgent to ...

[休暇]
夏期休暇中の待機スタッフ ………………… 76
the standby staff for the annual summer holidays

全社休暇の間 ……………………………… 76
during the company wide holiday period

休暇を取り、オフィスを留守にします …… 77
will be away from the office on vacation

休暇で留守にします ……………………… 77
will be away for vacation

休暇中の連絡先の住所と電話番号 ………… 77
your leave contact address and phone number

[休日]
素晴らしい休日をお過ごしください ……… 147
have a wonderful vacation

[教授]
ご教示いただきたい ……………………… 125
please instruct us

[恐縮]
大変恐縮ですが …………………………… 103
I am really sorry to bother you, but

[強調]
強調してもしすぎることはない ………… 177
I cannot stress enough

〜ということを強調したい……………… 177
would like to emphasize that ...

〜ことの重要性を、我々は特に強調したい… 177
we would like to lay special emphasis on the importance of ...

[興味]
〜に興味があり、それを勉強したいと
思っています ……………………………… 95
I am interested in ... and want to learn it

〜に非常に興味があり …………………… 95
I am really interested in ...

〜に大変興味があります………………… 95
very interested in ...

ご興味があるようでしたら ……………… 163
if you are interested

[協力]
ご協力、ありがとうございます ………… 37
thank you for your cooperation

一致協力して臨む必要があります ……… 121
your unanimous cooperation is absolutely needed

ぜひともご協力ください………………… 121
your cooperation will be really appreciated

あなたのご協力に深く感謝します ……… 152
we would greatly appreciate your assistance

[許可]
〜する許可をいただきたいのですが、
いかがでしょうか ………………………… 153
May I ask your permission to... ?

もし許可がいただければ〜したいと思う … 153
would like to get your permission to ...

〜する許可をいただきたいと存じます …… 153
please allow me to ...

〜する許可を与えます …………………… 167
I grant you permission to ...

許可することにしました ………………… 167
have decided to grant

〜を〜から外すことを許可することに
しました ………………………………… 167
have decided to let ... be removed from ...

[記録]
当方の記録用として ……………………… 65
for our records

[緊急]
特別な緊急事態として …………………… 155
as one of the special urgency cases

く

[苦情]
苦情を申し上げたく、このメールを差し上げて
います ……………………………………… 199
I am sending this email to complain

〜ことを指摘したく、この苦情メールを
書いています …………………………… 199
I am writing this email to complain to you that ...

[ください]
〜してください ………………………… 154
we would like you ...

〜してください ………………………… 154
we request that ...

[クリスマス]
楽しいクリスマスと新年を……………… 147
a Merry Christmas and a Happy New Year

[詳しい]
さらに詳しいことを知りたい…………… 96
want to learn more about it

〜についてもっと詳しく伺いたい ……… 96
I am interested in hearing more about ...

もう少し詳しく
ご説明願えませんでしょうか …………… 96
Could you be more specific?

～に詳しい方をご存じでしたら …………… 97
if you know someone who is familiar with ...

何か詳しい資料はあります…………………… 117
have any detailed information (material) regarding it

け

警告
あらかじめ警告しておきます………………… 196
let this serve as fair warning

掲載
詳細が掲載されています……………………… 161
we have posted detailed information

経由
クレーム対応は～経由で行います ………… 133
we will deal with this claim through ...

経歴書
自分の経歴書に箔が付く……………………… 216
will look good on my resume

怪我
交通事故で怪我を負ってしまった ………… 141
was injured in a traffic accident

結果
データマイニングの結果……………………… 220
the results of the data mining

欠勤
当分の間、欠勤いたします ………………… 141
will be off from work for some time

結構
～の案で結構です……………………………… 193
...'s plan is acceptable

欠席
欠席される方のみ……………………………… 137
if you are not attending

決定
決定次第、メールをいただきたい ………… 125
please email us as soon as you have made a decision

～ことに決定しました……………………… 126
I have decided to ...

結論
結論を早急に出して…………………………… 125
make your decision as soon as possible

軽率な結論を下してはなりません ………… 164
we shouldn't draw a hasty conclusion

懸念
懸念しています ……………………………… 164
are concerned

件
～する件についてですが……………………… 118
with regard to ...

原因
～が原因です ……………………………… 36
it was due to ...

～が原因で ……………………………… 175
because of ...

見解
残念ながら我々は見解が違います ………… 186
I am afraid we don't see things the same way

元気
元気づけられました…………………………… 146
it cheered me up

その日は本当に元気が出ました …………… 146
really made my day

健康
ご健康を心からお祈りいたしております … 138
I am wishing you the very best of health

原稿
～というテーマで原稿を執筆 ……………… 120
write an article for us with a title like ...

～までに原稿を送って……………………… 120
send your article by ...

健康診断
定期健康診断……………………………… 92
annual physical examination

233

[検索]
どんな情報が検索できますか ……………… 208
What kind of information can I find?

[建設的]
資料が不十分なので建設的な意見が
言えない ……………………………………… 173
don't have enough information to give a
constructive opinion

[検討]
検討するために ……………………………… 104
to examine

検討結果をまとめて報告………………… 115
report a summary of your analysis

よくよく検討してみた結果………………… 123
after careful consideration of it

これらの２つのオプションの
両方を検討して ……………………………… 211
consider these two options

こ

[ご愛顧]
この１年のご愛顧に ………………………… 147
for your patronage this year

[光栄]
非常に光栄に思う …………………………… 124
honored and pleased

[高速化]
〜をカスタマイズして高速化する ………… 212
to customize ... and speed it up

[香典]
香典は絶対に送らないように …………… 143
wishes no donations to be sent

[考慮]
ご考慮いただくために ……………………… 65
for your consideration.

重要な要素を考慮に入れていない ………… 190
doesn't take into account certain important factors

[声]
声をかけていただき ………………………… 124
for asking

[ゴーサイン]
〜にはゴーサインを出せません …………… 168
I cannot give the green light to ...

[誤解]
多少の誤解があったのではないかと思う … 203
I am afraid that there seems to have been a
slight misunderstanding

〜について誤解があるようです …………… 203
there seems to be some misunderstanding
about ...

[心当たり]
心当たりのある人は ………………………… 88
if it rings a bell

[心遣い]
心のこもった ………………………………… 146
in which you expressed kind words
of sympathy

[後日]
後日送ることができます …………………… 67
I can send you at a later date

[語数]
語数は 2000 ワード前後で ………………… 120
the number of words of your article
around 2000

[ご足労]
皆様にご足労いただけますでしょうか …… 103
Can I ask everybody to come here?

[ご存じ]
すでにご存じのように ……………………… 32
as you already know

〜はご存じでしょうか ……………………… 165
I am wondering if you could tell me ...

〜かご存じですか …………………………… 165
Do you have any idea about... ?

[答える]
〜の方が私よりも答えるのに適任 ………… 100
... is more qualified to answer it than I am

お答えします ………………………………… 217
our answer is ...

[言葉]
言葉もありませんでした ……………………… 198
I was speechless

[断る]
心苦しいのですが、お断りせざるを
得ません ………………………………… 123
we are afraid we must decline it

[ご無沙汰]
長いことご無沙汰しております ……………… 28
I haven't seen you for a long time

[コミュニケーション]
正確にコミュニケーションしていない …… 203
not communicating with each other accurately

[コメント]
コメントをいただきたいから ………………… 65
because we want you to give us some comments

コメントをお聞かせください ………………… 88
please let me know your comments

コメントするのは困難です …………………… 173
it is difficult for us to comment

[今後]
今後ともよろしくお付き合い
くださいませ ……………………………… 112
am looking forward to a good working relationship with you

今後もご連絡させていただきたい ………… 136
will try to keep in touch

[困難]
～ことは困難だと思います ………………… 181
I think it will be difficult to ...

さ

[最悪]
最悪のオプションです ……………………… 191
would be the worst option

[在庫]
在庫はあるでしょうか ……………………… 117
Do you have ... in your stock?

[最終]
～がそちらの最終的な申し出であるなら … 194
if ... is your final offer

[最新]
最新のデータを～にアップしました ……… 87
I have placed the latest data

[再度]
再度ご連絡いたします ……………………… 129
this is to inform you again

[最優先]
～が我々の最優先課題だ …………………… 162
... is our first priority

[採用]
～として、あなたを採用したい …………… 140
very pleased to offer you the position of ...

～を採用したいと思います ………………… 140
we would like to hire ...

すでに採用が決定しております …………… 140
the position has already been filled

採用する予定はございません ……………… 140
has no plan to hire

～として採用するには不十分です ………… 140
is not quite enough for us to offer you the position of ...

～を採用いただきたく ……………………… 161
to inquire whether you would be interested in using ...

[避ける]
～こそ我々が避けるべき～である ………… 191
... is precisely the kind of ... we need to avoid

[差し上げる]
申し訳ありませんが～を差し上げることは
できません ………………………………… 123
we are sorry to tell you that we cannot grant ...

[早急]
早急にメールでお知らせください ………… 33
please let us know by email promptly

早急に返信してください …………………… 132
please respond right away

参加
参加希望者は、ご連絡ください 92
those who wish to participate, please contact us

参考
ご参考までに 65
for your information

お話を伺って大変参考になりました 112
your talk was really informative

参照
ご参考までに参照していただくため 65
for your reference

賛成
100％賛成です 182
agree one hundred percent

〜に私はまったく賛成です 182
I am in total agreement with ...

〜の大部分に私は賛成します 183
I agree with most of ...

〜については賛成しかねます 183
I find it difficult to agree with you on ...

あなたの意見に賛成したい 183
would tend to agree with your opinion

あなたに賛成したい 183
I am inclined to agree with you

〜に大賛成です 184
... has my full support

あなたの意見には賛成だとは言えません ... 186
I can't say that I share your idea

あなたの意見に私は賛成できません 186
I really can't agree with

残念
〜と伺い、とても残念です 31
I am sorry to hear that ...

残念ですが〜です 69
I regret to report that ...

残念ですが、ご連絡いたします 69
I am sorry to inform you

〜と知り、大変残念に思っております 145
are saddened to learn that ...

し

支援
今後ともご支援のほど、
よろしくお願いします 39
we appreciate your continued support

資格
あなたの資格は非常に素晴らしいのですが ... 140
although your qualifications are excellent

時間
検討に数日余計にかかってしまいました ... 27
took us a couple of days longer

〜ほどお時間をいただけますでしょうか ... 102
Could you spare about ... with me?

〜程度なら時間を割くことができます 106
I think I can spare about ...

もう少し時間をいだけませんか 115
Could I have more time?

時間をかけて考えた方がいい............... 164
we should take time to think

以下の時間帯以外なら............... 108
except for the following hours

資源
〜に記述されているリソースが必要です ... 218
you need the resources described in ...

指示
〜について、ご指示をいただきたい 125
have your instructions about ...

あなたの指示をお待ちしている 125
await your instruction

以下の指示に従ってほしい 126
please follow the following instructions

私の指示は次の通りです............... 126
my instructions are as follows:

私の指示は〜だ 126
my instructions to you are to ...

支持
最後まで支持する............... 184
will support all the way

|実施|
~を100%支持します……………………… 184
I am behind ... 100％

固く支持する …………………………… 184
firmly support

|事実|
事実関係を確認して …………………… 133
look into the matter

|自信|
自信を持ってお勧めできます ………… 161
we can certainly recommend with confidence

~という自信があります ……………… 179
we are confident that ...

100％の自信はありません …………… 164
I am not 100％ confident

|したい|
~したいと思っております …………… 160
I prefer ...

もしできれば~したいのですが ……… 160
I would rather ... if I could

~してほしいのですが、どうでしょうか … 160
I would prefer that ... How about it?

~したい、と考えています …………… 162
we are hoping to ...

|辞退|
辞退させていただきます ……………… 106
I am afraid I must decline

辞退させていただきます ……………… 123
I am afraid that we must decline

|下回る|
我々の期待を大きく下回っています ……… 199
I am afraid that it was far below our expectations

|実行|
~を実行することにしました ………… 159
has decided to carry out ...

明らかに実行されなければならないこと … 210
what must clearly be done

|実施|
以下の変更が実施されます ………………… 70
the following changes will be implemented

|質問|
この件に関して質問があります …………… 25
about which I have some questions

ご質問がありましたら …………………… 40
if you have any questions

~については、どなたに質問すればよいか … 98
who we should ask regarding ...

質問をメールしてみてはいかがですか …… 100
Why don't you email your question?

1つだけ質問があるのですが ……………… 165
my only question is

~とのご質問ですが ………………………… 217
in answering your question of ...

|指摘|
~ことを指摘させていただきたい ………… 174
allow me to point out that ...

|自動化|
ビジネスプロセスを自動化する …………… 206
automating the business processes

|自明|
~のは自明だ ……………………………… 179
it is self-evident that ...

|締め切り|
締め切りは~ですので、厳守してください … 120
please be reminded that your deadline is ...

最初の締め切り期限をあと1カ月延長 …… 213
one-month extension of the original deadline

|充実|
これまで以上に充実させていく ………… 147
expand ... than we did in the past

|住所|
新しい住所は以下の通りです ……………… 138
our new address is as follows

237

[就職]
〜で就職活動するのに有利 ………………… 216
a big advantage for a person who wants to find a job in ...

[重要]
重要な点は〜です ………………………… 174
the important point is that ...

〜ことが重要だと私は思います …………… 176
I believe that it is important for us to ...

〜することは重要です ……………………… 176
it is important to ...

〜に関して重要なのは ……………………… 176
what is important about ...

最も重要だと私は思います ………………… 177
I consider it most important

〜の問題が非常に重要です ………………… 177
the issue of ... is very significant

〜が重要だとは、私には思えません ……… 178
I'm afraid I'm not convinced of the importance of ...

さほど重要ではない ………………………… 178
it is not so important

〜の重要性が私にはわかりません ………… 178
I don't see the importance of ...

〜がそれほど重要だとは思いません ……… 178
I really do not think ... is all that important

あなたが考えるほど〜が重要だとは
思いません ………………………………… 178
I don't think ... is as important as you think it is

[熟知]
〜は熟知しております ……………………… 161
very familiar with ...

[受信]
〜以上のメール添付はうまく受信できない … 43
cannot handle any email whose size exceeds ...

[受諾]
妥協案は受諾しかねます …………………… 194
we won't be able to accept the compromise

[出荷]
もう出荷されて ……………………………… 117
been shipped already

[出欠]
出欠を〜までご連絡ください ……………… 137
please advice ... if you will attend

[出社]
〜には出社の見込みです …………………… 75
expected to return after ...

しばらく出社しません ……………………… 75
not expected to be back for some time

[出席]
〜へのご出席を心よりお待ち申し上げます … 78
you are cordially invited to attend ...

出席の確認を〜までお願いします ………… 79
I would appreciate it if you confirm your attendance at ... with ...

出欠をご確認いただけますか ……………… 79
would you please confirm your attendance

残念ですが〜には出席できません ………… 80
I regret to inform you that I won't be able to make it to ...

残念ですが、先約がございますので
出席できません …………………………… 80
I must decline as I have a previous engagement

商用で〜に出張しておりますので、
出席できません …………………………… 80
I will not be able to attend ... as I will be visiting ... on business

〜に出席できなくなりました ……………… 111
I cannot make it to ...

〜に出席できなくなりました ……………… 111
I will be unable to attend ...

[出張]
現在出張中で ………………………………… 75
is out of town on a business trip right now

私の出張日程は以下の通り ………………… 75
my itinerary is as follows

[順調]
問題なく進んでいます ……………………… 114
progressing without a hitch

[準備]
〜の準備ができ次第 ………………………… 22
as soon as ... is ready

使用

来月から使用できなくなります …………… 87
will be closed permanently starting next month

ご使用になりたい方は …………………… 87
those who would like to use it

現在使用中でないPC …………………… 89
a PC that is not being used right now

紹介

〜に私を紹介していただけないでしょうか… 97
can you introduce me to ...

どなたかにご紹介いただければありがたいです
………………………………………………… 97
I would appreciate it very much if you could introduce me to someone

御社のことは〜にご紹介いただきました … 99
your company's name was given to us by ...

〜を紹介するために …………………… 104
so that I can introduce you to ...

〜をご紹介いたします …………… 113, 147
this is to introduce ...

使用許諾
使用許諾をいただきたい…………………… 101
would like to get your permission

使用を許可していただければ …………… 101
if you allow me to use

条件

〜を条件に全力を尽くします …………… 193
will try our best provided that ...

〜ということを条件に〜することにします … 193
prepared to ... on the condition that ...

詳細

詳細をお知らせするためのもの …………… 26
to provide the details

正直

君の正直な意見を知りたい………………… 170
would appreciate your honest opinion

招待

ご招待券がお手元に届いていましたら、
その旨ご連絡いただけますでしょうか …… 79
if the invitation reached you

ご招待を喜んでお受けいたします ………… 80
we are delighted to accept your invitation

記念夕食会へご招待できる ……………… 85
you are cordially invited to attend a banquet to commemorate the occasion

承認

貴社のご承認をいただくため …………… 65
for your approval

〜する計画を承認します………………… 167
approve of the plan to ...

ここに承認します ………………………… 167
I hereby give my approval

承認されませんでした …………………… 168
was not approved

申し訳ありませんが、〜は承認できませんので、お知らせいたします………………… 168
I am sorry to inform you that we cannot approve of ...

仕様変更

仕様変更については ……………………… 212
about changing the specifications

情報源

このニュースの情報源の方 ………………… 98
who you got this news from

情報源を明らかにしていただく …………… 98
reveal the source of this information

情報源と、その方の連絡先 ………………… 98
the source of this information and who I should contact to get it

何か良い情報源 …………………………… 98
any good information sources

どんな情報源に当たればよいか …………… 98
which information sources we should look into

助言

さまざまな助言をいただき ……………… 148
all the advice you gave me

〜に関して、
助言をいただければ幸いです……………… 156
your advice on ... would be greatly appreciated

ご助言ください …………………………… 156
please advise me

239

～についてご助言いただけますか ………… 156
Could you advise me... ?

[処理]
～はどれくらいのデータを
処理できますか ……………………… 208
How much data can ... process?

[知らせる]
すでにお知らせしたように …………………… 26
as I have already informed you

申し訳ございませんが、お知らせできません … 68
I am sorry, but I can't tell you

ことをお知らせできるのをうれしく思います … 69
I am pleased to inform you

～ことをお知らせします ……………………… 69
this is to inform you that ...

オープンしたことをお知らせします ………… 70
I would like to announce the opening

～ことのお知らせです ………………………… 70
this is to announce ...

～のでお知らせします ………………………… 70
this is to announce that ...

ご注意ください ………………………………… 70
please make note of ...

～をお知らせください ………………………… 71
please inform us of ...

私に直接知らせてください …………………… 71
please advise me directly of ...

すぐに知らせてもらえますか ………………… 71
will you let me know soonest?

必ず知らせてほしい …………………………… 71
I want you to ensure that ... are brought to the attention of ...

私にもCCで知らせてください ……………… 133
please include me in the CC

[調べる]
～を調べていただけませんか ………………… 152
Could you help us find... ?

[資料]
下記の新着資料が入りました ………………… 92
the following technical books have newly arrived

～に関する資料を送ってください ………… 94
please send me information concerning ...

～に関する詳しい資料 ……………………… 94
the details regarding ...

～に関する資料をメールで
お送りいただくことは可能ですか ………… 94
Is it possible for you to email me information concerning ...

～に関する資料はありませんか …………… 94
Do you have any information regarding ... ?

どんな資料でも、お送りいただければ
ありがたいです ……………………………… 94
any information you could provide would be greatly appreciated.

～について、もう少し資料を ……………… 96
a little more information about ...

[知る]
～のか知りたいのですが …………………… 165
would like to know if ...

あなたがどのようにお考えかを知りたい … 170
interested to know what you think

[しれない]
～かもしれません …………………………… 172
it could be that ...

[人員]
追加で人員をつける ………………………… 115
add more people

追加で人員をつける ………………………… 115
bring in more people

[信じる]
～なんて信じられません …………………… 198
I can't believe that ...

[診断書]
医師の診断書を提出 ………………………… 141
present your doctor's report

[進捗]
現在の進捗状況をお知らせください ……… 114
please inform me how ... is coming on

240

[進展]
進展はいかがでしょうか………………… 114
How is everything coming on?

[新年]
素晴らしい新年を………………………… 147
wonderful new year

[心配]
心配しています…………………………… 164
it concerns us

私の心配は〜かということです ………… 164
my concern is whether ...

心配する必要はまったくありません……… 166
you don't have to worry about it at all

[信頼]
信頼できる〜をご存じでしたら …………… 97
if you know a reliable ...

す

[図]
グラフは〜で作成………………………… 120
draw graphs using ...

[推奨]
〜ことを勧めます………………………… 157
I recommend that ...

[推薦]
これは〜を推薦する書状です …………… 139
this letter recommends ...

〜を推薦いたします……………………… 139
I am happy to have this opportunity to recommend ...

〜を推薦いたします……………………… 139
I am happy to recommend ...

〜を自信をもって推薦したいと思います … 139
I would like to recommend ... without reservations

[推測]
〜と推測してよろしいのでしょうか ……… 127
Am I correct in assuming that ... ?

[優れる]
〜という点で、特に優れています ………… 161
is superb in that ...

技術面で優れて…………………………… 208
technical advantages

[スケジュール]
今後の概略スケジュール………………… 113
the rough schedule for ...

今週のスケジュールは以下の通り ………… 113
this week's schedule is as follows

今後数週間のスケジュールは〜です ……… 113
schedule over the next few weeks includes ...

[勧める]
〜ことを強く勧めます…………………… 158
I strongly advise you to ...

[素晴らしい]
〜は素晴らしい、と思います ……………… 149
I think ... is excellent

[済みません]
お詫びいたします………………………… 36
please accept my apologies

せ

[請求]
ご請求の資料……………………………… 118
the information you requested

[精密検査]
病院で精密検査がある…………………… 141
need to undergo a thorough medical examination

[整理]
2、3の点を整理させてください …………… 26
clarifying a few things

[接続]
Web接続する場合 ………………………… 219
to connect to the Web

[絶対]
絶対に反対………………………………… 191
absolutely opposed

241

［説明］
メールを送り、〜を説明してください …… 71
please send an email ... and explain

ご説明するために ………………………… 104
so that I can explain ...

［世話］
いろいろお世話になり ………………… 148
for all the help you gave me

［全体的］
全体的には賛成です …………………… 185
our overall reaction is favorable

［全面的］
〜に全面的に賛成します……………… 167
I entirely approve of ...

全面的に賛成です ……………………… 184
give my total support

全面的に支持することを表明する ……… 184
express my total support

〜に全面的に賛成するわけではありません … 186
I don't completely agree with ...

そ

［葬儀］
葬儀は〜で執り行われます…………… 142
funeral will take place at ...

葬儀は親族の方だけで行われる ……… 142
there will be a private funeral service attended by the family and relatives only

［増設］
電話回線がもう１本増設されました ……… 72
an additional telephone line has been installed

増設されました ……………………………… 87
has been added

［相談］
〜についてご相談したいと思います ……… 102
would like to consult with you about ...

そちらに伺って、ご相談したい …………… 104
would like to come see you to discuss

［送付］
送付先の住所と電話番号を返信で
お知らせください ………………………… 64
please indicate your shipping address and phone number

［送別会］
〜の送別会にご招待 …………………… 137
invited to attend a farewell party for ...

〜の送別会を行います ………………… 137
we are planning a farewell party for ...

［即時］
即時に〜できない理由があれば ……… 155
if there is any reason why you cannot ... right away

［属性］
属性を追加しました …………………… 212
have added attributes

［続報］
〜をお知らせしたく、続報として ………… 26
as a follow-up to remind you that ...

［訴訟］
訴訟に訴えざるを得ません…………… 196
will be forced to take the matter to the court

［率直］
率直なご意見を ………………………… 170
your honest opinion about it

［沿って］
〜に沿って仕事を進めます …………… 113
plan to go forward with the project in line with ...

［外側］
〜の外側にある ………………………… 215
located outside ...

た

［対応］
適切な対応をしてください……………… 133
please take appropriate action

早急な対応をお願いします ……………… 133
please respond right away

対処
問題に対する対処法 …………………… 133
what to do to deal with the problem

～することでこの問題に対処したい ……… 211
we would like to take care of this
problem by ...

代替案
提案した代替案は非常に妥当だ …………… 193
the alternative solution we suggested is very
reasonable

妥協
～に同意して、貴社と妥協させてください … 193
let us agree ... to meet you halfway

妥協案で結構だ ………………………… 193
the compromise solution would be perfectly
acceptable

～の妥協案が有効な解決策かどうか ……… 194
whether ...'s compromise is a viable solution

託す
どんな情報を託すことができますか ……… 208
What kind of information can I entrust?

確か
～のは確かでしょう ……………………… 158
we will surely ...

助ける
～していただき助かりました ………… 45, 156
very thoughtful of you to ...

～していただけると助かる ……………… 152
be so kind as to have ...

～していただけると助かります ………… 154
it would be helpful if you would ...

～していただけると助かります …………… 35
I would be grateful if you could ...

きっと助けてもらえると思います ………… 100
I think he will be able to help you on that matter

私どもが手助けできることが何かあれば … 40
if there is something we can do for you

尋ねる
～までメールでお尋ねください …………… 87
please contact us by email at ...

訪ねる
どなたを訪ねればよろしいでしょうか …… 109
who should I visit

直ちに
直ちに取りかかります …………………… 58
I will get on to it right away

直ちに～してください …………………… 155
I want you to ... right away

立場
～は意見を述べる立場にはないと思います … 173
I don't think that ... is in a position to comment

あなたの立場はわかりますが ……………… 188
I can see your point of view, but

妥当
～の提案は妥当のように私には思えます … 193
... 's proposal seems to me to be reasonable

楽しみ
お会いできるのを楽しみにしています …… 38
I am looking forward to seeing you

～でご一緒できるのを楽しみにしております … 39
I look forward to working for ...

～さえあれば楽しめます ………………… 217
you only need ... to enjoy

頼む
質問に答えるように頼んでおきました …… 100
asked him to answer it

ため
～のためになる、と思います …………… 157
I think that it would be in the best interest of ...

試す
何ができるか試してみる ………………… 209
to try to see what ... can do

担当
ご担当 …………………………………… 97
let me know who is in charge of ...

〜についての担当者 ……………………… 122
who is in charge of ...

ち

知恵
お知恵を拝借したい ……………………… 88
would like to get his/her advice

力
皆さんのお力添え ………………………… 121
your cooperation

ひとつ力を貸してはくれないだろうか …… 121
Could I request your help?

中止
中止になりました ………………………… 119
has been called off

注目
〜に注目していただきたい……………… 174
would like to draw your attention to ...

注文
〜の注文書です …………………………… 116
this is our order sheet for ...

弔詞
〜に対し丁重なご弔詞をメールでいただき … 146
your email with expressions of sympathy upon ...

著作権
著作権上、問題があるでしょうか ………… 101
Would it be copyright infringement?

御社が著作権を持つ ……………………… 101
to which your company holds the copyrights

つ

追加
プラグイン形式で追加できます …………… 207
you can plug-in

この新機能の追加によって ………………… 212
with the addition of this new feature

ついで
ついでですがご連絡しておきます ………… 128
I would like to take this opportunity to inform you

使い勝手
使い勝手を大きく高めるために ………… 212
in order to greatly enhance the usability

都合
ご都合はいかがですか …………………… 102
I wonder if it would be convenient for you

どちらがご都合よろしいでしょうか ……… 107
which place you prefer

どちらがご都合よろしいでしょうか ……… 107
Which will be convenient for you?

こちらの都合で ……………………………… 110
placing my convenience ahead of yours

伝える
〜にお伝えください ……………………… 130
please inform ...

あなたに伝えるように頼まれました ……… 130
asked me to tell you

て

手
〜から手を引く …………………………… 119
pull ourselves out of ...

提案
ご提案、大変感謝しております …………… 24
I really appreciate your suggestion

提案ですが ………………………………… 118
about your proposal for ...

〜ことを提案します ……………………… 157
I suggest that ...

〜ことを強く提案します ………………… 158
I suggest strongly that ...

あなたの提案に従って …………………… 159
as you suggested

〜ことを提案します ……………………… 189
would like to propose that ...

私の提案は〜です ………………………… 189
my proposal is that ...

提案したいと思う ………………………… 189
would like to put forward a proposal

~の提案を支持できません ……………… 190
cannot support ...'s proposal

提供
喜んでご提供いたします …………………… 34
we will be happy to provide you with

このシステムは~を提供できますか ……… 208
Can this system provide ... ?

付け加えて提供してください ………………… 212
please add and provide

停止
停止します ………………………………… 87
will be shut down

システムを停止させる必要があります …… 211
need to take the system down

社内ネットワークを停止する ……………… 221
shut down the in-house network system

提示
別の案をご提示 …………………………… 123
come up with an alternative plan

できる
もしできることなら ………………………… 160
if I may

~することができるのでしょうか ………… 165
I wonder whether we could ...

~ことができます …………………………… 167
we grant that ...

撤退
~から弊社は撤退する ……………………… 119
forced to withdraw ourselves from ...

手伝う
お手伝いはできません ……………………… 123
am unable to help you

お手伝い ……………………………………… 124
give you a hand

手伝ってもらえませんか …………………… 152
Could I ask you to help me out?

では
では、そういうことでしたら ……………… 58
OK, in that case

手配
ホテルの手配のお手伝い …………………… 86
your assistance in arranging hotel

ように手配しておきます …………………… 109
I will make an arrangement so that ...

デバイス
どんなデバイスに対して …………………… 214
to what kind of devices

出迎え
出迎えを~に寄越してください …………… 81
have someone come to pick him up

転勤
~に転勤することになりました …………… 136
I will be transferred to ...

伝言
~からの伝言で~とのことでした ………… 130
... asked me to communicate to you that ...

転載
転載使用したい ……………………………… 101
would like to reproduce it as ...

転送
ご参考までに転送します …………………… 55
I am forwarding to you for your information

データ転送をサポートする ………………… 221
support data transfer

添付
このメールに添付します …………………… 42
I am going to attach it to this email

添付しましたのは~です …………………… 42
attached is ...

~のファイルを添付いたしました ………… 42
please find attached a file of ...

ファイルを添付せずに ……………………… 44
without attaching the file

245

言及されているファイルが添付されていません … 44
without the attached file you were talking about

[電話]
お電話ありがとうございました ……………… 24
thank you for your call

と

問い合わせ
〜日付けのお問い合わせを受け取りました … 25
I have received your inquiry of ...

〜についての問い合わせ先………………… 98
where to send my inquiry about ...

お問い合わせいただいた ………………… 118
you inquired

〜に関してのお問い合わせですが ………… 118
in response to your inquiry about ...

問い合わせ先 ……………………………… 122
the contact information

[同意]
〜というあなたの意見に同意します ……… 182
agree with your opinion that ...

〜には同意しかねます……………………… 183
I can't agree with ...

あなたの考えには残念ながら同意しかねます 186
I am afraid I do not share your view

〜という考えに私は同意できません ……… 187
I can't agree with the idea that ...

[同意見]
〜と同意見です ……………………………… 182
is of the same opinion as ...

[どうしても]
どうしても〜させなければなりません …… 169
we absolutely must ...

[同情]
ご同情に耐えません ………………………… 145
let you know how sorry I am

[どうする]
どうしてほしいのですか…………………… 125
What do you want me to do?

[同席]
〜も同席させたい ………………………… 106
I would like to bring ... with me to the meeting

[届く]
本日、私の元に届きました ………………… 66
today, I received

このメールが届きましたら………………… 132
if this email reaches you

[留める]
皆さん、心にお留めおきください ………… 32
everybody, I would like to draw your attention to the fact that ...

[取り急ぎ]
このメールは取り急ぎお知らせするための
ものです …………………………………… 29
this brief email is just to inform

[取り消す]
約束を取り消さなければならなく
なりました ………………………………… 111
I am afraid that I have to cancel the appointment

な

[内線]
内線123番をお呼び出しください ………… 109
please dial extension ...

[内容]
内容はご覧の通りです ……………………… 63
which should be self-explanatory

[亡くなる]
〜で突然お亡くなりになった …………… 142
suddenly passed away with ...

[なる]
〜ことになりました ……………………… 126
it has been decided that ...

に

[二次的]
二次的な問題です ………………………… 178
is of secondary importance

[日時]
ご都合のよい日時の候補 …………………… 108
a couple of dates that will be convenient for you

ご希望の日時を …………………………… 110
when you would like to meet

別の日時を提案 …………………………… 110
suggest an alternative date

別の日時を提案 …………………………… 110
come up with a different date

[入院]
入院する必要 ……………………………… 141
needs to be hospitalized

[入手]
その情報は〜で入手できます ……………… 58
you can obtain that information at ...

入手可能 …………………………………… 117
available for delivery

[人数]
人数を把握するため ………………………… 85
in order to finalize numbers

ね

[願う]
〜ことを心より願っています ……………… 131
it is our sincere hope that ...

[値引き]
値引きのご用意がございます ……………… 206
we are willing to grant you a reduction

さらに値引きさせていただくつもりです … 206
we are prepared to offer you another reduction

[寝耳]
寝耳に水でした …………………………… 198
I have been caught off guard

の

[納期]
納期はどれくらい ………………………… 117
rough estimate for the delivery date

[望む]
〜ことを望むだけです …………………… 131
we can only hope that ...

は

[パーティー]
ささやかなパーティーを開催する ………… 85
have a small party

[拝借]
〜を拝借できれば ………………………… 152
would like to have the benefit of ...

[配信]
ネットワーク配信する …………………… 218
to network deliver

[配布]
データをどうやって配布する計画か ……… 218
how our company plans to distribute data

[配慮]
すぐにご対応いただければ
ありがたく存じます ……………………… 35
please give your attention to

〜へのご配慮に、感謝いたします ………… 35
we would appreciate your attention to ...

〜を、ご配慮ください …………………… 35
your prompt response ... will be appreciated

好意あるご配慮に感謝いたします ………… 35
we appreciate your favorable consideration to ...

すぐにご配慮いただけることを望んで
おります …………………………………… 35
I hope you will give them your consideration without delay

ご配慮をいただくために ………………… 65
for your attention

[励まし]
励ましのお言葉をいただき〜 …………… 146
for the encouragement

励まされました …………………………… 146
meant a lot to me

派遣
直ちに〜を派遣していただければ
感謝します ………………………… 155
would appreciate having ... right away

始める
〜で始めてみませんか ……………………… 211
Why don't we start with ... ?

場所
適当な場所を探しています……………… 137
I am looking for a good place

パターン
同じパターンを素早く見つける ……………… 220
find a matcing pattern very fast

発送
本日発送いたします ………………………… 62
we will ship ... today

直ちに再発送いたします ……………………… 62
we will immediately reship

発展
ますますのご発展を ……………………… 147
a Happy and Prosperous New Year

発表
〜ことを発表できるのをうれしく思います … 70
I am pleased to announce ...

花
花は送らないように …………………… 143
no flowers should be sent

お花は受け取りたい …………………… 143
the family will accept flowers

話し合う
〜はもっと話し合うべきでしょう ………… 183
... should be discussed further

早い
できるだけ早く ………………………… 22
as soon as possible

予定よりも少し早いペースで …………… 114
a little ahead of schedule

反対
〜には大反対です ………………………… 168
I am strongly against ...

〜という考えに反対しない…………………… 185
would not oppose the idea of ...

反対しなくてはならない、と思います …… 186
I feel that I really must disagree

まったく反対 ……………………………… 187
in total disagreement

あなたに反対するつもりはありませんが … 188
I don't mean to disagree with you, but

判明
〜ということが判明しました …………… 201
it has come to our attention that ...

ひ

比較的
比較的小さな ……………………………… 178
a relatively minor

引き合い
お引き合い、どうもありがとうございます … 124
thank you for your inquiry

引き続き
引き続き知らせてもらえますか …………… 71
will you please keep us informed

久しぶり
久しぶりです ……………………………… 28
I haven't seen you for ages

久しぶり …………………………………… 28
long time no see

ビジネス手法
ビジネス手法を変えさせる………………… 208
change the way we do business

ビジネスモデル
どんなビジネスモデルを提供できますか … 208
What kind of a business model can ... provide?

必要
必要な場合は ……………………………… 40
if you require (need) ...

| 〜する必要がある 169
it is necessary for you to ...

必要なのは〜ことです 169
what is necessary for you is to ...

メモリはどれだけ必要 214
how much memory is needed

必要なだけしかメモリを 214
memories only as much as needed

人手
人手が必要であれば 163
if you need some helping hands

一肌
一肌脱ぐことにしましょう 121
I will help you out

費用
費用はどのくらいかかりますか 210
how much do you charge for it

■ ふ

フォロー
〜に対するメールのフォローアップです ... 26
this is just a follow-up to ...

不可欠
〜ことは不可欠だ 177
... is a vital issue

不公平
〜はいくぶん不公平だと私は思います 194
I feel that ... is somewhat unfair

ふさがる
すべてふさがっていて、空いているところが
ありません 108
occupied and have no opening

復帰
職場には〜から復帰できます 141
can get back to work on ...

復旧
さきほど復旧しました 87
it came back a while ago

不都合
不都合をお詫びします 36
I am sorry for the inconvenience caused

分担
役割分担（仕事のアサイン） 121
job assignment

■ へ

閉鎖
社屋改装のため閉鎖されます 76
will be closed for remodeling

〜いっぱい閉鎖されます 76
is closed throughout ...

閉鎖せざるを得なくなった 119
have been forced to close

別便
別便にて送ります 67
I will send in a separate email

明日、別便にて送ります 67
will send in a separate email tomorrow

返却
至急返却してください 89
please return them immediately

変更
変更されることをお知らせします 72
I would like to advise you that ... will change

〜に変更になりました 72
please note that ... has been changed to ...

〜以外、連絡先の詳細は変更ありません ... 72
all the communication details other than ...
remain unchanged

返事
早速お返事いただき、ありがとうございます... 24
thank you for your prompt reply to ...

これは、〜に対する返事です 25
this is to reply to ...

すぐに返事をすることができませんでした ... 27
I could not respond to your email right away

すぐにお返事をすることができず 27
I was unable to reply sooner

249

お返事をいただきたく、お待ちしております … 33
I look forward to your reply

お返事をお待ちしています……………… 33
we look forward to hearing from you as soon as possible

ほ

報告
ご報告が遅れて ………………………… 36
that I didn't report to you sooner

ご報告いたします ……………………… 129
this is to report

法的手段
法的手段をとらざるを得ません …………… 196
will be forced to take legal action

訪問
〜を訪れます ……………………………… 81
will be visiting ...

〜を訪問し、当地に３日間滞在します …… 81
will visit ... and stay there for three days

保管
保管用の ………………………………… 65
for your retention

欲しい
ほしいものがあれば …………………… 163
if you need anything

保証
〜ことを保証します …………………… 166
I assure you that ...

〜ことを保証します …………………… 166
I guarantee that ...

〜上での動作は保証していません ………… 217
we don't guarantee to work properly on ...

保存
XML形式で顧客データを保存する ………… 220
saves our customer data in the XML format

褒める
君のことをいつも褒めている ……………… 149
I have heard nothing but praise for you

〜を褒めたいと思います ……………… 149
I want to commend you for ...

ま

前
〜分前には ……………………………… 22
... minutes before

〜の前までに …………………………… 22
before ... starts

まずい
まずい考えだと思います ……………… 187
I think that it's a bad idea

間違い
間違って送られてきたと思われます ……… 44
apparently forwarded to me by mistake

〜のは間違いありません ……………… 169
there is no question that ...

間違っているかもしれませんが …………… 172
I could be mistaken, but

〜ことは間違いない …………………… 179
there is no doubt that ...

あなたは間違っていると
思わざるを得ません …………………… 186
I can't help feeling that you are not quite right

〜によれば、重大な間違いがありました … 201
based on ... , a serious error has been made

申し訳ありません、〜の間違いが
ありました ……………………………… 201
please excuse me, but there has been a ... error

〜と考えるのは間違っています ………… 201
it is a mistake to think that ...

待
２、３日、お待ちください ……………… 58
please wait for a couple of days

まったく
まったく賛成できません ……………… 191
don't agree at all

〜をあなたが支持する理由がまったく
わかりません …………………………… 191
see no reason for you supporting ...

間に合う
期限に間に合いそうもありません ………… 115
we cannot make it to the deadline

回す
〜に回してください ……………………… 122
please forward to ...

満足
〜に非常に満足しております ……………… 149
we couldn't be more pleased with ...

み

見過ごす
〜という事実を見過ごしてはなりません … 174
we should not overlook the fact that ...

見せる
貸していただけませんか ……………………… 88
Could anyone let me take a look at it?

見つける
見つけた方はメールでご連絡ください …… 90
if you find it, please let me know by email

見つけられた方はすぐにご連絡ください … 90
please contact me immediately if you find it

見積もり
〜からの見積もりのコピー ………………… 63
a copy of the quotation from ...

おおまかな〜を見積もってもらえますか … 117
Could you give us your rough estimate of ... ?

認める
〜は認められません ………………………… 168
I cannot grant ...

〜ことを認めません ………………………… 168
you do not have my permission to ...

見逃す
見逃すべきでないと思う …………………… 169
I think we should not overlook

〜という事実を見逃してはなりません …… 176
we should not overlook the fact that ...

む

無条件
全面的かつ無条件で支持します …………… 184
total and unconditional support

難しい
難しいのは〜ことです ……………………… 202
the difficulty lies in ...

無理
〜のは無理でしょう ………………………… 181
there is very little likelihood of ...

無理のようです ……………………………… 181
it is very unlikely

まったく無理です …………………………… 187
just isn't feasible

無料
無料で自由に使える ………………………… 215
which you can use for free

め

明白
〜のは明白だ ………………………………… 179
it is obvious that ...

迷惑
ご迷惑をおかけした ………………………… 36
inconvenienced you

ご迷惑をおかけして ………………………… 200
any inconvenience it may have caused you

メール
〜日付けのメールに関し …………………… 25
in reference to your email of ...

メールを最後に交わしたのは ……………… 28
when we exchanged our emails last

〜までメールしてください ………………… 64
please email them to ...

メールアドレス
あなたのメールアドレスは〜に
教えてもらいました ………………………… 57
I got your email address from ...

〜であなたのメールアドレスを知りました … 57
I found your email address on ...

アドレス帳の更新をよろしくお願い
いたします ……………………………… 74
update your address book information

旧アドレスは〜をもって使用中止になります … 74
the old address will no longer be active as of ...

今後、メールは新しいアドレスである〜に
お送りください ………………………… 74
send your email to my new email address
from now on

私の旧アドレスはもう使われていません … 74
the old email address of mine is no longer in use

[メリット]
御社が〜を利用するメリットの1つ ……… 206
one of the merits for your company to use ...

[面会]
ご面会いただければ大変喜ぶと思います … 105
would enjoy meeting you very much

■ も

[申し上げる]
〜を申し上げたく、このメールを
書いています …………………………… 29
I am writing this email to express ...

[申し訳]
〜とのご連絡をメールでいただき、
大変申し訳なく思っております …………… 200
we are very sorry to learn from your email that ...

[目的]
〜の主目的は〜です ……………………… 82
the main purpose of ... is to ...

第一の目的は〜にある …………………… 162
the primary goal is to ...

〜の目的は〜です ………………………… 162
the purpose of ... is to ...

〜が主目的です …………………………… 207
the main scope is ...

[目標]
〜ことが我々の目標です ………………… 162
we aim to ...

[もっとも]
〜の意見はごもっともだと思いますが …… 188
we think that ... has a point, but

あなたのご指摘はもっともですが ………… 188
I understand your point, but

[問題]
問題ないでしょうか …………………… 101
Would that be all right with you?

大きな問題はありません ………………… 114
haven't encountered any big problems

問題が出てきました ……………………… 114
have encountered problem (s)

特に問題はありません …………………… 124
foresee no particular problems

〜のは問題だと思います ………………… 164
it is cause for my concern that ...

問題が2、3あるように思います ………… 190
there seem to be a couple of problems

いくつかの問題が予測されます ………… 190
I can see some problems

唯一の問題は〜ということです ………… 202
the only problem is that ...

〜に問題があるようだ …………………… 202
there seems to be a problem with ...

1つだけ問題がある ……………………… 202
there is only one problem

■ や

[約束]
アポイントメントを取る ………………… 102
set up an appointment with you

〜ことをお約束します …………………… 166
you have my word that ...

〜ことを約束します ……………………… 166
I promise you that ...

[役立つ]
もし我々でお役に立てることがあれば、
ぜひお知らせください …………………… 34
if we can be of any assistance

お役に立ちたいのはやまやまなのですが … 68
I wish I could help you, but

私にお役に立てることがあれば ……… 163
to assist you in any way

あなたのお役に立てれば ……………… 163
to help you in any way I can

お役に立つとお思いでしたら ………… 163
if you think it would be helpful

休む

お休みさせていただいてもよろしい
でしょうか ……………………………… 141
Could I stay home from work?

今日１日休みを取る …………………… 141
I will take a day off today

できれば休ませてください …………… 141
I would like to take a day off, if I could

〜がひどいので今日は休む …………… 141
won't be coming to work today because he has a severe ...

宿

〜にあるホテルに、宿の手配を ……… 86
arrange accommodation at a hotel located ...

宿を取っていただける ………………… 86
if you could arrange accommodation at a hotel

当地での宿の手配 ……………………… 86
arrange hotel accommodation for him in the area

山場

今が山場です …………………………… 115
now we are at a crucial point

■ **ゆ**

唯一

唯一の方法は〜ことです ……………… 195
the only way I could do it would be to ...

有意義

有意義な議論ができ …………………… 112
having a productive discussion

有効

唯一の有効なソリューション ………… 158
the only viable solution

この新しい機能は非常に有効です ……… 206
this new function is quite effective

優先

転送優先度の問題 ……………………… 221
the problems of transmission priority

誘導

入場者を誘導する ……………………… 121
steer visitors to show them the way

有能

〜にとって有能な人材となることを
確信しております ……………………… 139
I am sure he would be a great asset to ...

有用

非常に有用です …………………………… 66
will help me a lot

行方不明

行方不明で困っています ………………… 89
I am in trouble because I cannot locate

行方不明の〜を探しています …………… 89
I am looking for ... that is missing

許す

〜をお許しください …………………… 31
please forgive me for ...

どうぞお許しください ………………… 36
please forgive

■ **よ**

要件

システムの要件についてまとめたもの …… 209
supposed to show the system requirements of

要請

直ちに対応するように要請します ……… 155
require your immediate action on it

要素

要素をいくつ使うべきですか …………… 220
How many elements should we use?

[要点]

〜の要点を確認します ……………… 127
this is to confirm the main points of ...

主要点を確認させていただきますと ……… 129
to confirm the main points

[用命]

今後またご用命いただければ幸いです …… 38
we look forward to the possibility of serving you again

[予測]

予測より多少時間がかかる ……………… 213
it is going to take a little longer than I estimated

[予約]

使用するには予約が必要です ……………… 87
those who want to use it need to register themselves

〜を予約してくださいますか ……………… 116
Could you reserve ... ?

予約してください ……………………… 116
please reserve

予約はできますか ……………………… 116
Can I make a reservation?

予約してくれてありがとう ……………… 148
many thanks for booking

[喜ぶ]

〜できることは、我々の喜びです ………… 38
it would be our pleasure to be able to ...

〜と聞いて喜んでいます ………………… 150
I was delighted to hear that ...

〜と聞いて、大変喜んでおります ………… 150
it was with great pleasure that I learned of ...

〜と伺って、大いに喜んでおります ……… 150
I was overjoyed at the news that ...

喜んでそうします ……………………… 163
I would be happy to do so

[よろしい]

よろしいでしょうか ……………………… 153
Would it be all right with you... ?

[よろしく]

〜に、どうぞよろしくお伝えください …… 39
please give my best regards to ...

〜に、よろしくお伝えください …………… 39
please give my regards to ...

〜によろしく ……………………………… 39
my best to ...

よろしくお願いします …………………… 39
thank you very much for your help

ら

[来社]

ご来社いただければ幸いです……………… 107
would appreciate it if you could visit us

お忙しい中わざわざご来社いただき ……… 112
taking your busy time to come to our office

[落胆]

〜には落胆した、と私は言わざるを
得ません ……………………………… 197
I must say that ... disappointed me

り

[理解]

〜との理解でよろしいですね ……………… 127
... Is my understanding correct?

〜に関して理解が同じである ……………… 127
we have the same understanding about ...

〜を理解していただくのに役立つ ………… 128
will help you understand ...

あなたの考えは理解できます……………… 182
can understand your thoughts

あなたの仰りたいことは理解できますが … 188
I see your point, but

[履修]

〜の履修を科しています …………………… 216
requires ... to learn

[理由]

このメールを書いている理由は〜です …… 29
the reason (why) I am writing this email is ...

理由の1つ ……………………………… 175
one reason why

254

以下の理由で ……………………………… 175
for the following reason

〜する理由はたくさんあります …………… 175
there are a number of reasons for ...

[療養]
自宅で療養します ………………………… 141
I will stay home and take it easy

[旅程]
詳細旅程を添付いたします ………………… 81
I am attaching detailed proposed itinerary

[リリース]
リリースするつもりです ……………………… 218
we intend to release

る

[留守]
オフィスを留守にします ……………………… 77
I will be away from the office

れ

[連絡]
近いうちにまたご連絡します ……………… 38
I will be in touch with you soon

メールでご連絡ください ……………………… 40
please contact us by emai

準備が整ったら連絡します ………………… 58
we will contact you when we are ready

ご連絡いたします ……………………… 69
I'm pleased to inform you

〜をご連絡いたします ……………………… 69
I would like to inform you of ...

できるだけ早く連絡いただけますか ……… 71
will you let us know as soon as possible

メールでの連絡はいつでも可能です ……… 75
cannot be reached by email

連絡先は以下の通りです …………………… 77
my contact information is as follows

私の不在中は、〜が各種連絡を担当すること
になっております ……………………………… 77
while I am away, ... is responsible for handling my correspondence

〜についてご、連絡いただけると
助かります ……………………………………… 94
I would appreciate it if you could inform us as to ...

連絡先を教えてください…………………… 97
please let me know his contact information

本人から直接連絡させます ……………… 105
I will instruct him to get in touch with you

こちらから連絡を差し上げたい …………… 122
would like to contact you

〜に連絡するよう ……………………… 122
to get in touch with ...

〜かどうかをご連絡ください ……………… 125
please let me know whether ...

新しい連絡先は以下の通りです …………… 136
my new contact information is as follows

もし私だったら〜に連絡を取ります ……… 157
I would get in touch with ... if I were you

わ

[わかる]
私ではわかりかねます ……………………… 68
I am not sure

私にもさっぱりわかりません……………… 68
I am as confused as you are

〜かどうか私にはわかりません …………… 190
I am not sure if ...

[忘れる]
〜を置き忘れた方 …………………………… 90
anybody who left ...

〜ことをどうぞお忘れなく ………………… 128
this is just to remind you that ...

〜ことをお忘れなく ………………………… 128
I would like to remind you that ...

〜ことをお忘れなく ………………………… 174
let me remind you that ...

〜ことを忘れてはならない ………………… 174
we should not forget that ...

255

用語索引

数字
24時間緊急サービス ……………… 76
3D ……………………………………… 215

アルファベット
CC ……………………………………… 133
CST …………………………………… 21
EST …………………………………… 21
had better ………………………… 14
IPアドレス ………………………… 221
MST …………………………………… 21
PST …………………………………… 21
Quote ………………………………… 54
Salutation ………………………… 16
should ……………………………… 14
smiley ……………………………… 55
Subject ……………………………… 17
Unquote ……………………………… 54
Webアプリケーション …………… 219
Web接続 …………………………… 214
would ……………………………… 154

あ
挨拶 ……………………………………… 147
曖昧 …………………………………… 172
悪影響 ……………………………… 179
アクセス …………………………… 220
アクセス数 ………………………… 211
アスタリスク ……………………… 48
圧縮 …………………………………… 43
　－効率 …………………………… 161
　－フォーマット ………………… 43
アップ ………………………………… 87
宛先複数 …………………………… 49
アドバイス ………………………… 156
アドレス帳 ……………………… 73, 74
アポイントメント ……………… 102
アンケート ………………………… 50
暗号化 ……………………… 217, 221

い
胃潰瘍 ……………………………… 141
以下略 ……………………………… 52
遺憾 …………………………………… 33
　－なメール ……………………… 31
意見 …………………………………… 133
　－交換 ……………………… 88, 170
　－調整 …………………………… 115
遺失物室 …………………………… 90
異常動作 …………………………… 67

移植 …………………………………… 156
一時中止 …………………………… 159
一般消費者 ………………………… 217
移転 …………………………………… 72
　－先 ……………………………… 165
異動 ………………………… 136, 137
イベント …………………………… 78
イメージアップ ………………… 162
依頼 …………………………………… 154
祝い状 ……………………………… 150
インターネット接続 …………… 220
インデント ………………………… 47
インフルエンザ ………………… 141
引用 ……………………………… 51, 132
　－文 ……………………………… 51

う
請け合う …………………………… 166
受け取り確認 ……………………… 66
売り込む …………………………… 161
運賃の見積もり ………………… 64

え
栄転 ………………………… 137, 150
婉曲 ……………………… 153, 160, 165
　－的 ……………………………… 123
援助 ……………………… 118, 152, 163
遠慮 …………………………………… 40

お
お客さま相談室 ………………… 133
お悔やみ ………………… 144, 146
送る …………………………………… 62
お知らせ …………………………… 70
おせっかい ………………………… 163
お世話 ……………………………… 136
落ち度 ……………………………… 36
お問い合わせ …………………… 118
驚き ………………………………… 198
オフィス …………………………… 72
オブジェクト …………………… 221
オプション ………………………… 211
お見舞い ………………… 144, 146
お礼 ……………………… 112, 138
オンライン ………………………… 218

か
会議 …………………………………… 78
　－室 ……………………………… 87
解雇 ………………………… 167, 191

会合場所	107
開催	78, 189
会社案内	92
開設	72
解説記事	120
解凍	43
回答	211
開発会議	22
開発計画	183
開発契約	32, 39, 198
開発作業	187
開発者	216
-会議	126
開発チーム	182
開発予算	156, 175
価格表	62
書き出し	24
確実	179
確認	127, 129
箇条書き	45, 46
稼動	38
可能性	180, 181
上半期	21
枯れている	215
環境	214
関係	38, 44
歓迎会	85
関係者	121
感謝	148
感情的表現	59
関数サンプル	42
簡素化	82
関知	186
観点	206
感服	149
願望	38
カンマ	20
簡略化	10

き

企業決済	206
期限の延長	213
帰国	136
技術情報	34
技術的詳細	209
技術文書	154, 195
機種番号	218
機種名	218
議事録	83, 84
-原稿	64
既存	220
期待	131
議題	82

期待感	38
記念パーティー	80
記念品	137
記念夕食会	85
機能の追加	212
起筆	16
寄付	143
希望	131
-的観測	181
基本仕様	184
基本設計	161, 187
-変更	210
疑問	165
キャンセル	111, 119
キャンペーン	91
休暇	76, 77
休業	76
究極の解決策	181
休憩	182
急成長	174
急用	111
今日中	21
恐縮	103
業績	144
強調	177
共同開発	38
興味	95
業務連絡	32
業務を簡素化	70
共有設備	87
協力	37, 40
許可	153, 167
緊急メール	17
緊急要員	76
緊急要件	76
近隣地図	72

く

空白	50
苦情	133, 199
くだけた表現	12, 13
句読点	20
組み込みシステム	161
クリスマス	147
グリッドコンピューティング	88
クレーム	122, 133

け

経緯	29
計画	162
-立案	213
警告	196
経済状態	181

掲示板	87
罫線	48
継続性	131
契約	203
－書	175
－発注	58
経歴書	155
下旬	21
欠陥プロダクト	69
欠勤	141
結語	16
月末	21
懸念	164
献花	143
言及	44
権限	172
原稿	120
現時点	22
研修	92
－講座	92
譴責する	158
建設的	173
現地時間	21
件名	17

こ

ご愛顧	39
高圧的	196
好意	35
公開鍵暗号方式	221
交換	158
攻撃	219
構築	35
交通事故	141
後任	136
高熱	141
候補	139
広報部	92
効用	208
効率	149
ご栄進	150
誤解	127, 203
互換性	97
顧客	
－管理システム	87, 161
－情報	220
－データベース	220
国外	212
告知	91
国内	212
誤作動	200
ご支援	38, 39
語数	120

コスト	
－効果	161
－効率	207
－削減	174
骨折	141
断る	194
好ましいメール	30
ご無沙汰	28
ご迷惑	33
コメント	51
顧問弁護士	158
雇用市場	170
コラボレーション	178
コロン	20, 46
懇親会	85
混乱	36

さ

サーバー構成	96
在庫	117
再考	192
最終決定	188
再送	43
催促	132, 155
採用	140, 186
探し物	89
作業工程	115
作業の効率	215
削減	175, 180
削除	52
早急	33
作法	57
些末	178
参加希望者	92
残業	145, 167, 176
－手当	35, 177
賛成	182
参入	186
サンプル一覧	63

し

資格	140, 216
時間関係	22
時間帯	108
自己紹介	57
仕事ぶり	199
字下げ	47
指示	125, 126
支持	184, 185
市場シェア	162
自信	179
システム開発契約書	42
システム構築	180

辞退	106
実験モデル	215
実行時の制約	215
実績のある	215
実装計画	183
質問	165
失礼	199
自動決済	62, 71, 209
－機能	158, 181
品切れ	31
締め切り	120, 213
下半期	21
謝意	24, 37
社屋改装	76
謝罪	171
社内IT研修セミナー	97
社内便	89
社内報	101, 120
就業時間	21
住所	72
重職	150
周知	130
周辺機器	97
重要性	176, 177
重要メール	17
修理費用	196
宿泊	85
主題	29
出荷ミス	36
出欠	50, 79
出欠通知	64
出席	79
出張	75
－計画書	63
－日程	75, 152
－費用	64
－旅費	70
主任プログラマー	30
紹介	97, 105
障害	145
紹介元	99
奨学金基金	143
昇級	192
上級職	85
状況	210
使用許諾	101
条件付き	195
条項	175
詳細	26
召集	67
上旬	21
昇進	32, 70, 150
招待	80

－券	79
－状	79
承諾	106
承認	167, 168
仕様変更	212
情報	34, 68
－源	98
－交換	88
－収集	94
助言	37, 156
所定外費用	179
署名	19
処理速度	162
資料	62, 68, 94, 117
新規事業	91
進行表	78
人材	139
－採用	139
人事異動	136
新住所	138
申請書	169
新着技術書	92
進捗状況	114
進捗報告	176, 177
－書	90, 200
新年	147
新聞記事	94
人脈	100

す

推奨	214
推進	186
推薦	139
－状	163, 169
数日中	21
スキル	216
スケジュール	113
勧める	158
頭痛	141
ストリーミング	217
スピード	10
スペース	20
スペック	218

せ

制作会社	97
生産性	149
精算伝票	64
精通	100
製品発表	78, 79
セキュリティ	218, 219
是正	197
設計ツール	199

絶対	179
設定ファイル	218
セットアップ	163
説明員	121
セミコロン	20
選択肢	50
専門	206
先約	80
全力	193

そ

葬儀	142
送受信	42
相談	152
早朝レクチャー	92
送付先	64
送付の目的	65
送付ミス	44
送別会	137
双方向性	219
続報	26
粗雑	172
組織変更	136
訴訟	198
即刻	155
損傷部品	62
尊大な表現	14

た

第1四半期	21
対案	189
退院	141
対応	218
－策	133
－製品	218
待機要員	76
太鼓判	166
大至急	33
代替案	193
タイムフレームワーク	96
代理店契約	122
妥協案	193
打診	108
立ち上げ	155
立場	173
脱落	84
断定的	172

ち

致命的	201
注意	174
中国時間	21
中止	119

抽出	220
中旬	21
注文	116
－書	63
中略	52
長期出張	75
直属の上司	30
著作権	101
陳謝	200

つ

追加	115
追加情報	96
月中	21
月初	21
都合	110
伝える	69

て

提案	189
定員	117
定期健康診断	92
定時	160
丁寧な表現	12
データ転送	212, 221
データベース	220
データマイニング	220
テーマ	120
適任	100
手作業	211
手付金	195
デバッグ情報	63
出迎え	81, 148
転勤	136
伝言	130
電子掲示板	87
転職	136
転送	37, 51, 55
－の目的	55
－優先度	221
添付ファイル	42, 43

と

問い合わせ	117
同意	182
投稿	120
動作環境	214
同時に	221
盗難	145
同報	49, 72
特殊機能	208
特定の操作	221
滞りなく	69

トラブルメーカー	174
取り交わし	203
取り消し	119
取り引き	206

な
内線	109
並び換え	212

に
日時	21, 108
日程	113
日本語能力	140
日本時間	21
入場料	69
認証方式	219
認定資格	178, 216

ね
ネック	209
ネットワーク	221
−障害	210
−トラブル	221
−パフォーマンス	221
年初	21
年度始め	21
年末	21
念を押す	35, 128

の
納期	117, 177, 179
納入期限	213

は
パーティー	78
拝借	152
配信システム	152
配布資料	22
ハイフン	48
励まし	145, 146
派遣社員	89
外す	167
発信者	56
発送スケジュール	166
発送手数料	67
パッチプログラム	40
パフォーマンス	207, 209, 218
払い戻し	64, 69, 70, 199
反対	186, 187
−意見	188
販売契約	125
販売支援ツール	161

ひ
引き合い	157
非生産的	191
引っ越す	180
必要性	169
秘密保持誓約	22, 195
病気療養中	141
標語	91
ピリオド	20

ふ
ファイアウォール	96, 153, 215
ファイル共有サーバー	87
不安	164
不一致	186, 187
フェースマーク	55
フォローアップ	26
部外者	196
不可欠	177
不具合	209
腹痛	141
不在	75
−中	77
不採用	140
不支持	190
不測の事態	111
二日酔い	141
不能	181
部分的に合意	183
不便	200
訃報	142
不法侵入	153
不本意	197
プレゼン	39
プログラマー研修	197
プロポーザル	40
紛失物	90

へ
閉鎖	198
変更	119
返事	25, 27, 33
返信	27, 50, 51, 58
−文	53

ほ
報告	69
方法論	183
訪問	81
保守契約	123
保守契約書	128
ホテル	86
本文	18

ま
前金 ･････････････････････････････････ 169
前払い ･･･････････････････････････････ 195
間違い ･･･････････････････････････ 44, 201
窓口 ･････････････････････････････････ 122
間に合わせる ･･･････････････････････ 181

み
見落とし ･････････････････････････････ 201
見過ごし ･････････････････････････････ 36
見積もり ･････････････････････････ 35, 63
未払い ･･･････････････････････････････ 198
未払金 ･･･････････････････････････････ 196
身元 ･････････････････････････････････ 163

む
結び ･････････････････････････････････ 33
無能 ･････････････････････････････････ 168

め
迷惑 ･････････････････････････････････ 200
メーリングリスト ･･･････････････････ 49
メールアドレス ･････････････････････ 73
面会 ･････････････････････････････････ 102
　－手順 ･････････････････････････････ 109
　－の目的 ･･･････････････････････････ 104
面接 ･････････････････････････････････ 148
面倒 ･････････････････････････････････ 152

も
申し出 ･･････････････････････････ 123, 124
盲腸 ･････････････････････････････････ 154
目的 ･････････････････････････････････ 162
目標 ･････････････････････････････････ 162
物知り ･･･････････････････････････････ 100
モバイル機器 ･･･････････････････････ 219
モバイル技術 ･･･････････････････････ 88
問題解決策 ･････････････････････････ 210
問題点 ･･･････････････････････････････ 202

や
役員会 ･･･････････････････････････････ 168
約束 ･････････････････････････････ 110, 166
役割分担 ････････････････････････････ 121

ゆ
ユーザーサポート ･････････････ 217, 218
ユースケース図 ･･･････････････････ 209

よ
用件 ･････････････････････････････････ 10
要人 ･････････････････････････････････ 81
要素 ･････････････････････････････････ 211
要望 ･･････････････････････････ 133, 160, 211
容量 ･････････････････････････････････ 43
予算 ･･････････････････････････････ 166, 178
予想 ･････････････････････････････････ 131
予約 ･････････････････････････････････ 116
よろしく ･････････････････････････････ 39

ら
来社 ･････････････････････････････････ 103
来週中 ･･･････････････････････････････ 21
落胆 ･････････････････････････････････ 197

り
理解 ･････････････････････････････････ 182
略語 ･････････････････････････････････ 19
略式歓迎会 ･････････････････････････ 85
理由 ･････････････････････････････････ 175
了解 ･････････････････････････････････ 53
旅程 ･････････････････････････････ 64, 81
履歴書 ･･････････････････････････ 140, 216

れ
例外扱い ････････････････････････････ 171
例文 ･････････････････････････････････ 11
レガシーシステム ･････････････ 158, 207
レコード ････････････････････････････ 220
連絡先 ･･･････････････････････ 73, 122, 138
連絡住所 ････････････････････････････ 77

ろ
ログファイル ･･･････････････････････ 157
論拠 ･････････････････････････････････ 175

わ
割り当てる ･････････････････････ 178, 221
論拠 ･････････････････････････････････ 175

わ
割り当てる ･････････････････････ 178, 221

■倉骨彰
　（くらほね あきら）

早稲田大学卒業。テキサス大学オースチン校大学院言語学研究科博士課程修了。数理言語学博士。同校で自然言語処理などを研究、自動翻訳システムのR&Dを専門とする。共著に、『10分間で超速スキルUP！　ビジネス英文メールの鉄則』(日経BP社)、『怪我と病気の英語力　病院・医院で役に立つ文例2800』(日本経済新聞出版社)、『実践的UML入門　IIOSSで始める新世紀プログラミング』(アスキー) などがある。訳書に、アーサー・ブロック『マーフィーの法則』(アスキー)、ウェンディ・ゴールドマン・ローム『マイクロソフト帝国　裁かれる闇』、ジャレド・ダイアモンド『銃・病原菌・鉄』(以上、草思社)、ジャレド・ダイアモンド『昨日までの世界　文明の源流と人類の未来』、ニック・ボストロム『スーパーインテリジェンス　超絶AIと人類の命運』(以上、日本経済新聞出版社)、マーク・スウェル他『職業としてのソフトウェアアーキテクト』(ピアソン・エデュケーション) など多数。

■トラビス・T・クラホネ
　（Travis T. Kurahone）

米国ユタ州生まれ。全米各地で4000超のリテールストアを展開するホームセンター企業の国際物流スペシャリスト。幼少期より電子通信メディアを活用。共著に、『英文Eメール文例ハンドブック　ビジネスですぐ使える！』(日本経済新聞出版社)、『そのまま使える！ビジネスメール英文集』(PHP) などがある。

本書は小社から2003年に発行した『説得できる英文Eメール　200の鉄則』を改題、再編集したものです。

英文ビジネスメール　200の鉄則

2018年4月16日　初版1刷発行

著　者	倉骨彰、トラビス・T・クラホネ
発行者	村上広樹
発　行	日経BP社
発　売	日経BPマーケティング
	〒105-8308　東京都港区虎ノ門4-3-12
装　幀	岩瀬聡
編　集	鈴木亨、長友真理
制　作	クニメディア株式会社
印刷・製本	中央精版印刷株式会社

ISBN978-4-8222-5562-6　　©2018 Akira Kurahone & Travis T. Kurahone
Printed in Japan

本書の無断複写・複製（コピー等）は著作権法上の例外を除き、禁じられています。購入者以外の第三者による電子データ化及び電子書籍化は、私的使用も含め一切認められておりません。
本書籍に関するお問い合わせ、ご連絡は下記にて承ります。
http://nkbp.jp/booksQA